LIBRARY OF HISTORICAL JESUS STUDIES

Editor
Robert L. Webb

Published under
LIBRARY OF NEW TESTAMENT STUDIES
327

formerly the Journal for the Study of the New Testament Supplement Series

Editor
Mark Goodacre

WHO DO MY OPPONENTS SAY I AM?

An Investigation of the Accusations against Jesus

Edited by

Scot McKnight
Joseph B. Modica

t &t clark

Published by T&T Clark International
A Continuum imprint
The Tower Building, 11 York Road, London SE1 7NX
80 Maiden Lane, Suite 704, New York, NY 10038

www.tandtclark.com

British Library Cataloging-in-Publication Data
A catalog record for this book is available from the British Library.

ISBN-10:   0-567-03126-8
ISBN-13:   978-0-567-03126-6   (hardback)

Typeset by ISB Typesetting, Sheffield
Printed on acid-free paper in Great Britain by Biddles Ltd, King's Lynn, Norfolk

Dedicated to

Alliance Theological Seminary, Nyack, NY

Trinity Evangelical Divinity School, Deerfield, IL

CONTENTS

ACKNOWLEDGMENTS

We would like to thank Professor Robert L. Webb for facilitating the process of allowing us to contribute a volume to this prestigious series. We would like to extend our gratitude to Haaris Naqvi, T & T Clark Senior Editor, and his staff for guiding this project to completion. It was also a privilege to collaborate with such a distinguished group of scholars. We learned much from their engagement with each accusation.

Finally, we deeply appreciate the institutions that we dedicate this book to. Each seminary has had a profound influence on our thinking about the historical Jesus (Modica, Alliance Theological Seminary; McKnight, Trinity Evangelical Divinity School). May each continue to expound a Christology that comes from *all* sides.

ABBREVIATIONS

AB	Anchor Bible
ABD	*Anchor Bible Dictionary* (Ed. D.N. Freedman; 6 vols; New York: Doubleday, 1992)
ABRL	Anchor Bible Reference Library
ANRW	*Aufstieg und Niedergang der römischen Welt: Geschichte und Kultur Roms im Spiegel der neueren Forschung* (Ed. H. Temporini and W. Haase; Berlin: W. de Gruyter, 1972–)
BBR	*Bulletin for Biblical Research*
BDB	F. Brown, S.R. Driver, and C.A. Briggs, *A Hebrew and English Lexicon of the Old Testament* (Oxford: Clarendon Press, 1907)
BDF	F. Blass, A. Debrunner, and R.W. Funk, *A Greek Grammar of the New Testament and Other Early Christian Literature* (Chicago, 1961)
BIS	Biblical Interpretation Series
BR	*Biblical Research*
BTB	*Biblical Theology Bulletin*
ConBNT	Coniectanea biblica: New Testament Series
CBQ	*Catholic Biblical Quarterly*
CBQMS	Catholic Biblical Quarterly Monograph Series
DJG	*Dictionary of Jesus and the Gospels* (Ed. J.B. Green and S. McKnight; Downers Grove: InterVarsity Press, 1992)
DNTB	*Dictionary of New Testament Backgrounds* (Ed. C.A. Evans and S.E. Porter; Downers Grove: InterVarsity Press, 2000)
DLNT	*Dictionary of the Later New Testament and Its Developments* (Ed. R.P. Martin and P.H. Davids; Downers Grove: InterVarsity Press, 1997)
ETL	*Ephemerides theologicae lovanienses*
EvQ	*Evangelical Quarterly*
HUCA	*Hebrew Union College Annual*
ICC	International Critical Commentary
ITC	International Theological Commentary
JBL	*Journal of Biblical Literature*
JSHJ	*Journal for the Study of the Historical Jesus*
JSJ	*Journal for the Study of Judaism in the Persian, Hellenistic, and Roman Periods*
JSNT	*Journal for the Study of the New Testament*
JSNTSup	*Journal for the Study of the New Testament*, Supplement Series
JSOT	*Journal for the Study of the Old Testament*
JSOTSup	*Journal for the Study of the Old Testament*, Supplement Series
JSP	*Journal for the Study of the Pseudepigrapha*
JSSR	*Journal for the Scientific Study of Religion*
JTS	*Journal of Theological Studies*
NIBCNT	New International Biblical Commentary on the New Testament

NIBCOT	New International Biblical Commentary on the Old Testament
NICNT	New International Commentary on the New Testament
NIGTC	New International Greek Testament Commentary
NovT	*Novum Testamentum*
NTS	*New Testament Studies*
PRSt	*Perspectives in Religious Studies*
RAC	*Reallexikon für Antike und Christentum* (Ed. T. Kluser *et al.*; Stuttgart, 1950–)
SBLDS	Society of Biblical Literature Dissertation Series
SJLA	Studies in Judaism in Late Antiquity
SNTS	Society of New Testament Studies
SNTSMS	Society for New Testament Studies Monograph Series
SupNovT	Supplements to Novum Testamentum
TDNT	*Theological Dictionary of the New Testament* (Ed. G. Kittel and G. Friedrich; trans. G.W. Bromiley (10 vols; Grand Rapids: Eerdmans, 1964–76)
TZ	*Theologische Zeitschrift*
WBC	World Biblical Commentary
WUNT	Wissenschaftliche Untersuchungen zum Neuen Testament
ZAW	Zeitschrift für alttestamentliche Wissenschaft

CONTRIBUTORS

MICHAEL F. BIRD is Tutor in New Testament at the Highland Theological College (Dingwall, Scotland). He holds a PhD from the University of Queensland, Australia.

DWIGHT D. SHEETS is an Associate Professor of New Testament at Evangel University (Springfield, MO). He taught at Valley Forge Christian College in Phoenixville, PA for the last ten years. Sheets holds a PhD from Fuller Theological Seminary.

JOSEPH B. MODICA is University Chaplain and Associate Professor of Biblical Studies at Eastern University (St Davids, PA). He holds a PhD from Drew University.

DARRELL L. BOCK is Research Professor of New Testament Studies and Professor of Spiritual Development and Culture at Dallas Theological Seminary (Dallas, TX). He holds a PhD from the University of Aberdeen.

JAMES F. MCGRATH is an Assistant Professor of Religion at Butler University (Indianapolis, IN). He holds a PhD from the University of Durham.

LYNN H. COHICK is an Associate Professor of New Testament at Wheaton College (Wheaton, IL). She holds a PhD from the University of Pennsylvania.

SCOT MCKNIGHT is the Karl A. Olsson Professor in Religious Studies at North Park University (Chicago, IL). He holds a PhD from the University of Nottingham.

INTRODUCTION

Scot McKnight and Joseph B. Modica

> The Son of Man came eating and drinking, and they say, 'Look, a glutton and a drunkard, a friend of tax collectors and sinners!'.... (Mt. 11.19ab)

> Sticks and stones may break my bones, but names will never hurt me (Childhood saying).

Although this well-known apocryphal saying has been used by children on playgrounds for decades, it reinforces a misconception that this book hopes to challenge. Calling people names does indeed impact how one understands and acts towards those persons.

One of the most memorable sayings of Jesus in the synoptic gospels is 'Who do people say that the Son of Man is?' (Mt. 16.13 and pars Mk 8.27, Luke 9.18, NRSV). Much scholarship has been written about the Christological impact of Jesus' self-referential question. Notably, the prompt response by Peter is also quite memorable: 'You are the Messiah, the Son of the living God' (Mt. 16.16). Thus, in Peter's brief reply, he attributes a name, so to speak, to Jesus ('Messiah'); one that will inevitably cause Him anguish and death. Names can indeed hurt people.

In this book, we attempt to further what Bruce J. Malina and Jerome H. Neyrey deftly did nearly twenty years ago in *Calling Jesus Names: The Social Value of Labels in Matthew* (Sonoma, CA: Polebridge Press, 1988), namely, to formulate a 'Christology from the side'—by examining the various accusations (vis-à-vis 'names') against Jesus in the gospels. Often Christological investigations, as noted by Malina and Neyrey, begin either from 'above' (i.e., early church council assessments of Jesus) or from 'below' (assessments of Jesus with an emphasis on his humanity). Therefore, Malina's and Neyrey's approach is novel, since to posit a 'Christology from the side,' one must recognize and appreciate the value of social labels placed on Jesus because they offer 'the human perspective and social arrangement marked by the relation of inside and outside, center and periphery' (p. x). Simply put, these social labels demonstrate 'how Jesus was evaluated by his enemies and followers' (p. x).

Malina and Neyrey utilize the late anthropologist Mary Douglas' social-scientific theory on deviance. Their methodology is to examine the deviant 'names' ('labels') given to Jesus in the Gospel of Matthew using as the backdrop the ancient Mediterranean culture. Their premise is that the social-scientific model 'attends precisely to the interpretations of Jesus by those who assessed him in terms of the socially perceived and appreciated lines that produced the culture of Jesus and Matthew' (p. xvi).

This is not to suggest, of course, an uncritical approach to their methodology (see J.B. Modica's essay, n. 6), yet we believe Malina's and Neyrey's approach can be broadened to include other 'names' – what we will call 'accusations' – beyond Matthew's gospel.

The impetus and structure for this book originate in a recent article by one of the co-editors and contributors, who unearthed seven accusations against the historical Jesus (see S. McKnight, 'Calling Jesus *Mamzer*', *JSHJ* 1.1 [2003]: 73-103). Simply stated, they are: (1) Jesus as Law-breaker, (2) Jesus as Demon-Possessed, (3) Jesus as a Glutton and Drunkard, (4) Jesus as Blasphemer, (5) Jesus as False Prophet, (6) Jesus as King of the Jews and (7) Jesus as a *Mamzer* ('Illegitimate Son').

Each contributor was given the task to examine a specific accusation and offer how this accusation might lend itself to a more comprehensive Christological understanding of the historical Jesus.

JESUS AS LAW-BREAKER

Michael F. Bird

Introduction

As one who teaches New Testament studies in a Christian College of the Reformed tradition, it has become apparent to me that Pharisees and Presbyterians share at least two things in common. First, both groups regard themselves as the true representatives of Israel. Second, the most heinous and vitriolic accusation that could be oppugned against either group would be to call them *antinomian*, that is, to insinuate that one of their members lives without proper respect for and submission to the law of God.

My point is not to equate Presbyterians with Pharisees (heaven forbid), but to suggest that an accusation of being 'lawless' or a 'law-breaker' functions in certain sociological contexts as a form of deviant labelling.[1] In such a context, one group ostracizes another by asserting that the beliefs and practices of a group defy the patterns of behaviour prescribed by a network of shared expectations. Thus to make the charge of being a law-breaker against a certain individual or group is to signify a challenge to the legitimacy of that individual's or that group's claim to participate in a shared identity. Furthermore, the gravity and rhetoric that the challenge is embellished in is heightened in socio-religious contexts that emphasize the importance of orthopraxy over orthodoxy.

For example, in a Jewish context where the law or Torah functions as the constitution for a community (formative horizon), where Torah observance operates as an prerequisite for membership and as a boundary-marker for fellowship in the community (sociological horizon), and even comprises the basis for the eschatological vindication of the community (eschatological horizon), the significance of the label 'law-breaker' becomes exceedingly acute. Violation of Torah meant incurring the curses of Deuteronomy

---

1. Bruce M. Malina and Jerome H. Neyrey, *Calling Jesus Names: The Social Value of Labels in Matthew* (Sonoma, CA: Polebridge, 1988).

28. In prophetic, wisdom, and apocalyptic traditions, a failure to observe the Mosaic statutes resulted in punishment by pagan nations.[2] It is the prevention of such dire consequences that led the author of the *Epistles to Aristeas* to say that the law was given to 'surround us with unbroken palisades and iron walls to prevent our mixing with any other peoples in any matter, being thus kept pure in body and soul, preserved from false beliefs, and worshipping the only God omnipotent over all creation' (*Ep. Arist.* 139). Likewise, the rabbinic oral law was a further fence around the written law to guard against lawlessness (*m. 'Abot.* 1.1; 3.14).

There are numerous examples in Second-Temple Jewish literature where rival groups raise charges against another group's practices. Accusations are then issued to denounce compromisers as law-breakers. In the Qumran Scrolls the Pharisees are regarded as 'seekers after smooth things' (4Q169 2.4; 3.3, 6-8). In the Damascus Document one reads: 'they had sought flattery, choosing travesties of true religion; they looked for ways to break the law; they favoured the fine neck. They called the guilty innocent, and the innocent guilty. They overstepped the covenant, violated the law; and they conspired to kill the innocent'[3] (CD 1.18-20). In the Maccabean writings, the Jewish Hellenizers are described with disdain and contempt. Menelaus, the high priest, is called 'a traitor of the laws and the fatherland' (2 Macc. 5.15). He is denounced as a 'law-breaker' (παρά-νομος) who appropriately 'died without burial' (2 Macc. 13.7). Another high priest, Jason brother of Onias, is reported to have 'destroyed the lawful ways of living and introduced new customs *against the law* (παράνομος)' (2 Macc. 4.11) and 'changed the nation's way of life and altered its form of government in *every lawless way* (ἐπὶ πᾶσαν παρα-νομίαν)' (*4 Macc.* 4.19). Josephus narrates how the High Priest Ananus was able to have James the brother of Jesus and his companions summarily executed on a charge of being 'breakers of the law (παρανομέω)' (*Ant.* 20.200). In Justin's *Dialogues with Trypho* 108, he reports a Jewish charge that Christianity was a 'godless and lawless heresy' (αἵρεσίς τις ἄθεος καὶ ἄνομος) and Jesus was accused of teaching 'godless and lawless and unholy doctrines' (ἄθεα καὶ ἄνομα καὶ ἀνόσια). In the Gospels Jesus provokes opposition over issues pertaining to the Sabbath (e.g.,

---

2.   Cf. Neh. 9.26-29, 34; Pss. 78.10-11; 89.30-32; Isa. 5.24; 42.24; Jer. 6.19; 9.13; 16.11; 32.23; 44.10-23; Hos. 8.1; Amos 2.4; Dan. 9.11-13; Wisd. 6.4; *4 Ezra* 1.8; 4.23; 7.24, 72, 79-81; 8.56; 9.11, 32; 14.30.

3.   Translation from Michael Wise, Martin Abegg and Edward Cook, *The Dead Sea Scrolls: A New Translation* (London: HarperCollins, 1996).

Mk 2.24; Lk. 13.14; 14.1-6) and food laws (Mk 7.1-23) and his fidelity to the Torah was regarded as suspect to the point that Jesus and his disciples were regarded as performing unlawful acts (Mk 2.24; 3.4). It appears that Jesus also responded in kind (Mt. 24.12; cf. Mt. 5.20; Lk. 11.42-52/Mt. 23.1-36). But Jesus was not alone as other Jews could also condemn the Pharisees for their practices. In the *Testament of Levi* there is a possible anti-Pharisaic remark: 'You shall set aside the Law and nullify the words of the prophets by your wicked perversity' (*T. Levi* 16.2). The *Testament of Moses* contains a similar opprobrium: 'Then will rule destructive and godless men, who represent themselves as being righteous, but who will (in fact) arouse their inner wrath, they will be deceitful men, pleasing only themselves, false in every way imaginable... They, with hand and mind, will touch impure things, yet their mouths will speak enormous things, and they will even say, "Do not touch me, lest you pollute me in the position I occupy"' (*T. Mos.* 7.3, 9-10). These vitriolic remarks are part and parcel of intra-Jewish polemics about Torah and Jewish identity.

The same phenomenon occurs in the early church with Christians using labels of law-breaker and related terms to describe non-believing Jews and even competing Christian factions. Stephen's speech in Acts 7 climaxes with the accusation against the Jewish leaders that: 'You are the ones that received the law as ordained by angels, and yet you have not kept it' (Acts 7.53). Paul makes a vehement remark about nomistic Jewish-Christians that 'even the circumcised do not themselves obey the law, but they want you to be circumcised so that they may boast about your flesh' (Gal. 6.13). The Johannine Jesus accuses his interlocutors of failing to keep the law (Jn 7.19). One also finds traces in the New Testament of authors responding to allegations that Christians are law-breakers, including James (1.25; 2.8-12; 4.11) and Paul (Rom. 2.13-16; 3.8, 31; 6.14-15; 7.7-25). The distinctive aspect of the Matthean Jesus is that he upholds and fulfills the entire law (Mt. 5.17-20; 7.12)[4] and this portrayal functions as an important christological belief for Jewish Christian groups still in some proximity to Judaism.[5] Strewn throughout the New Testament are exhortations and

---

4. On this passage Joachim Jeremias (*New Testament Theology* [trans. John Bowden; London: SCM, 1971], p. 207) writes: 'The charge of antinomianism, says Jesus in Matt. 5.17, is not completely without foundation, but it is a misinterpretation; Jesus is not concerned with destroying the law but with fulfilling it to its full eschatological measure'.

5. One extra-canonical tradition that also attempts to absolve Jesus from being a law-breaker is *P. Eger.* 2.1-4: 'Then Jesus said to the lawyers, "Punish everyone that behaves unjustly and is lawless, but do not punish me"'.

warnings against ἀνομία, or lawless actions and persons (Mt. 7.23; 13.41; 23.28; 24.12; Rom. 6.19; 2 Cor. 6.14; 2 Thess. 2.3, 7; Heb. 1.9; 1 Jn 3.4). The pejorative sense of lawlessness in early Christianity differs markedly from later gnostic writings where freedom from the law was a characteristic of those enlightened by *gnosis* and Jews and Christians were derided as remaining enslaved to the law (e.g., *Apoc. Pet.* 82.26; *Treat. Seth* 65.14-17; *Test. Truth* 29.22-25; *Gos. Eg.* 65.18-19).[6]

It is apparent that disputes and divisions about the Torah were central in shaping the character of Judaism and early Christianity. It is equally true that Jesus' approach to the Torah aroused suspicion, indignation and finally accusations as a 'law-breaker' from his Jewish contemporaries. Jesus' disputes with the Pharisees recorded in the Gospels represent a form of intra-Jewish legal debate that demonstrates Jesus' basic convictions about the Torah, the kingdom of God, and Jewish identity – convictions that proved to be notorious. The umbrage prompted by Jesus' actions and teachings in relation to Torah derived from a radical challenge to his interlocutors as to what it meant to be faithful to God in light of the dawning eschatological age. At the same time, the historical Jesus' view of Torah is highly disputed, both in terms of the authenticity of traditions and the question as to whether Jesus deliberately abrogated the Mosaic commandments.[7] Therefore, it is the aim of this study to investigate how

6. Carl B. Smith, *No Longer Jews: The Search for Gnostic Origins* (Peabody, MA: Hendrickson, 2004), pp. 210-13.

7. J.D.M. Derrett, *Law in the New Testament* (London: Darton, Longman & Todd, 1970); Klaus Berger, *Die Gesetzesauslegung Jesu: Ihr historischer Hintergrund im Judentum und im Alten Testament. Teil I* (WMANT, 40; Neukirchen-Vluyn: Neukirchen, 1972); Robert Banks, *Jesus and the Law in the Synoptic Tradition* (SNTSMS, 28; Cambridge: Cambridge University Press, 1975); Stephen Westerholm, *Jesus and Scribal Authority* (ConBNT, 10; Lund: Gleerup, 1978); D.J. Moo, 'Jesus and the Authority of the Mosaic Law', *JSNT* 20 (1984), pp. 3-49; Peter Fiedler, 'Die Tora bei Jeus und in der Jesusüberlieferung', in *Das Gesetz im Neuen Testament* (ed. Karl Kertelge; QD, 108; Freiburg: Herder, 1986), pp. 71-87; Roger P. Booth, *Jesus and the Laws of Purity: Tradition History and Legal History in Mark 7* (JSNTSup, 13; Sheffield: Sheffield Academic Press, 1986); James D.G. Dunn, *Jesus, Paul and the Law: Studies in Mark and Galatians* (Philadelphia: Westminster/John Knox, 1990), pp. 10-86; Ingo Broer (ed.), *Jesus und das Jüdische Gesetz* (Stuttgart: W. Kohlhammer, 1992); William Loader, *Jesus' Attitude towards the Law: A Study of the Gospels* (WUNT, 2.97; Tübingen: Mohr/Siebeck, 1997); John P. Meier, 'The Historical Jesus and the Historical Law: Some Problems within the Problem', *CBQ* 65 (2003), pp. 52-79; Dale C. Allison, 'Torah, *Urzeit, Endzei*', in *Resurrecting Jesus: The Earliest Christian Tradition and Its Interpreters* (New York: T&T Clark/Continuum, 2005), pp. 149-97.

the perspective of Jesus' opponent's illuminates Jesus' understanding of Torah and also his own mission.

The Problem of Torah and Nomos

The study must be prefaced with several preliminary observations. First, the role and function of Torah in Second-Temple Judaism[8] and early Christianity[9] are all widely disputed in scholarship. What is clear, however, is that there was a multiplicity of views about the law in Judaism and primitive Christianity. Diversity provides a catalyst for dispute and rivalry to ensue between religious parties.

Second, the terms Torah (תורה) and *nomos* (νόμος) require definition.[10] Torah could refer to general instruction but most frequently signifies the

---

8. E.P. Sanders, *The Jewish Law, Five Studies* (London: SCM, 1990); Peter Richardson and Stephen Westerholm *et al.* (eds), *Law in Religious Communities in the Roman Period: The Debate over Torah and Nomos in Post-Biblical Judaism and Early Christianity* (SCJ, 4; Waterloo, ON: Wilfrid Laurier University Press, 1991); Fredrich Avemarie and Hermann Licentenberger (eds), *Bund und Tora: Zura-theologischen Begriffsgeschichte in alttestamentlicher, frühjüdischer und urchristlicher Tradition* (WUNT, 135; Tübingen: Mohr/Siebeck, 1996); Heinrich Hoffmann, *Das Gesetz in der frühjüdischen Apokalyptik* (Gottingen: Vandenhoeck & Ruprecht, 1999); Reinhard Weber, *Das Gesetz' bei Philon von Alexandrien und Flavius Josephus: Studien zum Verständnis und zur Funktion der Thora bei den beiden Hauptzeugen des hellenistischen Judentums* (Frankfurt am Main: Peter Lang, 2001).

9. Heikki Räisänen, 'Freiheit vom Gesetz im Urchristentum', *Studia Theologica* 46 (1992), pp. 55-67; Meinrad Limbeck, *Das Gesetz im Alten und Neuen Testament* (Darmstadt: Buchgesellschaft, 1997); Markus Bockmuehl, *Jewish Law in Gentile Churches: Halakhah and the Beginning of Christian Public Ethics* (Edinburgh: T&T Clark, 2000); Peter Stuhlmacher, 'The Law as a Topic of Biblical Theology', in *Reconciliation, Law and Righteousness* (Philadelphia: Fortress Press, 1986), pp. 110-33; Raymond E. Brown and John P. Meier, *Antioch and Rome* (New York/Ramsey: Paulist, 1983), pp. 1-9; Veronica Koperski, *What Are They Saying about Paul and the Law?* (New York: Paulist, 2001); James G. Crossley, *The Date of Mark's Gospel: Insights from the Law in Earliest Christianity* (JSNTSup, 266; London: T&T Clark/Continuum, 2004), pp. 125-58.

10. Cf. Stephen Westerholm, '*Torah, nomos,* and Law: A Question of "Meaning"', *SR* 15 (1986), pp. 327-36; Philip S. Alexander, 'Jewish Law in the Time of Jesus: Towards a Clarification of the Problem', in *Law and Religion: Essays on the Place of the Law in Israel and Early Christianity by Members of the Ehrhardt Seminar of Manchester University* (ed. Barnabas Lindars; Cambridge: Cambridge University Press, 1988), pp. 44-58.

Mosaic legislation or Pentateuch. Although the Greek word *nomos* has a broader meaning, it is ordinarily used to translate *Torah*. In the Gospels one finds the reference to the 'Law of Moses' (Lk. 2.22; 24.44; Jn 7.23) directly associating *nomos* with the Mosaic precepts. Additional designations of the Jewish law include 'Scripture', 'commandment', 'decree', 'Moses', and 'it is written'.[11] The doctrine of dual Torah, one written and one oral, belongs to the rabbinic era. However, the Pharisees possessed a body of oral traditions that stood beside the written Torah and in an authoritative relation to them. This 'tradition' formed the bedrock of the oral Torah of later rabbinic thought.[12]

The oral tradition of the Pharisees was authoritative in so far as it was bound up with applying Torah. Pharisaic hermeneutics seems to have anticipated postmodern literary theory by pointing out that the lines between text, tradition, and interpretation are not so easily removed from one another. For some Pharisees the divinely given Torah is accompanied by a divinely given *Tradition* so that the difference between *Text* and *Interpretation* is blurred. Texts have no utility apart from interpretation and when it comes to the proper interpretation of Torah the Pharisees claim to speak for God in their tradition. By effect, if not by design, the Pharisaic *halakhah* was an extension of Torah itself.[13]

Jesus' Disputes with the Pharisees (Authenticity)

The benefit of reconstructing the viewpoint of Jesus' opponents is that it enables us to confirm aspects of his teaching and behaviour that cannot be attributed to the interests of the Evangelists. E.P. Sanders and M. Davies write: 'Once we can discern both favourable and unfavourable portraits of Jesus, we can ask what is common to both portraits and we may have considerable confidence that what is common is historically sound'.[14] There were several areas of disputation that arose between Jesus and his contemporaries regarding Torah.

---

11. Cf. D.J. Moo, 'Law', in *DJG* (eds Joel Green, *et al.*; Downers Grove, IL: InterVarsity Press, 1992), p. 451.

12. *b. Šabb.* 31a; *m. 'Abot.* 1.1; cf. 'tradition of the elders' in Mk 7.3, 5, 8, 9, 13 and Josephus, *Ant.* 13.297-98, 408; 18.15; Gal. 1.13-14; Acts 22.3.

13. Also Martin Hengel and Roland Deines, 'E.P. Sanders' "Common Judaism", Jesus, and the Pharisees', *JTS* 46 (1995), p. 31.

14. E.P. Sanders and Margaret Davies, *Studying the Synoptic Gospels* (London: SCM; Philadelphia: Trinity Press International, 1989), p. 302.

Topic	Mark	Q	'M'	'L'	John	Other
Sabbath	2.1-12			13.10-17	5.1-18	Gos. Thom. 27
	2.23-28			14.1-6	7.10-24	Gos. Naz. § 10[15]
	3.1-6				9.1-41	
food laws	2.15-17			7.36-50		P.Oxy. 1224 §1
(fellowship)	7.1-23					P.Oxy. 840 § 2
						Gos. Thom. 14
fasting	2.18-22		6.16-18			Gos. Thom. 14
						Gos. Thom. 27
						Gos. Thom. 104
divorce	10.2-12	Q 16.18	5.31-32			1 Cor. 7.10-11
	12.18-27		19.10-12			
taxation	12.13-17		17.24-27			Gos. Thom. 100
circumcision					7.22	Gos. Thom. 53
burial of		Q 9.59-60				
parents						

Some scholars advocate that Jesus did not really oppose the Pharisees. Moreover, there were no Pharisees in Galilee for Jesus to confront and the Gospel authors have projected their own post-70 CE debates with Pharisaic Judaism onto Jesus.[16] Sanders complains that the Gospel narratives are unrealistic since:

> Pharisees did not organize themselves into groups to spend their Sabbaths in Galilean cornfields in the hope of catching some transgression (Mark 2.23f.), nor is it credible that scribes and Pharisees made a special trip to Galilee from Jerusalem to inspect Jesus' disciples' hands (Mark 7.1f.). Surely stories such as these should not be read as describing actual debates between Jesus and others.[17]

Despite the genuine possibility these pericopae owe their origin to debates between Jews and Christians (pre- and post-70 CE), I remain convinced that such traditions do go back to a setting in Jesus' lifetime. First, in the

15. = Jerome, *Comm. Matt.* 2 (on Mt. 12.13).
16. Rudolf Bultmann, *History of the Synoptic Tradition* (trans. John Marsh; New York: Harper & Row, 2nd edn, 1963), p. 16; Morton Smith, *Jesus the Magician* (San Francisco: Harper & Row, 1978), pp. 153-57; E.P. Sanders, *Jesus and Judaism* (London: SCM, 1985), pp. 264, 270-93; idem, *The Historical Figure of Jesus* (London: Penguin, 1993), pp. 205-37; Paula Fredriksen, *From Jesus to Christ: The Origins of the New Testament Images of Jesus* (London: Yale University Press, 1988), pp. 102-10; idem, *Jesus of Nazareth, King of the Jews* (New York: Vintage, 1999), pp. 10-11.
17. Sanders, *Jesus and Judaism*, p. 265; idem, *Historical Figure of Jesus*, p. 214.

Gospels the Pharisees and scribes have an obvious literary function as the agents of the Jerusalem authorities and are a foil for controversy in the various pronouncement stories. Even so, Richard Horsley notes, 'they would have no credibility in either function unless they did, historically, on occasion at least, appear outside of their focus of operations in Jerusalem'.[18] The fact that the Jerusalem authorities sent a Pharisaic delegation to take control of the region at the outbreak of hostilities in 66 CE renders the portrait of the Pharisees as delegates of the Jerusalem authorities to Galilee entirely plausible (Josephus, *Life* 191-93, 197). Johanan ben Zakkai relocated the Sanhedrin to Galilee in the aftermath of the Jewish revolt. We know of at least two other Pharisees who were active outside of Jerusalem and enforcing strict observance of Torah in Saul of Tarsus (Acts 9.1-3; Gal. 1.13-14; Phil. 3.6; 1 Cor. 15.9) and Eleazar (Josephus, *Ant.* 20.43-45). Josephus narrates how the Pharisees took measures to transmit their traditions to the common people (Josephus, *Ant.* 13.297-98; 18.15), while Philo records that persons (probably Pharisees) took it upon themselves to guard their ancestral traditions and reacted against those that might subvert them (*Spec. Leg.* 2.253) – this is far beyond a concern for introspective piety but expresses an agenda to disseminate and regulate Torah observance to some degree.[19] Archaeological discoveries of white stone vessels, bone ossuaries, and ritual baths throughout Galilee are also telltale signs of the adoption of a distinctly Pharisaic *halakhah* in some quarters of the Galilee.[20] Pharisaic influence on Galilee and an attempt to monitor Torah practice by the inhabitants cannot be rejected as implausible.[21]

Second, Sanders thinks that since it was not Jesus but his disciples that are censured for disobeying the law, the stories are in fact allegories of Gentile churches that did not keep the law and have retrojected their own

18. Richard A. Horsley, *Galilee: History, Politics, People* (Valley Forge, PA: Trinity Press International, 1995), pp. 70 and 150-52.

19. Cf. John P. Meier, *A Marginal Jew: Companions and Competitors* (ABRL; New York: Doubleday, 2001), pp. 315-16.

20. J.F. Strange, 'Galilee', in *DNTB* (eds Craig A. Evans and Stanley E. Porter; Downers Grove, IL: InterVarsity Press, 2000), p. 396; Jonathan L. Reed, *Archaeology and the Galilean Jesus* (Harrisburg, PA: Trinity Press International, 2000), pp. 49-51, 125-31.

21. For a fictional but realistic story of two Sabbath 'police' in Capernaum see Gerd Theissen, *The Shadow of the Galilean* (trans. John Bowden; Philadelphia: Fortress Press, 1989), pp. 100-103.

debates with Pharisaic Judaism onto Jesus.[22] It is true that the accusation about handwashing is directed against Jesus' disciples in Mark 7.2-4, but in Luke 11.38 it is directed against Jesus personally. This view also over-looks a further problem: Pharisaic opposition to Christianity precedes the entrance of Gentiles into the church as indicated by the persecution of Christians by Saul of Tarsus. Pharisaic opposition to the Jesus movement in the early to mid-30s renders plausible Pharisaic antagonism towards Jesus in the late-20s. One cannot take all the radical sayings about the law and lay them at the door of the Gentile churches. There is nothing to say that the radical directions of Jesus' teachings were consistently followed in their radicalism by his followers.[23] When it comes to the Temple, the early Christian community in Jerusalem exhibits an attitude to it far more positive than that of Jesus (Acts 1-5). It is the Hellenistic circle associated with Stephen that urged a return to Jesus' radical position vis-à-vis the Temple (Acts 6.13-14). The Gentile churches affiliated with Paul (esp. Antioch, Galatia, and Rome) did not, as far as we know, radicalize Paul's teachings on the law as much as they felt constrained to acquiesce to a more conservative Jewish position.

Third, the types of debates about the law in early Christianity are not found in the Synoptics. The canonical Gospels do not provide any dominical ruling by Jesus on matters that were a cause of division in the early church including circumcision (Gal. 2.3-9; 5.1-12; 6.12-13; Phil. 3.3; Acts 15.1-5; 21.21) and Jew-Gentile table-fellowship (Gal. 2.11-14; Acts 10–11). Also debates about fasting, Sabbath observance, and hand washing have no immediate application for resolving matters of disagree-ment in the early years of the Christian movement. To be sure, Paul rejected the imposition of Sabbath observance upon Gentiles (Gal. 4.10; Col. 2.16), but he never claimed that Jesus abrogated the Sabbath or that Sabbath keeping was a bad thing. Paul even acknowledged that Sabbath observance was all right if undertaken as a voluntary act (Rom. 14.5-6). Maurice Casey argues for the authenticity of two Sabbath controversy stories in Mark 2.23-3.6 on similar grounds:

> The Sitz im Leben of these disputes is in the life of Jesus. Jesus lived in first-century Judaism, where the question of how to observe the Law was a permanent focus of Jewish life ... These disputes have no Sitz im Leben in the early church, which was concerned about whether Christians, especially

---

22. Sanders, *Jesus and Judaism*, pp. 266, 292; idem, *Historical Figure of Jesus*, pp. 217-18; Bultmann, *History of the Synoptic Tradition*, p. 16.

23. Joachim Gnilka, *Jesus of Nazareth: Message and History* (trans. S.S. Schatz-mann; Peabody, MA: Hendrickson, 1997), p. 216.

Gentile Christians, should observe the Law at all. These detailed disputes do not speak to that major issue.[24]

Thus, the reasons for rejecting the authenticity of the controversy stories between Jesus and the Pharisees are not as convincing as they might appear to be.[25]

Jesus and the Food Laws

Space does not permit a rigorous study of all the areas of legal dispute between Jesus and his adversaries.[26] Hence I will focus on the food laws as an example of Jesus' disputes about Torah with his opponents. In broaching this topic we must approach them on their own terms and bracket out Christian theological concerns about *Law and Gospel* as well as avoid sifting the Jesus tradition for answers to the quandary of Paul and the law.[27]

The purpose of the purity laws in the Levitical code was to maintain Israel's chosen status so as to protract her capacity to serve and worship God.[28] The laws are linked closely with Israel's election and call to

24. Maurice Casey, *Aramaic Sources of Mark's Gospel* (SNTSMS, 102; Cambridge: Cambridge University Press, 1998), pp. 192, and 138-92, 257.

25. Cf. Edward Schillebeeckx, *Jesus: An Experiment in Christology* (trans. Hubert Hoskins; London: Collins, 1979), pp. 233-34; Arland J. Hultgren, *Jesus and His Adversaries: The Form and Function of the Conflict Stories in the Synoptic Tradition* (Minneapolis: Augsburg, 1979), pp. 198-99; Gnilka, *Jesus of Nazareth*, p. 268; Gerd Theissen and Annette Merz, *The Historical Jesus: A Comprehensive Guide* (trans. John Bowden; Minneapolis: Fortress Press, 1998), p. 225; Hengel and Deines, 'E.P. Sanders', p. 11; Jürgen Becker, *Jesus of Nazareth* (New York: Walter de Gruyter, 1998), p. 278.

26. On Jesus and the Sabbath commandment see Sven-Olav Back, *Jesus of Nazareth and the Sabbath Commandment* (Åbo: Åbo Akademi University Press, 1995).

27. Cf. Meier, 'Historical Law', p. 53.

28. For recent studies on purity see E.P. Sanders, *Jewish Law from Jesus to the Mishnah: Five Studies* (London: SCM, 1990); Hannah K. Harrington, *The Impurity Systems of Qumran and the Rabbis* (SBLDS, 143; Atlanta: Scholars Press, 1993); Walter Houston, *Purity and Monotheism: Clean and Unclean Animals* (JSOTSup, 140; Sheffield: Sheffield Academic Press, 1993); Hyam Maccoby, *Ritual and Morality: The Ritual Purity System and its Place in Judaism* (Cambridge: Cambridge University Press, 1999); Eyal Regev, 'Pure Individualism: The Idea of Non-Priestly Purity in Ancient Judaism', *JSJ* 31 (2000), pp. 176-202; Jonathan Klawans, *Impurity and Sin in Ancient Judaism* (Oxford: Oxford University Press, 2000); idem, *Purity, Sacrifice, and the Temple: Symbolism and Supersessionism in the Study of Ancient Judaism* (Oxford: Oxford University Press, 2005); John C. Poirier, 'Purity beyond

national holiness.[29] The food laws rigorously detailed which consumables were suitable and which were not.[30] The connection of food with election is evident in 1 Maccabees which tells how 'many in Israel stood firm and were resolved in their hearts not to eat unclean food. They chose to die rather than to be defiled by food or to profane the holy covenant; and they did die.'[31] Philo tells a similar story of a Jewish woman who, during the anti-Jewish riots in Alexandria, was tortured because she refused to eat pork.[32] Observing kosher food came to express Israel's separateness from other nations in that it distinguished the Jewish diet from others, but was also a sign of faithfulness to the Covenant. In practical terms it meant that a Jew could not eat with a Gentile without being contaminated since there was no guarantee that the food was kosher and had been appropriately prepared. Hence table fellowship with Gentiles was often (but not always) taboo. In Daniel and Tobit the protagonists refuse to defile themselves by eating Gentile food.[33] *Jubilees* urges: 'Separate yourself from the Gentiles, and do not eat with them, and do not perform deeds like theirs. And do not become associates of theirs.'[34] Jews in the Diaspora attempted to acquire native food.[35] The Jewish refusal to dine with non-Jews was duly noted by Greco-Roman authors.[36] There are also indications of post-biblical expansions of food laws. According to Josephus, some priests who were imprisoned in Rome ate only figs and nuts.[37] The Qumran scrolls forbid a member of the community from accepting food from a Gentile.[38] Josephus records how those who were expelled from the Essenic order starved to death because they would not eat impure food.[39]

---

the Temple in the Second Temple Era', *JBL* 122 (2003), pp. 247-65; Thomas Kazen, *Jesus and Purity Halakhah: Was Jesus Indifferent to Impurity?* (CBNT, 38; Stockholm: Almqvist & Wiksell, 2002).

29. Lev. 11.45; 20.24-26; Deut. 7.6; 14.1-4, 21.

30. Lev. 11.1-47; Deut. 14.3-21; cf. Josephus, *Apion* 2.173-74, 282; Philo, *Spec. Leg.* 4.100-20; *Agric.* 131-32; *m. Hullin*.

31. 1 Macc. 1.62-63; cf. 2 Macc. 11.31; *4 Macc.* 5.1-38; 6.16-22; 8.2, 12, 29; 13.2.

32. Philo, *Flacc.* 95-96.

33. Dan. 1.5-16; Tob. 1.10-11.

34. *Jub.* 22.16.

35. Josephus, *Ant.* 14.261.

36. Tacitus, *Hist.* 5.5.2; Diodorus, *Bib. Hist.* 34.1.1; Philostratus, *Vit. Ap.* 33.

37. Josephus, *Life* 13-14.

38. 4Q394 frags 3-7.

39. Josephus, *War* 2.129, 139, 143-44, 152; *Ant.* 18.22; on food and purity 1QS 5.12-16; 6.16; CD 10.10-13; 12.8-22; 4Q284.

Purity in relation to food was a particular concern of the Pharisees as the 'separated ones' (Heb. פרושים; Aram. פרישיא; Gk. Φαρισαῖοι) who formed a purity-dining fellowship where they could eat with other Jews who observed similar scruples.[40] The rationale for engaging in extra-temple purity by the Pharisees is disputed, and a vigorous debate has taken place between Neusner and Sanders on the topic. According to Neusner, the Pharisees pursued purity in order to apply the priestly code to their own lives.[41] In contrast, Sanders believes that purity was pursued for its own sake as something intrinsically good.[42] Many scholars (with qualification) have followed Sanders' view.[43] Still, Sanders' concession that the Pharisees made a 'minor gesture'[44] towards priestly purity opens the door for Neusner in some way since a gesture, full of symbolism and loaded with polemic, can constitute a point of division. For many Jewish groups the practice of purity was the attempt to realize the conditions necessary for the restoration of Israel and the arrival of the eschaton.[45]

The food laws were an equally contentious topic in the primitive Christian movement, aroused by table-fellow between Jews and non-Jews. Luke depicts Peter as breaking down the traditional barriers between Jews and Gentiles in the episode with Cornelius (Acts 10–11) while later in Antioch Peter consciously withdrew from contact with Gentile believers at the behest of 'certain men from James' (Gal. 2.11-14). In the Pauline churches food proved to be a divisive topic.[46] Paul asserts that he is 'convinced by the Lord that nothing itself is unclean' (Rom. 14.14). The Colossians are

---

40. Cf. Emil Schürer, *The History of the Jewish People in the Age of Jesus Christ* (rev. and ed. G. Vermes, F. Millar and M. Black; 3 vols; Edinburgh: T&T Clark, 1973–87), II, pp. 396-98; John P. Meier, *A Marginal Jew: Rethinking the Historical Jesus: Companions and Competitors* (ABRL; New York: Doubleday, 2001), pp. 366-67.

41. Jacob Neusner, *The Idea of Purity in Ancient Judaism* (SJLA, 1; Leiden: Brill 1973).

42. Sanders, *Jewish Law*, pp. 29-42, 131-254 (esp. 192, 235); idem, *Judaism: Practice and Belief 63 BCE – 66 CE* (London: SCM, 1992), pp. 214-30.

43. Hengel and Deines, 'E.P. Sanders', pp. 41-51; Maccoby, *Ritual and Morality*; Regev, 'Pure Individualism', pp. 176-202; Poirier, 'Purity beyond the Temple in the Second Temple Era', pp. 247-65; but see Klawans, *Impurity and Sin in Ancient Judaism*; James D.G. Dunn, 'Jesus and Purity: An Ongoing Debate', *NTS* 48 (2002), p. 454, n. 23.

44. Sanders, *Jewish Law*, p. 235.

45. Steven M. Bryan, *Jesus and Israel's Traditions of Judgment and Restoration* (SNTS, 117; Cambridge: Cambridge University Press, 2002), p. 153.

46. Rom. 14.1–15.6; 1 Cor. 8.1-13; 10.20-33.

urged not to submit to Jewish purity laws arguably stemming from some who were insistent on their observance of it (Col. 2.20-23). The Apostolic council in Acts 15 presents James as offering somewhat of a *via media* through his interpretation of Amos 9.11-12 as he exhorts Gentiles to live in accordance with the Noachide commandments with a view to abstaining from pagan religious festivals.[47] There is then a discernible tension between Paul, Peter and James on matters of food and purity in early Christianity.[48]

Several studies propose that Jesus was highly critical of the Jewish purity statutes. Marcus Borg thinks of purity and compassion as mutually exclusive with Jesus urging an abandonment of the former, while John Dominic Crossan regards the Jewish purity system as a weapon of the Jewish aristocracy that exploits or discriminates against others and Jesus viciously attacked it in want of a more egalitarian ethic.[49] It is often overlooked that purity regulations were not confined to Judaism since Greco-Roman cults possessed their own purity regulations; indeed, Philo attempts to argue for the superiority of the Jewish rites over pagan ones.[50] Purity and ritual was part and parcel of the religious practice of the ancient world.

I am persuaded by Harvey's historical 'constraint of the law' whereby a Jewish Jesus implies a Torah devout Jesus.[51] Yet we must appreciate a tension that is reflected in the Gospels as Jesus is portrayed as both a legal radical in some matters (e.g., fasting, Sabbath keeping, and food laws) but

47. Gen. 9.4; Lev. 17.10; Deut. 12.16, 23-25; cf. *b. Sanh.* 56a-b; 1QapGen 12.17; Philo, *Quaest. in Gen.* 2.59.

48. Cf. Bruce D. Chilton, 'Purity and Impurity', in *DLNTD* (eds Ralph P. Martin and Peter H. Davids; Downers Grove, IL: InterVarsity Press, 1997), pp. 988-96; idem, 'Jesus, Levitical Purity, and the Development of Primitive Christianity', in *The Book of Leviticus: Composition and Reception* (eds Rolf Rendtorff and Robert A. Kugler; Leiden: Brill, 2003), pp. 358-82; Scot McKnight, 'A Parting within the Way: Jesus and James on Israel and Purity', in *James the Just and Christian Origins* (eds Bruce Chilton and Craig A. Evans; NovTestSup, XCVIII; Leiden: Brill, 1999), pp. 83-129.

49. Marcus Borg, *Conflict, Holiness and Politics in the Teachings of Jesus* (Harrisburg, PA: Trinity Press, 2nd edn, 1998), pp. 112-13, 135-55; John Dominic Crossan, *The Historical Jesus: The Life of a Mediterranean Jewish Peasant* (San Francisco: HarperCollins, 1991), p. 323; see the critiques by Paula Fredriksen, 'Did Jesus Oppose the Purity Laws?' *Bible Review* 11 (1995), pp. 20-25, 42-47 and Chilton, 'Jesus, Levitical Purity', p. 358.

50. Philo, *Spec. Leg.* 1.263-66.

51. A.E. Harvey, *Jesus and the Constraints of History* (London: Duckworth, 1982), p. 37 (see esp. pp. 37-51) and also Geza Vermes, *Jesus and the World of Judaism* (London: SCM, 1983), pp. 45-46.

also as pious and Torah obedient (esp. toward the Temple).[52] Consequently, I am inclined to identify Jesus as essentially Torah compliant, but also recognize the fact that he challenged and flouted many of the legal interpretations of his contemporaries.[53] One particular area of disagreement appears to be in matters relating to purity, witnessed by several episodes in the Gospels including: (1) Jesus' table fellowship with 'sinners' and tax collectors.[54] By eating with such people Jesus became ritually impure since the *am'hares* were presumed to neglect levitical law.[55] (2) Within the course of his healing ministry Jesus touched lepers[56] and dead persons,[57] both of which rendered him impure due to the transmission of impurity.[58] (3) Jesus is reported in Mark 7.15 as saying that only things going out of a man defile and Mark draws the conclusion in Mark 7.19c that by saying this Jesus 'declared all foods clean'. For the sake of brevity I shall not attempt a rigorous study of all these incidents but focus on Mark 7.15 since it the passage most likely to express Jesus' central convicts about Torah in general and purity in particular.

In Mark 7.1-23 Jesus is confronted by the Pharisees as to why his disciples eat with 'defiled' (κοινός) hands. After a sharp rejoinder to their question the pericope climaxes in the pronouncement of Mark 7.15: 'There is nothing outside a person that by going into him can defile him, but the things that come out of a person are what defile him'.[59] There

---

52. Cf. Allison, 'Torah, *Urzeit, Endzeit*', pp. 149-97.

53. Cf. Harvey, *Constraints*, pp. 37-51; Booth, *Jesus and the Laws of Purity*, pp. 109-12; Geza Vermes, *The Religion of Jesus the Jew* (London: SCM, 1993), pp. 11-25.

54. Mk 2.15-17; Lk. 7.34/Mt. 11.19; Lk.15.1-2; 19.2-7.

55. Booth, *Jesus and the Laws of Purity*, p. 110; Gnilka, *Jesus of Nazareth*, p. 216.

56. Mk 1.41; 14.3; Lk. 7.22/Mt. 11.5; Lk. 17.11-19; cf. Lev. 13.1-46.

57. Mk 5.35-43; Lk. 7.22/Mt. 11.5; Lk. 7.11-17; Jn 11.1-45; cf. Num. 19.13, 20; Josephus, *Ant.* 18.36-38; Philo, *Spec. Leg.* 3.205-207.

58. One may argue that contraction of impurity would not be a big deal since impurity was part of every day life and cleansing was available through the Mosaic regulations (e.g., Sanders, *Jesus and Judaism*, pp. 182-85). Even so, in an honor-shame culture one's status in the community was assigned by a variety of factors including 'purity'. Thus, in order to maintain one's perceived social status and to protract one's capacity for worship it was advisable to avoid all forms of unnecessary impurity. In light of this Jesus' lack of concern about contracting impurity is shocking and anti-social.

59. In terms of the shift from the question about hand washing to an answer about food, Banks (*Jesus and the Law in the Synoptic Tradition*, p. 140) believes that Jesus takes the debate to a higher level. Alternatively, Booth (*Jesus and the Laws of*

seems a reasonable probability that Mark 7.15 is an authentic utterance of Jesus.[60] It terms of its historical plausibility it makes sense amidst a Jewish context with its concern for food laws and debates about purity and morality. Chilton suggests that the logion can be easily retroverted into Aramaic, which intimates the possibility of an Aramaic source beneath the Marcan text.[61] The thought is verbalized elsewhere[62] and, in Holmen's estimation, 'cross-referenced' by Jesus' conduct of dining with sinners.[63]

On the Jewish background of the logion, the hand washing specified in Mark 7.1-5 looks much like the attempt to make the regulations for priests in Leviticus 22.1-6 (cf. Exod. 30.19-20) applicable to others. Several factors suggest that some Pharisees adopted this custom and were keen for others to do so as well. (1) Despite the fact that the Mishnah tractates *Yadaim* and *Hullin* reflect stipulations pertaining to hand washing and food in the post-70 CE era, they may reflect an earlier halakhic concern. (2) Sanders admits that the Pharisees washed hands prior to Sabbath and festival meals. If so, it is not a long step to washing hands before communal meals, particularly given traditions about the susceptibility of hands to uncleanness.[64] Moreover, Neusner thinks that all Pharisees washed hands before eating ordinary food in the first century.[65] (3) Other texts

Purity, p. 219), Loader (*Jesus' Attitude towards the Law*, p. 76) and R.T. France (*The Gospel of Mark* [NIGTC; Carlisle: Paternoster, 2002], pp. 277-78) think that Jesus responds to a narrow point with a wide principle. Robert H. Gundry (*Mark: A Commentary on His Apology for the Cross* [Grand Rapids, MI: Eerdmans, 1993], p. 354) sees a progression from *how* to eat to *what* to eat.

60. Bultmann, *History of the Synoptic Tradition*, p. 105; Vincent Taylor, *The Gospel According to St. Mark* (London: MacMillan & Co, 1952), pp. 342-43; Norman Perrin, *Rediscovering the Teaching of Jesus* (London: SCM, 1967), p. 70; Banks, *Jesus and the Law in the Synoptic Tradition*, pp. 138-39; Booth, *Jesus and the Laws of Purity*, pp. 108-12; Sanders, *Jewish Law*, p. 28; Loader, *Jesus' Attitude towards the Law*, p. 75; Borg, *Conflict*, pp. 110-11; Theissen and Merz, *Historical Jesus*, pp. 365-67; Tom Holmén, *Jesus and Jewish Covenant Thinking* (BIS, 55; Leiden: Brill 2001), pp. 248-49; Gerd Lüdemann, *Jesus after 2000 Years* (London: SCM, 2000), p. 49.

61. Chilton, 'Jesus, Levitical Purity', p. 359.

62. Lk. 11.39-40/Mt. 23.25-26; *Gos. Thom.* 89 and Mt. 5.8.

63. Holmén, *Jesus and Jewish Covenant Thinking*, pp. 248-49.

64. *m. Ber.* 8.2, 4; *m. Mik.* 1.5-6; James D.G. Dunn, *Jesus Remembered: Christianity in the Making* (Grand Rapids, MI: Eerdmans, 2003), I, p. 572, n. 127; Sanders, *Jewish Law*, p. 31.

65. Neusner, *Purity in Ancient Judaism*, p. 3; idem, *From Politics to Piety*, pp. 83-86; cf. Booth, *Jesus and the Laws of Purity*, pp. 185-86; Gundry, *Mark*, pp. 358-59.

point to a concern about washing hands in relation to prayer that is not mandated in the Hebrew Scriptures.[66] (4) The presence of stone jars used for purification (cf. Jn 2.6) may point to a wider adherence to such washing regulations. (5) The connection between the washing of hands and eating of food is that unclean hands could transmit *derived* impurity to food and render it unclean.[67] (6) Sanders think that although the *haberim* undertook special purity rules, there is no evidence that they expected others to do so.[68] Yet Mark 7.1-5, at face value, should be taken as evidence that some did. The question posed to Jesus may then be a veiled exhortation addressed to another religious leader to undertake a more strenuous form of law observance. In this way, one finds a suitable context for Mark 7.15.[69]

One implication of the logion is supplied by Mark's editorial aside in 7.19c, 'And he declared all foods clean' (καθαρίζων πάντα τὰ βρώματα, lit. 'cleansing all food'). Such a statement is nothing short of radical and at face value implies the entire undermining of not only the purity code but even the invalidity of many (if not most) of the Old Testament regulations.[70] Matthew deliberately omits it due to his Jewish sensitivity. On the

---

66. *Sib. Or.* 3.591-92; 4.165-66; *Ep. Arist.* 305-306; Jdt. 12.7-8.

67. *m. Zab.* 5.12; *m. Yad.* 3.1-2; *m. Tohar.* 2.2.

68. Sanders, *Jesus and Judaism*, pp. 185-86, 264-66; idem, *Jewish Law*, pp. 39-40, 261-63; cf. Booth, *Jesus and the Laws of Purity*, p. 202.

69. Booth, *Jesus and the Laws of Purity*, p. 202; Crossley, *Date of Mark's Gospel*, p. 184.

70. Crossley (*The Date of Mark's Gospel*, pp. 191-93,) thinks that Mk 7.19 does not imply the abolishment of the food laws which forms part of his thesis that Mark was composed in an era when Christians remained law-observant (i.e., early 40s CE). He surmises that Mk 7.15, 19 is a follow up from 7.1-13 which attacks the role of handwashing, so the point of the episode is that food eaten with unwashed hands does not render one unclean. Crossley's attempt to take Mark anything other than 'literally' on this point is problematic for several reasons: (1) If the statement about food in Mk 7.19 only concerns the consumption of food *without* handwashing, then it would hardly offend Jewish scruples and Matthew's omission of the phrase is needless. Crossley acknowledges that Matthew omits Mk 7.19 precisely to avoid the conclusion that the purity laws are rejected. Matthew apparently does this because Christians in his day were not law-observant (p. 201). Perhaps so, and maybe one of those Christians was Mark. In which case Mt. 15.20 ('but eating with unwashed hands does not make him unclean') is not an elaboration of Mark, but more likely an urgent qualification that strives to avoid the implication that Jewish Christians no longer have to honour the food laws. (2) The attempt to demonstrate that the 'all' of 'all foods' is merely rhetorical fails. True, texts like *Ep. Arist.* 234

assumption that Mark was writing for Gentile readers (hence his explanation of the customs in 7.3-4), such a statement could arguably be taken to mean: 'For you *Gentiles*, he declares all foods clean so you do not have to follow Jewish customs'.[71] The coherence with Romans 14.14, 20 would see Mark adopting a Pauline perspective on Gentiles and the food laws and not an abrogation of the law *in toto*, at least not for Jewish believers.[72]

However, some see in Mark 7.15 a deliberate abrogation of the purity laws.[73] This is unlikely on both the horizon of Mark's theology and of the historical Jesus. If annulling the food laws were the intended purpose of

and Sir. 36.23 are radical but need to be understood in their broader context. But Mk 7.19 lacks the comparative or dialectic structure of these sayings meaning that its radicality is not qualified. (3) It is not certain that the remarks about food in Mk 7.15, 19 relate back directly to comments about washing in Mk 7.1-13. The link between food and washing can be made in other ways (see esp. Gundry, *Mark*, p. 354). (4) The coherence between Mk 7.19 and Rom. 14.14, 20 is evidence that such statements were taken to mean that the 'strong' (i.e., Gentiles or Jewish Christians like Paul) did not have to obey the food laws if they did not want to. (5) Crossley thinks that if Mark wanted to abrogate the food laws he would have chosen a much more direct way of doing it. But for many others and myself, Mk 7.19 is rather direct indeed.

71. Banks, *Jesus and the Law in the Synoptic Tradition*, p. 145-46; Booth, *Jesus and the Laws of Purity*, pp. 220-21; Gundry, *Mark*, p. 348; Sanders, *Historical Figure of Jesus*, p. 223; Loader, *Jesus' Attitude towards the Law*, p. 71; Holmén, *Jesus and Jewish Covenant Thinking*, pp. 245-46; Dunn, *Jesus Remembered*, p. 575.

72. Taylor, *St. Mark*, pp. 346-47; Booth, *Jesus and the Laws of Purity*, p. 221; Jesper Svartvik, *Mark and Mission: Mk 7:1-23 in its Narrative and Historical Contexts* (ConBNT, 32; Stockholm: Almqvist & Wiksell, 2000), pp. 344-47; France, *Mark*, p. 278; David J. Rudolph, 'Jesus and the Food Laws: A Reassessment of Mark 7:19b', *EvQ* 74 (2002), pp. 304-308; Vermes, *Jesus and the World of Judaism*, p. 46.

73. Joseph Klausner, *Jesus of Nazareth: His Life, Times, and Teachings* (trans. Herbert Danby; London: Allen & Unwin, 1929), p. 291; Ernst Käsemann, 'The Problem of the Historical Jesus', p. 39; Eduard Schweizer, *Jesus* (trans. David E. Green; London: SCM, 1971), pp. 32-33; Gundry, *Mark*, p. 356; Loader, *Jesus' Attitude towards the Law*, pp. 74-79; John Riches, *Jesus and the Transformation of Judaism* (London: Darton, Longman & Todd, 1980), p. 136; Joel Marcus, *Mark 1–8* (AB; New York: Doubleday, 2000), pp. 453-54; Moo, 'Law', p. 454. Bank's (*Jesus and the Law in the Synoptic Tradition*, p. 141) contention is that Jesus neither attacks the law nor affirms it, but his remark moves in a complete different reality regarding what does or does not constitute defilement. However, as Booth (*Jesus and the Laws of Purity*, p. 104) points out, it is difficult to impose a new definition of purity without somehow criticizing a pre-existing one.

the saying then it would be an anomaly in the Jesus tradition.[74] It would also seem that Mark has not failed to notice the incongruity of having Jesus attack the Pharisees for nullifying the law in favour of their tradition, only to have Jesus nullify the law in reference to food regulations. Mark's concern is probably not a total sweeping away of the law. The parenthesis in 7.19c probably indicates the significance of the saying for Gentiles and his remark would indicate that his position is a logical step from Jesus' utterance. Furthermore, the pervasiveness to which the purity code was followed by Jews in the Mediterranean and the 'constraint' of Jesus' general adherence to the law make such an abrogation by him improbable. Additionally, if the historical Jesus had spoken so clearly on the issue of abrogating the food laws then why was food such a disputed topic in the early church and why didn't they simply refer back to sayings of Jesus to settle the matter? The most reasonable solution is because Jesus never said such a thing.[75]

A better way to understand Mark 7.15 is in a comparative sense whereby the point is 'not only...but also'.[76] Understood this way, what matters is not only cultic purity, but also moral purity. The point is that cultic impurity does not harm someone as much as moral impurity can. A similar dialectic structure is found in *Aristeas* where it is reported that Jews 'honour God not only with gifts and sacrifices, but also with a purity of heart'.[77] On the one hand, the logion maintains a unity between internal

---

74. Jeremias, *New Testament Theology*, p. 210.

75. Cf. Banks, *Jesus and the Law in the Synoptic Tradition*, pp. 140-41; Harvey, *Constraints*, p. 39; Sanders, *Jesus and Judaism*, pp. 246, 249-50, 266; idem, *Historical Figure of Jesus*, pp. 220-22; Vermes, *Religion of Jesus the Jew*, pp. 25-26; Fredriksen, 'Did Jesus Oppose the Purity Laws?' p. 25; idem, *Jesus of Nazareth*, p. 108; N.T. Wright, *Jesus and the Victory of God* (Minneapolis: Fortress, 1996), pp. 380-82; Holmén, *Jesus and Jewish Covenant Thinking*, p. 243.

76. Ben F. Meyer, *The Aims of Jesus* (London: SCM, 1979), p. 149; Booth, *Jesus and the Laws of Purity*, pp. 69-71, 84-85, 218; Sanders, *Jewish Law*, p. 28; idem, *Jesus and Judaism*, p. 260; idem, *Historical Figure of Jesus*, 219; Loader, *Jesus' Attitude towards the Law*, pp. 215-16; McKnight, 'A Parting within the Way', p. 93, n. 15; Svartvik, *Mark and Mission*, pp. 203, 406; Holmén, *Jesus and Jewish Covenant Thinking*, p. 241; Rudolph, 'Jesus and the Food Laws', p. 298; BDF § 448, n. 1. Against this perspective is Ben Witherington, *Christology of Jesus* (Minneapolis: Fortress Press, 1990), p. 64; Gundry, *Mark*, p. 365; Theissen, *Shadow of the Galilean*, p. 102; Theissen and Merz, *The Historical Jesus*, p. 366; and France, *Mark*, p. 289.

77. *Ep. Arist.* 234; cf. Pseudo-Phocyclides 228; Philo, *Spec. Leg.* 3.208-209; and the tradition attributed to Johanan ben Zakkai in *Num. Rab.* 19.8.

disposition and outward acts.[78] But on the other hand, the element designated by 'but also' (moral purity) is elevated in importance over the first
element (ritual purity). Purity is not negated by shifting it from cultic to
moral realms,[79] but is redefined or prioritized in terms of relations of persons rather than exclusively by ritual contamination through objects and
space. Such a redefinition is memorialized powerfully in the parable of
the Good Samaritan (Lk. 10.30-37).[80]

The saying, then, is probably an attempt to articulate the relationship
between morality and purity. Was impurity sinful?[81] In one sense impurity
was simply part of daily life whether it was from menstruation for women
or burying a deceased relative and for that reason it was not intrinsically
sinful. Torah allowed for the reintegration of persons who were temporar-
ily impure for a time. However, it should be borne in mind that ancient
cultures, Judaism in particular, did not always know of a rigid distinction
between ethics and purity or belief and ritual.[82] Moral and ceremonial
impurity were not always distinguished. Ritual language for cleansing is
frequently used of sin.[83] On the Day of Atonement the high priest made
amends for the impurity *and* transgressions of the people (Lev. 16.16,
30). Furthermore, ritual impurity could be seen as sinful to that extent that
ritual expressed one's piety and adherence to purity laws was com-
manded.[84] Religious observance while in a state of impurity was sinful.[85]
The equation of ritual with moral impurity was heightened in some
contexts such as Qumran.[86] Philo saw a philosophical connection between

78. Scot McKnight, *A New Vision for Israel: The Teachings of Jesus in National
Context* (Grand Rapids, MI: Eerdmans, 1999), p. 214.

79. Chilton, 'Jesus, Levitical Purity', p. 363.

80. McKnight, 'A Parting within the Way', p. 94.

81. Contrast Holmén, *Jesus and Jewish Covenant Thinking*, pp. 224, 230-31 with
Sanders, *Jesus and Judaism*, pp. 182-83; Fredriksen, 'Did Jesus Oppose the Purity
Laws?' pp. 22-24; Svartvik, *Mark and Mission*, pp. 354-75. Kazen (*Jesus and
Purity Halakhah*, 219) argues that there was '*some* sort of interaction or link between
sin and bodily impurity'. John Dominic Crossan and Jonathan L. Reed (*Excavating
Jesus: Beneath the Stones, Behind the Texts* [San Francisco: Harper, 2001], pp. 166-68)
argue that one cannot equate pure and impure with virtue and vice, but purity and
justice do go hand in hand.

82. Neusner, *Purity in Ancient Judaism*, p. 2; Holmén, *Jesus and Jewish Covenant
Thinking*, p. 230, n. 213.

83. Lev. 16.30; Num. 8.7; Zech. 13.1; Prov. 20.9; *Pss. Sol.* 8.12; 1QS 3.7-8.

84. Lev. 19.8; 22.9; *Num. Rab.* 19.8; Josephus, *Ant.* 3.262; Philo, *Spec. Leg.* 3.209.

85. Isa. 6.7; *1 En.* 5.4; *Pss. Sol.* 8.12-13.

86. Klawans, *Impurity and Sin in Ancient Judaism*, pp. 108-109; for an example:

moral and ritual purity.[87] Early Christianity retained the similar ideas pertaining to purification and the removal of sin.[88] The use of the language of impurity to describe immorality is more than metaphorical because transgression of the law produces a genuine defilement with consequences of the cultus, people, priesthood, land and the perpetrator.[89] It is arguably this nexus between morality and purity that Jesus addresses.

It is misleading and inaccurate to suppose that Jews divided the law into civil, ceremonial, and moral components and to think that Jesus abrogated the ceremonial aspects in favour of the moral code.[90] For the Jews, law was law, an indissoluble unity. The Torah was divinely given and had to be obeyed in its entirety. Even so, there was in existence a tradition of criticizing merely outward forms of religious display, in both the Hebrew sacred scriptures and in intertestamental literature.[91] The interiorizing of the commandments was nothing new to Judaism (e.g., 'circumcise your hearts').[92] Thus, a purely outward or ceremonial expression of Jewish religion performed in isolation from morality is censured in prophetic, rabbinic, sapiential and apocalyptic writings. The *Tannaim* arguably 'compartmentalized' ritual and moral purity to some extent.[93] That means (contra Sanders) that it is possible to make a distinction within the law even if such a distinction cannot be expressed in anachronistic terms like civil, ceremonial and moral.[94] As such, Mark 7.15 (and the citation of

'He said to me, Carefully avoid all ritual impurity and every kind of sin' (1Q121 B.8-9).

87. Philo, *Migr.* 89; *Spec. Leg.* 3.208-209; cf. Booth, *Jesus and the Laws of Purity*, pp. 84-85; Klawans, *Impurity and Sin in Ancient Judaism*, pp. 64-65.

88. Acts 15.9; 2 Cor. 7.1; Heb. 10.1-4; Jas. 4.8; 1 Jn 1.9

89. Bryan, *Jesus and Israel's Traditions*, p. 144.

90. Cf. Moo, 'Law', p. 454; and Kazen, *Jesus and Purity Halakhah*, pp. 218-19 against Neusner's difference between literal and metaphorical impurity and Klawans' difference between ritual and moral purity.

91. Hos. 6.6; Jer. 7.22-24; Zech. 7.4-14; *Num. Rab.* 19.8; Prov. 21.3; Sir. 34.25-26; 1QS 3.2-12; Josephus, *Apion* 2.173; *Jub.* 23.21; *T.Mos.* 7.7-9; Philo, *Spec. Leg.* 3.208-209; Mt. 9.13; 12.7; Heb. 10.8. Cf. Holmén, *Jesus and Jewish Covenant Thinking*, pp. 230-31, n. 213.

92. Vermes (*Jesus and the World of Judaism*, p. 47) contends that while interiority was not unique to Jesus, it did play a greater role in his ministry due to his stress on 'eschatological finality'.

93. Klawans, *Impurity and Sin*, pp. 93-94.

94. Sanders, *Jesus and Judaism*, p. 247. We could add that the Nazoreans or Nazarenes kept the law but noted valid and invalid parts of it (Epiphanius, *Adv. Haer.* 39.5.4). If we knew which parts they thought were invalid and why, it would potentially illuminate our understanding of law in early Christianity. But this

Isa. 29.13 in Mk 7.6-8) fits neatly into Second-Temple Judaism and can be understood as warning against elevating purity over morality. Such a statement corresponds with other complexes in the Jesus tradition such as the beatitudes, 'Blessed are the pure in heart'[95] and the woe against the Pharisees who 'clean the outside of the cup and plate, but inside they are full of greed and self indulgence'.[96] In such statements Jesus is no more trying to abrogate the law than Hosea or Sirach.[97]

There is a measure of ambiguity, perhaps deliberately, in this Jesuanic *mashal*. Thus Mark interprets this saying in light of his Gentile audience with a view to their freedom from Jewish food laws, while Matthew perceives in the logion an affirmation of the superior morality of the Jewish law and a powerful critique of the Pharisees.[98] Holmén points out that Jesus' actions do not stem from a desire to abolish the distinction between clean and unclean, but they do reveal a marginalization of them in view of moral commands.[99] It is noteworthy that relativization can still yield the same practical outcome as abolishment: non-observance. Dunn goes so far as to state that the distinctive features of the Marcan version οὐδέν... ἔξωθεν...δύναται makes abandonment of the food laws inevitable.[100] That was a corollary not followed by all Jewish Christians, but the Pauline missiological principle of non-law adherence for Gentiles stands to some degree in continuity with the implications of Mark 7.15.[101]

---

demonstrates concretely that while Jews could talk about weightier matters of the law, some Christians (Gentiles and Jews) were discussing the validity of certain aspects of it in the post-Easter era.

95. Mt. 5.8; cf. *2 En.* 45.3.

96. Lk. 11.39-40/Mt. 23.25-26; *Gos. Thom.* 89.

97. Cf. Bockmuehl, *Jewish Law*, p. 10; Klawans, *Impurity and Sin*, p. 147.

98. Banks, *Jesus and the Law in the Synoptic Tradition*, pp. 145-46; Booth, *Jesus and the Laws of Purity*, pp. 220-23; Dunn, *Jesus Remembered*, p. 575.

99. Holmén, *Jesus and Jewish Covenant Thinking*, pp. 236-37; and see Klausner, *Jesus of Nazareth*, pp. 255, 367; Theissen and Merz, *The Historical Jesus*, pp. 230, 361; Kazen, *Jesus and Purity Halakhah*, pp. 256-60; Klawans, *Impurity and Sin*, pp. 146-50. The view of Gnilka (*Jesus of Nazareth*, p. 215) that Jesus saw the laws of cultic purity 'irrelevant' and Westerholm (*Jesus and Scribal Authority*, pp. 90-91) that Jesus was 'religiously indifferent' to them go too far.

100. James D.G. Dunn, *Jesus, Paul and the Law* (London: SPCK, 1990), p. 41.

101. Sanders (*Jesus and Judaism*, pp. 247-50) thinks that Jesus would not have said such a thing because he would have been aware that making a distinction within the law and elevating one part over another would lead to non-observance of the law in the future. Even if Jesus did foresee the implication that Mark draws (and let it be said that anything the historical Jesus believed let alone what he could have envisaged is shifting into the realm of speculation) there is nothing to say that he

The question remains as to what drove this radical new redefinition of purity. A portrait of the future Israel that emerges in Zechariah is that of an Israel purified by the eschatological outpouring of God's holiness on his people, and Jesus may have drawn upon this view. The eschatological hope of Zechariah is for a fountain that gushes forth water from Jerusalem in order to offer forgiveness and cleansing (Zech. 13.1; 14.8). The concluding scene in Zechariah is one where everything, even the most mundane of objects, becomes pure (Zech. 14.20-21).[102] This Zecharian vision of holiness has arguably become a controlling principle for Jesus' ministry where it drives the redefinition of purity *within Judaism* as it is holiness rather than impurity that acts as a *contagion*. Much like the gushing out of water from Jerusalem in Zechariah, 'Jesus, by touching people, turns them from impure Israelites into pure Israelites'.[103]

In sum, Jesus' critique of the Pharisees or *haberim* is twofold. First, he rejects their expansive interpretation of the purity laws, that is, eating food as priestly food and expecting others to do the same.[104] Second, Jesus refuses to make adherence to a distinctive application of food laws a test case for covenant loyalty.[105] The food laws functioned in many ways as a badge of Jewish identity, for the Pharisees and Qumranites their distinctive food practices operated to demarcate them from other Jews and perhaps were used to define themselves as the true keepers of the covenant. These criticisms are anchored in Jesus' understanding of morality and purity, his view of holiness rather than impurity acting as a contagion, and arguably influenced by ideas of eschatological holiness in prophetic literature.

would have opposed the idea of non-Jews joining his movement without submitting to the entire Mosaic code. In line with biblical literature, Jesus might have anticipated the eschatological pilgrimage of the Gentiles (e.g., Isa. 2.2-4; Mic. 4.1-4; Jer. 3.17-18; Zech. 8.21-23) who join the returning Jewish exiles in worshipping God but without first becoming proselytes to Judaism (cf. Mt. 8.5-13; Mk 4.32; Lk. 4.25-27). See Hengel and Deines, 'E.P. Sanders', p. 15.

102. Bruce D. Chilton, *The Temple of Jesus: His Sacrificial Program within a Cultural History of Sacrifice*. University Park, PA: Pennsylvania State University Press, 1992), p. 136; McKnight, 'A Parting within the Way', pp. 87-88.

103. McKnight, 'A Parting within the Way', p. 95.

104. Borg, *Conflict*, p. 112; Svartvik, *Mark and Mission*, p. 406; Theissen and Merz, *The Historical Jesus*, p. 229.

105. Holmén, *Jesus and Jewish Covenant Thinking*, pp. 236-37, 251; Dunn, *Jesus Remembered*, pp. 576-77.

Conclusion

Several pertinent observations can be drawn from this study about Jesus and Torah.

(1) Jesus and his followers were regarded as law-breakers by their Jewish contemporaries. The taunt of being a law-breaker continued to be used against Christians in the post-Easter period culminating in the martyrdom of James the Just.

(2) In the Gospels Jesus is depicted as both radical in setting aside elements of Torah but also conservative in intensifying some commands further. The more radical sayings about the Sabbath and disregarding the duty to bury of one's parents were not an attempt to abrogate Torah. Instead, they were issued out of Jesus' conviction that where the mission of the kingdom and Torah conflicted the Torah had to give way. The intensifications of certain commands (e.g., prohibition on divorce and antitheses) were anchored in the view that the kingdom would transform human existence to an edenic state that would render many of the Mosaic regulations redundant. What is more, Jesus ordered his followers to start living as if the edenic conditions were already a reality. Importantly, relaxation and intensification of the law is a standard feature of Jewish renewal movements.[106]

(3) The debate about purity in Mark 7.1-23 represents an interiorizing of purity by Jesus so that external purity is not abrogated but relativized. What Jesus opposed was the *halakhah* of the Pharisees and not Torah itself. Jesus' pronouncements about purity were not a pretext for condemning legalism and externalism.[107] Jesus would have censured self-righteousness if he encountered it (Mt. 23.1-39/Lk. 11.37-54; Lk. 18.9-14), but so would have other Jews (1QS 11.11-15; 15.18-20; Philo, *Sacr.* 54-57). Accordingly, Jesus refuses to make distinctive approaches to food and purity the markers of covenant identity and a criterion for participation in the eschatological kingdom.

(4) It is difficult to determine to what extent Jesus' reputation as a law-breaker contributed to his arrest, trial and death.[108] It was Jesus' Temple action that finally drove the authorities to seek his execution. Nevertheless,

106. Gerd Theissen, *The Sociology of Palestinian Christianity* (Philadelphia: Fortress Press, 1978), pp. 75-79; Bockmuehl, *Jewish Law*, p. 10.

107. The view that Jesus' disputes were mainly over legalism persists still (Gnilka, *Jesus of Nazareth*, pp. 216, 219-20).

108. Cf. Jeremias, *New Testament Theology*, p. 211.

Jesus' view of Torah and the Temple, two of the pillars of Judaism, were probably used against him at his trial in order to substantiate the charge that he was leading Israel astray.[109]

(5) Finally, the invective remark of Jesus being a law-breaker ultimately derives from a negative evaluation of Jesus' own eschatology and Christology. Jesus can set the kingdom against Torah or *halakhah* on certain occasions, but he does so only because he understands himself to be invested with unmediated divine authority and because he alone is the broker of the coming kingdom. Conflicts about Torah ensue out of Jesus' contention that the kingdom is in some sense present and is also ready to burst upon the world and transform the structures of human existence. It is Jesus' unique role in relation to the kingdom that propels him into intra-Jewish debates about what constitutes covenant fidelity in light of the current eschatological climate. What is more, Jesus' attitude towards the law reveals something of his sense of special authority. In Jewish thought, Torah embodies and reveals the *will* and *wisdom* of God (e.g., Sir. 24.1-23; Bar. 3.29–4.1; *4 Macc.* 1.16-17). Yet in the antitheses, 'You have heard it said...but I say to you' (Mt. 5.21-48), Jesus speaks not merely as one who fulfils Torah or who can provide the proper interpretation of Torah, but as one who is uniquely ranked and can mandate what God truly requires of his people. Similarly, in John 5.1-47, the charge of breaking the Sabbath shifts from an accusation of lawlessness to one of blasphemy. In other words, Jesus speaks about the law and acts towards the law as if he is, in some sense, to be identified with the God who legislated it. Debates about Jesus and the law (both during and after his lifetime) were indebted to the claim that Jesus was the eschatological fulfiller of the law, he provided its proper interpretation, and he spoke about it with a divine authority. This is paralleled by Paul, who announced that Christ was the 'end of the law' (Rom. 10.4); Jesus' teachings on discipleship are described as the 'law of Christ' (1 Cor. 9.21; Gal. 6.2), and Jesus himself embodies the heavenly Wisdom normally associated with the law (1 Cor. 1.30).

---

109. *b. Sanh.* 43a; Mk 14.58 (and par.); Lk. 23.2; Jn 11.47-48.

JESUS AS DEMON-POSSESSED

Dwight D. Sheets

Introduction

> Then they brought to him a demoniac who was blind and mute; and he
> cured him, so that the one who had been mute could speak and see. All
> the crowds were amazed and said, 'Can this be the Son of David?' But
> when the Pharisees heard it, they said, 'It is only by Beelzebul, the ruler
> of the demons, that this fellow casts out the demons.' (Mt. 12.22-24)

According to Morton Smith the accusation that Jesus cast out demons by
Beelzebul was the most important of all for understanding the complaints
against him. 'Take it away, and all that remains is a collection of unrelated complaints, most of them not very serious; introduce it, and the complaints can be seen as component elements of a comprehensive structure.'[1]
Indeed, in the setting of first-century Palestinian Judaism the accusation
would have been quite damning; the rumor alone would have been damaging to one's reputation. In the attempt to do Christology 'from the side' this
study will probe the question as to why Jesus' opponents made this particular accusation. The answer *seems* obvious; it was a malicious charge
intended to ruin him. To the believing reader, Jesus' accusers look far
worse than the one they accuse, for mistakenly or not they have attributed
his works to a wholly evil source. To this accusation Jesus responds that
they are in danger of blaspheming the Holy Spirit, something he deemed
unforgivable.

It is not the purpose of this study to understand Jesus' response to the
allegation made by his opponents. What Jesus may have meant by a sin
that 'will not be forgiven', is the subject of another study. The purpose is
to consider the underlying reasons that motivated Jesus' opponents to
make the accusation that he worked in league with demons. Why did the
scribes deem Jesus' exorcisms as participation with evil and yet consider

---

1. Morton Smith, *Jesus the Magician* (London: Gollancz, 1978), p. 31.

the work of other Jewish exorcists to be admirable Jewish therapy?[2] The question is important because it cuts to the heart of our subject: how did Jesus' opponents perceive him? Our goal is to understand the thought process that led Jesus, the messianic deliverer to his followers, to be seen as a minion of Satan by his opponents.

The accusation that Jesus worked in league with demons occurs in Q, Mark and John.[3] For reason of space the discussion will be limited to four Synoptic accounts, Matthew 9.32; 12.22, Mark 3.22, and Luke 11.14, sections commonly referred to as the *Beelzebul* controversy. The study will begin with analysis of the texts in question to ask the critical questions regarding their sources, context, and authenticity. The second section consists of a review and critique of Malina and Neyrey's very popular socio-anthropological interpretation of demon-possession accusations. The final section of the study explores a further idea, one that probes the development of Jewish eschatological themes and considers the possibility that the accusation may have its source in antecedent eschatological antagonist traditions. In this section the idea is put forward that Jesus' opponents had theological reasons for the accusation; their confrontation with Jesus' ministry advanced the conclusion that he, in league with Satan, was acting in ways similar to an eschatological antagonist.

Review of the Texts

Matthew 9.32-34	Matthew 12.22-24	Mark 3.20	Luke 11.14-15
'After they had gone away, a demoniac who was mute was brought to him. And when the demon had been cast out, the one who had been mute spoke; and the crowds were amazed and said, "Never has anything like this	'Then they brought to him a demoniac who was blind and mute; and he cured him, so that the one who had been mute could speak and see. All the crowds were amazed and said, "Can this be the Son of David?" But when the Pharisees heard it,	came together again, so that they could not even eat. When his family heard it, they went out to restrain him, for people were saying, "He has gone out of his mind". And the scribes who came down from Jerusalem said, 'and the crowd	'Now he was casting out a demon that was mute; when the demon had gone out, the one who had been mute spoke, and the crowds were amazed.

But some of them said, "He casts out demons by |

---

2. The question asked by Smith, *Jesus the Magician*, p. 143.
3. Mt. 9.32; 10.25; 12.24; Mk 3.22; Lk. 11.14; Jn 7.20; 8.48, 52; 10.20.

Matthew 9.32-34	Matthew 12.22-24	Mark 3.20	Luke 11.14-15
been seen in Israel". But the Pharisees said, "By the ruler of the demons he casts out the demons".'	they said, "It is only by Beelzebul, the ruler of the demons, that this fellow casts out the demons".'	"He has Beelzebul, and by the ruler of the demons he casts out the demons".'	Beelzebul, the ruler of the demons".'

The authenticity of the *Beelzebul* accusation is not often disputed.[4] Although redactional elements are present, it is generally agreed that the story reflects the *Sitz im Leben Jesu*. The name *Beelzebul*, although not found in the literature prior to the gospels, reflects the language of a Palestinian environment. The use of the name was not common to Judaism or the earliest Christian circles. The content of the accusation argues for its authenticity since the preservation of a tradition that accused Jesus of being demon-possessed would have been an embarrassment.[5] The fact that the *Beelzebul* accusation has multiple attestations in both its sources and literary forms (note Mt. 10.25) argues for its authenticity and for its frequency as an accusation made against Jesus.[6] The questions asked of these texts have not so much to do with their authenticity as they do with the explanation for accusation.

The relationship of the Synoptic accounts of the *Beelzebul* controversy is complex. Common to all is the remark 'By the ruler of the demons he casts out the demons' (Mt. 9.34, ἐν τῷ ἄρχοντι τῶν δαιμονίων ἐκβάλλει τὰ δαιμόνια). To this phrase Matthew 12.24 and Luke 11.14 insert the name *Beelzebul*, identifying him as the ruler of demons.[7] There are also

4. The Jesus Seminar lists the *Beelzebul* controversy as one of the ten authentic acts of Jesus. R. Funk, *The Acts of Jesus: The Search for the Authentic Deeds of Jesus* (San Francisco: Harper San Francisco, 1999), p. 566. Luke's account receives a red rating, Matthew and Mark a pink.

5. A point well argued by G. Stanton, *The Gospel and Jesus* (Oxford: Oxford University Press, 1989), pp. 174-77. R. Gundry, *Mark: A Commentary for His Apology of the Cross* (Grand Rapids, Eerdmans, 1993), p. 180, states: 'it seems likely that Christian piety would have kept Mark or an earlier tradition from fabricating such a charge'; see too J. Meier, *A Marginal Jew*. II. *Mentor, Message, and Miracles* (New York: Doubleday, 1994), p. 625.

6. Mt. 10.25 is a didactic pericope outside the controversy accounts which seems to reflect an independent tradition. W.D. Davies, D.A. Allison, *The Gospel According to Matthew* (ICC, 2; eds J.A. Emerton, C.B.E. Cranfield, and G.N. Stanton; Edinburgh: T&T Clark, 1991), p. 193, consider Mt. 10.25 to be dominical.

7. Matthew = ἐν τῷ Βεελζεβοὺλ ἄρχοντι...and Luke = ἐν Βεελζεβοὺλ τῷ ἄρχοντι...

distinct differences. Mark's account differs dramatically from the others in its context and wording. Although an exorcism occurs in Mark 3.11, unlike the others the exorcism of a mute in the immediate context is not that which elicits the charge of the scribes. Rather, in Mark the charge is elicited by the concern of Jesus' family that he was 'out of his mind' (ἐξέστη).[8] The scribes from Jerusalem agreed; their diagnosis was that 'he has *Beelzebul*' (Βεελζεβοὺλ ἔχει).[9] The reason for the visit of scribes from Jerusalem is debated. Lane seems correct that it 'suggests that the Galilean mission of Jesus had attracted the critical attention of the Sanhedrin'.[10] Their inclusion in the narrative implies that Jesus' ministry had become a crisis for both his family and also the religious authorities.[11]

Matthew has two independent exorcism accounts.[12] Matthew 9.32-34 appears to be from Q, and except for a few details, has much in common with Luke 11.14-15.[13] Luke lacks a comment of the amazed crowd ('Never has anything like this been seen in Israel') and identifies some of them as Jesus' accusers. Conversely, Matthew 9.32-24 lacks the name *Beelzebul* and identifies the Pharisees as Jesus' accusers. Matthew 12.22-24 differs in that his demoniac is both mute *and* blind and not exorcized but 'cured'. Like Matthew 9.32, the demoniac is brought to Jesus, but his cure brings a more focused response from the amazed crowd ('Can this be the Son of

8.   Gundry, *Mark*, p. 171. Polybius, *Histories*, 26.1a, notes a similar accusation against Antiochus IV who was called '*epimanes*' by his enemies rather than his title '*epiphanies*'.

9.   R. Guelich, *Mk 1–8.26* (WBC, 34a; ed. B.M. Metzger; Dallas: Word Books, 1989), pp. 171, 173, 'the presence of the charge makes the most sense when taken as Mark's redactional bridge from his inserted material regarding Jesus' ministry of exorcism (3:22c–29) to the previous context of 3:20–21 by linking "his people's" charge in 3:21b with that of the "scribes".'

10.   W. Lane, *The Gospel According to Mark* (NICNT; ed. F.F. Bruce; Grand Rapids: Eerdmans, 1974), p. 141. Note too Gundry, *Mark*, pp. 171-72, who adds that the scribes came from Jerusalem in response 'to the great multitude that flocked to Jesus "from Jerusalem"' (p. 172).

11.   Gundry, *Mark*, p. 172, suggests that the mention of scribes 'perhaps looks forward to the scribes in Jerusalem who will help engineer his crucifixion (8.31; 10.33; 11.18, 27-28; 14.1, 43, 53; 15.1, 31 cf. also 7.1)'.

12.   D.A. Hagner, *Matthew 1-13* (WBC; ed. R.P Martin; Dallas, TX: Word Books, 1993), p. 256, 'Probably we have here two originally independent stories of demon exorcism that have taken the same form'.

13.   J. Fitzmyer, *The Gospel According to Luke* (Anchor Bible 28-28A; 2 vol.; Garden City, NY: Doubleday, 1981–85), pp. 917-18, believes that Luke has 'by and large preserved the wording of "Q"'.

David?').[14] The Pharisees in both Matthean accounts are Jesus' accusers, but in 12.24 the Pharisees respond 'after hearing' (ἀκούσαντες) the disturbing question of the crowd.

It is significant that in Matthew and Luke the accusation against Jesus follows the response of the crowd. The charge does not appear 'out of thin air'; it was made because his opponents were distressed by the crowd's response to his miraculous works. Not unlike Mark, the response was to a crisis. Jesus' opponents perceived that the people were being led astray and were forced to render a verdict on the legitimacy of his works. They cannot deny the miracle; indeed, they never try, but are forced to give an explanation. It is necessary, then, to consider the origin and nature of their explanation.

Sociological Explanation: Demon-Possession Accusations as a Means of Controlling Social Deviants

An influential socio-anthropological study of the purpose and function of name-calling in Matthew was undertaken by Bruce Malina and Jerome Neyrey in their book *Calling Jesus Names: The Social Value of Labels in Matthew*.[15] Via the use of Mary Douglas'[16] social-scientific deviance model, the authors view the accusations of demon possession from the background of ancient Mediterranean 'witchcraft societies'. In these societies labeling someone a deviant (i.e., a 'witch') served as a medium of control. By attributing such evil to one's opponents, the hope was to lessen their influence and hopefully gain their expulsion from the group.[17]

The authors propose that the early Matthean community[18] reflected Douglas' sociological variables of a 'strong group' with a 'low grid'.

14. Note, however, the same theme in the blind men's cry in the preceding context of Mt. 9.32-34; 'Have mercy on us, Son of David!' (Mt. 9.27).

15. Bruce J. Malina and Jerome Neyrey, *Calling Jesus Names: The Social Value of Labels in Matthew* (Foundations and Social Facets; Sonoma, CA: Polebridge Press, 1988).

16. A list of Douglas' works can be seen at http.//www.unine.ch/ethno/biblio/2000douglas.html.

17. Malina and Neyrey, *Calling Jesus Names*, p. 4. In the gospels these accusations are made not only *against* Jesus, but also *by* Jesus and his followers against their opponents (Mt. 10.28; 12.43-46; 13.34; 23.15).

18. Malina and Neyrey, *Calling Jesus Names*, pp. 5-6, believe the witchcraft accusations against Jesus are 'found primarily in a stage of Matthew's history considerably earlier than its final form'. By this they refer to Q as being the most 'faction-focused' layer of tradition in Matthew.

'Group' refers to the pressure individuals within the community feel to conform to societal norms. A 'strong' group is a controlled system that values order and discipline, where an individual's primary identity is derived from the group. 'Grid' refers to 'the degree of ascent given to group norms, definitions and classifications of a cultural system'.[19] A 'low' grid indicates 'a poor degree of fit and match between individual experiences and stated societal patterns and experience'. The world 'is incomprehensible and fraught with contradictions'.[20] Strong group/low grid societies provide a cultural system fertile for witchcraft accusations.

Matthew's strong group/low grid society was defined according to the general social scientific categories of purity, ritual, personal identity, body, deviance, cosmology, and suffering and misfortune. The authors conclude that the community was a small tightly-controlled reform movement that considered purity and perfection its hallmark. Social stereotyping labeled individuals according to their group identity; boundaries were clear and strictly maintained. Its cosmology was 'profoundly dualistic'; the individual body and world at large were the arena of warring factions. Much energy was spent guarding against inner-group polluting elements. Deviants were exposed through discernment; their hypocrisy and evil made necessary their expulsion from the group.[21]

Further specific characteristics of witchcraft societies are also considered.[22] Within witchcraft societies competing groups lived in continuous close proximity to other rival groups. No one group possessed the power to silence or expel the other. Authority between groups and among group members was ill-defined, eliciting conflicting claims to power. Because of this intense disorderly confrontations were common, and yet no techniques had been established for regulating disputes and settling claims. Discernment was used to expose the presence of deviants who polluted the community.[23]

19. Malina and Neyrey, *Calling Jesus Names*, p. 8.

20. Malina and Neyrey, *Calling Jesus Names*, p. 8.

21. Malina and Neyrey, *Calling Jesus Names*, pp. 11-23. These social characteristics were those shared by Jesus' opponents; as such the social characteristics of Jesus' followers were those of his opponents.

22. Malina and Neyrey, *Calling Jesus Names*, p. 25. Douglas lists these categories as 'clearly drawn external boundaries, confused internal relations, close and continual interaction, poorly developed tension relieving techniques, weak authority and disorderly but intense conflict'.

23. Malina and Neyrey, *Calling Jesus Names*, p. 27, note that Jesus himself exercised the same type of discernment when he 'saw faith' and 'knew the thoughts' of his opponents.

Jesus was labeled a deviant because he acted outside of his social role by being physically mobile. Indeed, the Jesus-movement all witnessed to the fact that its central characters were deviants because of their physical mobility. Because stereotyping was inherent among strong group/low grid societies, a deviant status was applied to his entire group.[24] Jesus' deviance called for a social verdict. Some judged his mobility to mean that he was a wandering 'prophet' or 'teacher', while others (even his own family) as imbalanced or demon-possessed (in service of *Beelzebul*). Jesus was a deviant; therefore his words and actions were deviant. His exorcisms were not benevolent acts of kindness, but via 'discernment' deemed proof that he was a witch. Once the discernment was revealed, all of his activity – eating with sinners, exorcizing of demons, violating of Sabbath and washing rules – validated the charge. The function of the accusation was to bring about the eradication of Jesus. This was not possible in the highly contentious rivalry of the gospel setting since neither Jesus' followers nor his opponents possessed such authority. Nevertheless, name-calling was a means to control Jesus, call his authority into question, and hopefully have him expelled.

The social-anthropological model has become standard methodology for explaining demon-possession accusations in the gospels. Douglas' grid and group model provides a way to describe the character of social structures and explain the typical behavior of people within a particular setting. It helps us explain the social dynamic of demon-possession accusations. For this it is beneficial. It is also worthy of critique. Garrett is rightly critical of the common assumption that a sociological model is 'untainted by the ethnocentrism that it aims to circumvent'. 'The problem with the supposition is that the model is inevitably biased in favor of educated western categories and question about other cultures.'[25] In the quest to avoid imposing a modern social system on the text, it may be subjected to another just as foreign.

One must also question the amount to which social structures determine reality; do they describe what is or what is possible?[26] The advantage of a

24. Malina and Neyrey, *Calling Jesus Names*, p. 21. 'Every person is judged according to the features typical of the group to which he/she belongs'.

25. Susan Garrett, review of B.J. Malina, *Christian Origins and Cultural Anthropology: Practical Models for Biblical Interpretation* (Atlanta: John Knox, 1986), in *JBL* 107 (1988), pp. 532-34.

26. Bruce J. Malina, 'The Social Sciences and Biblical Interpretation', *Interp.* 36 (3.82), p. 238, suggests that 'from a social science point of view, human beings are socially determined'. Christopher Tuckett, *Reading the New Testament: Methods of Interpretation* (Philadelphia: Fortress Press, 1987), p. 147, considers sociological

sociological model becomes its greatest detriment when a text is interpreted through the lens of its underlying social structures only.[27] Sociological models are one of a number of interpretative aids. Surface level issues in the text must be allowed to speak with an equal voice. To suggest, for instance, that Jesus' mobility was that which caused him to be labeled a deviant seems strange considering that it is never an explicit issue to his opponents. A case might also be made that Jesus' journeys were non-deviant since he regularly returned home from his journeys, much like others who traveled for business and pilgrimage.[28] The *text* provides little link between Jesus' travels and deviance.

Most importantly, it must be asked of what Jesus was actually being accused. Jesus *is* accused of working in league with or having a demon, but he is *never* accused of being a witch, sorcerer, or magician.[29] This conclusion is contrary to that of Morton Smith,[30] who although using a different methodology than Malina and Neyrey concludes that if one takes into consideration Jesus' early life, his miraculous works and actions as compared to other magician figures, and the beliefs about him outside of the gospels, one must conclude that by first-century standards Jesus was a magician. He argues that the gospels are essentially a series of cover-ups to the real truth.

---

models as 'ideal types' not necessarily 'precise descriptions of empirical historical realities'.

27. Meier, *A Marginal Jew,* p. 551, directly referring to Malina and Neyrey, notes that 'Historians and social scientists may equate certain accusations (e.g., being in league with the devil or being a deceiver who led the Jewish people astray) with being a magician (or, alternatively, a witch); but that is a move made by modern scholars engaging in model building at a high level of abstraction'.

28. Mt. 4.13; 8.5; 13.54; 17.24-5; Mk 1.21; 2.1; 3.19; 6.1f; 9.33; Lk. 4.23, 31; 7.1; 10.15; Jn 2.12; 4.46; 6.17, 24, 59. Even if redactional, these passages work against the premise that early believers considered all of their founders as deviants because of their mobility.

29. Terms that were readily available: magician – μάγος or γόης; sorcerer, φαρμακεία. Graham Twelftree, *Jesus the Exorcist: A Contribution to the Study of the Historical Jesus* (Peabody, MA: Hendrickson, 1993), pp. 190-207, argues that Jesus was never accused of being a magician in his lifetime and that his miracles are clearly distinguished from magic; so too Meier, *A Marginal Jew*, p. 551, who further notes that the major flaw is that the accusation 'does reflect the precise vocabulary and immediate reaction of Jesus' fellow Jews in his own day or in the decades immediately following his death'.

30. M. Smith, *Jesus the Magician,* and more recently J.D. Crossan, *The Historical Jesus* (San Francisco: Harper & Row, 1991).

A number of scholars have been critical of this conclusion.[31] John Meier notes that in the gospels only certain types of miracles receive fierce opposition, those that are done on the Sabbath and some (not all) exorcisms (those thought to be done via the aid of demonic powers). The chorus of praise that Jesus received for most of his miracles argues against the idea that people saw him as a magician or witch. Meier finds no 'inextricable' link between magic and being in league with Satan. The latter, he says, was 'a much more serious issue'.[32] Indeed, something 'much more serious' underlies the accusation. What that might be is hinted at in Matthew 24.63 (cf. Jn 7.12, 47) where Jesus was charged with being ὁ πλάνος (a deceiver). Some have argued that πλάνος should also be translated 'magician', but within the New Testament this is problematic.[33] More significant is the fact that the πλάνος, πλάνη, πλανάω word group is linked to the work of false prophets throughout Jewish and Christian apocalyptic literature.[34] This concept appears in the antecedent traditions that would be used by the early church in the development of the Antichrist[35] figure but may be the traditions known and used by Jesus' opponents. If this is true, it may explain Jesus' appeal to the kingdom of God in his rebuttal, something not necessary if the only charge was that he was a witch or magician. This suggests that Jesus' words and deeds were of such an eschatological nature that to his opponents they could mean only one of two things; he was either an eschatological savior or an eschatological antagonist. The intense opposition to Jesus and the serious charge of demon possession are in part evidence that his opponents believed the latter of the two possibilities.

31. Note especially the rebuttal to Smith in Twelftree, *Jesus the Exorcist*, pp. 190-207.

32. Meier, *A Marginal Jew*, pp. 574-75, n. 74, refers to J. Lightstone, *The Commerce of the Sacred. Meditation of the Divine among Jews in the Greco-Roman Diaspora* (Brown Judaic Studies, 59; Chico, CA: Scholars, 1984), p. 56, who notes that Jewish magicians set up shop within the synagogue itself, something that would not have been allowed should magic and demon possession have been equated.

33. Twelftree, *Jesus the Exorcist*, pp. 201-202, refers to J. Samain, 'L'accusation de magie contre le Christ dans les Evangiles', *ETL* 15 (1938), pp. 449-90. Twelftree persuasively argues that in the New Testament πλάνος refers to deceptive words not magic.

34. The view of H. Braun, πλανάω, *TDNT*, pp. 233-53.

35. By the word 'Antichrist' we refer to a distinctly Christian development of an eschatological opponent of God and his people who in church tradition would appear bringing great trouble to believers just prior to the second coming of Christ. While it is anachronistic to speak of 'The Antichrist' with reference to pre-Christian Jewish literature, we may speak of an Antichrist idea lying within those traditions.

Eschatological Explanation: Demon-Possession Accusations and Antecedents of Eschatological Antagonist Tradition

A connection between the *Beelzebul* accusation and Jewish antecedents of eschatological antagonist traditions has not received much attention. In recent decades views have changed regarding the development of the theme. Following the conclusions of Bousset,[36] Charles,[37] and others, for some time scholars assumed that the concept of Antichrist had an historical development reaching far back into biblical history. It was commonly held that the idea was already highly developed for the writers of the apocalyptic books. [38] The origins were seen as early as ancient creation chaos mythology, which developed through the long history of Hebrew thought. Although early texts did not use the title 'Antichrist', scholars found the figure in them by first noting his characteristics in later Christian writings and then assuming his presence in figures appearing in earlier documents.[39] According to Bousset this methodology was valid because (1) eschatological traditions regarding the Antichrist remained relatively stable over the centuries, and (2) the Antichrist tradition circulated for some time in a secret and oral manner before it came into written expression by Christian writers.[40]

Recent studies have shown that a developed Antichrist tradition was

---

36. W. Bousset, *Der Antichrist in der Uberlieferung des Judentums, des Neuen Testament und der alten Kirche. Ein Beitrag zur Auselgung der Apokalypse* (Göttengen: Vandenhoeck & Ruprecht, 1895), in English, *The Antichrist Legend: A Chapter in Christian and Jewish Folklore* (London: Hutchinson, 1896).

37. R.H. Charles, *Revelation 1-14: A Critical and Exegetical Commentary on the Book of Revelation* (ICC, 2; Edinburgh: T&T Clark, 1920), pp. 76-87. G.C. Jenks, *Origins,* speaks of a Bousset–Charles 'consensus' that was reflected in the study of Antichrist by many commentators. Note the list on p. 51.

38. D.S. Russell, *The Method and Message of Jewish Apocalyptic: 200 BC – AD 100* (Philadelphia: Westminster, 1964). Russell traces the Antichrist theme well back into Israel's history on pp. 191ff.

39. Russell, *Method*, p. 277, states the Antichrist is 'identified with Antiochus Epiphanes'. See too, Charles, *Revelation*, II.2, p. 77.

40. Bousset, *Antichrist*, pp. 4, 8. Critical reviews of the earlier Bousset/Charles consensus are made by Jenks, *Antichrist*, pp. 5-13; L.J. Lietaert Peerbolte, *The Antecedents of Antichrist: A Tradio-Historical Study of the Earliest Christian Views on Eschatological Opponents* (New York: Brill, 1996), pp. 6-12; A. Yarbro Collins, *The Combat Myth in the Book of Revelation* (Harvard Dissertation; Missoula, MT: Scholars Press, 1976), pp. 166ff.

most probably a distinctly Christian phenomenon.[41] In his study of the Hellenistic Jewish literature from 200 BCE to 50 CE, Jenks concludes, 'numerous aspects of the later Antichrist myth...had parallels in the Hellenistic Jewish literature... [but] there is no evidence for an Antichrist myth tradition in these documents'.[42] Rather, the evidence indicates that Christian writers picked up antecedent themes from diverse and independent strands of Jewish tradition. One strand of tradition may have a figure who is a religious deceiver and in another a godless tyrant; in one he is a Gentile, and in another a Jew. The Christian concept of the Antichrist developed from a 'creative blending of [these] much older traditions of quite diverse origins'.[43]

Using different methodologies, dissertations by Jenks and Peerbolte come to somewhat similar conclusions regarding how the Antichrist figure developed in earliest Christianity. Although neither found a Jewish Antichrist figure in Hellenistic Jewish literature,[44] both acknowledge the presence of antecedent Antichrist themes that had not yet been combined into one idea or figure.[45] After the lifetime of Jesus, the earliest church developed the Antichrist figure from a 'christocentric adaptation of and blending of Jewish religious tradition'.[46] This happened as crisis events in the early church gave new meaning to earlier texts and allowed for the fusion of various independent traditions into a single figure.[47] Thus, during his lifetime Jesus' opponents had at their disposal antecedent Antichrist traditions.

---

41. J. Ernst, *Die eschatologischen Gegenspieler in den Schriften des Neuen Testaments* (BU, 3; Regensburg: Friedrich Pustet, 1967); Jenks, *Origin;* and also Peerbolte, *Antecedents.*

42. Jenks, *Origin,* p. 193.

43. Jenks, *Origin,* p. 121.

44. Jenks, Origin, pp. 117-98. This study included the works Daniel, *I Enoch, Jubilees, Martyrdom of Isaiah, Sibylline Oracles, Testament of Moses,* 1 and 2 Maccabees, *Psalms of Solomon,* and the Qumran texts. Peerbolte, *Antecedents,* pp. 225-39, adds the later texts of *4 Ezra* and *2 Baruch.*

45. Jenks, *Origin,* p. 193.

46. Jenks, *Origin,* pp. 358-63. 'The extent to which one or the other of these strands within the developing Antichrist tradition was emphasized seems to have depended on the immediate situation of the writer. In some circumstances the End-tyrant elements were of more relevance, and the development of those aspects was noted in some of the literature. In others, the need to combat false teaching led to the False Prophet traditions being drawn into play'. Similarly in Peerbolte, *Antecedents,* pp. 340-41.

47. Jenks, *Origins,* pp. 364-65, suggests events like Caligula's threat to the Jerusalem Temple in 40 CE, the fall of Jerusalem, the death of Nero, and other internal church crises, would have provided impetus for such development.

Something further is possible; the ministry of Jesus may itself have constituted a crisis event for Jewish leaders, not unlike the dynamic that led to the development of the Antichrist figure in the earliest church. The contemporary consensus regarding the Christian development of the Antichrist tradition makes this possible. Should the tradition have been as developed in the early first century as Bousset and Charles contend, linking the accusations made by Jesus' opponents to that tradition would be very difficult. Jesus' actions in the gospels cannot be paralleled to a fully developed Antichrist tradition. If, on the other hand, the antecedent strands of pre-Antichrist traditions were part of Jewish theological thinking in the early first century, these could easily be drawn upon as the basis of their accusations.

Jenks and Peerbolte also come to very similar conclusions regarding the content of the major antecedent strands of tradition from which the earliest church drew in the development of the figure. Although using slightly different terminology, the table below outlines the main streams of those traditions.[48]

Peerbolte	Jenks
False prophets	The False Prophet tradition
Eschatological tyrant	The Endtyrant traditions
Belial/Beliar	The Satan myth
Chaos Monsters	Chaoskampf traditions
Final assault of the Gentile nations	
Nero *redivivus*	
The climax of evil	

Of these traditions the two that were most important in the Christian development of the Antichrist were those of the Endtyrant and the False Prophet.[49] For reason of space, the remainder of our study will explore these two themes in relation to the *Beelzebul* controversy passages.

The Beelzebul *Controversy and Jewish Endtyrant Tradition*

Eschatological antagonist tradition may be seen in the name to which Jesus' accusers appeal as the source of his power. In the gospels the name

48. Peerbolte, *Antecedents*, p. 342; Jenks, *Origins*, p. 194, charts are given listing both the theme and the Jewish sources where the themes occurs.

49. Jenks, *Origins*, p. 363; Peerbolte, *Antecedents*, pp. 340-41; so too D. Aune, *Revelation 6–16* (WBC, 52b; ed. B.M. Metzger; Nashville: Thomas Nelson, 1998), p. 753. My use of the term 'Endtyrant' is from Jenks.

Beelzebul seems to have an established meaning as a synonym for Satan. How this occurred is unclear since the name does not occur in any literature prior to the gospels, a point that leads some to believe the name was coined on the spot.[50] The word Βεελ- is equivalent to the Hebrew בַּעַל, 'lord', 'owner', or 'master', and the name of the ancient god *Baal*.[51] The second half of the compound name, ζεβούλ, *Zebuîl* (זְבוּל), has puzzled scholars, yet may be a key as to why the title was used in the accusation.

Lloyd Gaston proposes that *Beelzebul* means 'lord of heaven' or 'lord of the temple'.[52] He suggests that Jesus may have indicated this in Matthew 10.25: εἰ τὸν οἰκοδεσπότην Βεελζεβοὺλ ἐπεκάλεσαν, πόσῳ μᾶλλον τοὺς οἰκιακοὺς αὐτοῦ ('If they have called the *head of the house* Beelzebul, how much more the members of his household!'). Jesus parallels οἰκοδεσπότης (head of the house) with Βεελζεβοὺλ (*Beelzebul*), giving assent to a derogatory taunt by indicating that he was truly the 'lord of the temple'.[53] If true, this may not only tell us something about Jesus' understanding of himself, it also suggests the meaning of the name *Beelzebul* and why Jesus' opponents chose to use it in their accusation.

The meaning of *Zebuîl* as 'heaven' or 'temple' can be inferred from occurrences of the word in the Hebrew text.[54] The noun זְבֻל in the Old Testament means 'elevation', 'height', or 'lofty abode'.[55] In its various contexts it refers to 'a lofty dwelling' such as heaven or the temple as God's dwelling place. This is seen in 1 Kings 8.13 (בָּנֹה בָנִיתִי בֵּית זְבֻל לָךְ מָכוֹן לְשִׁבְתְּךָ עוֹלָמִים, 'I have built you an exalted house, a place for you to dwell in forever'), where זְבֻל is parallel with בֵּית (house). The same is true of Isaiah 63.15 (הַבֵּט מִשָּׁמַיִם וּרְאֵה מִזְּבֻל קָדְשְׁךָ וְתִפְאַרְתֶּךָ 'Look down from

---

50. Lloyd Gaston, 'Beelzebul', *TZ* 18 (1962), p. 253, 'It is not a name otherwise known, because it was coined specifically for this situation'.

51. F. Brown, S.R. Driver, C.A. Briggs, *The New Brown-Driver-Briggs-Gesenius Hebrew and English Lexicon with an Appendix Containing the Biblical Aramaic* (Peabody, MA: Hendrickson, 1979), p. 127.

52. Lloyd Gaston, 'Beelzebul', pp. 247-55. See also E.C.B. MaClaurin, 'Beelzeboul', *NT* 20 (1978), pp. 156-60 (158).

53. MaClaurin, 'Beelzeboul', p. 157, argues that οἰκοδεσπότης *is* the Greek term representing Βεελζεβοὺλ. He further argues from Ugaritic parallels that the phrase ἄρχοντι τῶν δαιμονίων, 'ruler of the demons' (9.34; 12.24ff.; Mk 3.22; Lk. 11.15; 18ff.) also stands in parallel with the meaning of οἰκοδεσπότης and Βεελζεβοὺλ. MaClaurin equates the terms accordingly: ἄρχοντι = Βεελ-= δεσπότης whereas τῶν δαιμονίων = οἶκος= ζεβοὺλ (that is, οἶκος and ζεβοὺλ refer to a 'house' or 'temple' of demons).

54. Gaston, 'Beelzebul', p. 247, states that the etymology of the word comes from the Aramaic-Hebrew combination בְּעַל־זְבוּל.

55. *BDB*, p. 259.

heaven and see, from your holy and glorious habitation') where זְבֻל is a synonym for שָׁמַיִם (heaven). The four occurrences of זְבֻל in the Dead Sea Scrolls all refer to God's heavenly dwelling.[56] In Rabbinic Hebrew זְבֻל is not common but has the same meaning as the Old Testament and Dead Sea Scrolls. An example of this is *Hagigah* 12*b*, where זְבֻל is the name of the fourth heaven where the heavenly Jerusalem is found.

Gaston suggests the title *Beelzebul* reflects the situation of Antiochus IV Epiphanes and the Jewish struggle with his enforced worship of *Baal*. In the Hellenistic Age the chief rival of the Yahweh faith was 'the cult of the heavenly *Baal*, called in Greek Ζεὺς 'Ολύμπιος (Zeus Olympios) and in Aramiac בעלשמין, 'lord of the heavens'.[57] Among Gentiles the name בעל שמים, *Baal Shamayim* ('lord of the heavens') was an acceptable ascription for *Baal*, but among the Jews such a phrase could describe only Yahweh. This may explain why in the later writings of the Old Testament other phrases were substituted for *Baal*, reserving names meaning 'lord of the heavens' for Yahweh alone (for example מָרֵי שְׁמַיָּא in Dan. 5.23).[58] It may also explain the Latin variant[59] *Beelzebub*,[60] or 'lord of the flies', as 'an attempt to replace some honorific title by some disgraceful one'.[61] Derogatory terms were created via wordplay in order to cast aspersions toward

56. Gaston, 'Beelzebul', p. 249, notes that in 1QM 12.1, בזבול קודשדכה 'in thy holy dwelling', stands parallel with בשמים 'in heaven'; in 1QM 12.2 בזבול כבודכה 'in thy holy dwelling', is parallel with במעון קודשכה 'in thy holy habitation'; in 1QS 10.3 (cf. Hab. 3.11) the sun and moon shine מזבול קודש 'from the holy dwelling' and in 1QH 3.34 God 'thunders' זבול קודשו ('from his holy dwelling').

57. Gaston, 'Beelzebul', p. 252.

58. Ezra 1.2, 5.11; 12; 6.9, 10; 7.12, 21, 23; Neh. 1.4, 5; 2.4, 20; Ps. 136.26; Dan. 2.18, 19, 37, 44; 4.34; 5.23, Tob. 13.11; 2 Macc. 15.23.

59. c (ff¹) vg sy^{s.p}.

60. Kaufmann Kohler, 'Beelzebub', Jewishencyclopedia.com, holds that *Beelzebul* is a variant spelling of *Beelzebub* or 'lord of the flies', the god of Ekron whom the ailing King Ahaziah consulted in 2 Kgs 1.2-6. This view is rejected by Gaston, 'Beelzebul', p. 251; Twelftree, *Jesus the Exorcist*, p. 105. Bradley L. Stein, 'Who the Devil Is Beelzebul?', *BR* 13 (1997), pp. 42-48, believes that *Beelzebul* is a debased form of the Phoenician name *Baalazbul*. From this he concludes 'We should recognize *Beelzebul* as the Canaanite god Baal, reduced from deific grandeur to a malevolent spirit' (p. 45). Note too the various view in Fitzmyer, *Luke*, p. 920.

61. MaClaurin, 'Beelzeboul', p. 156. See also the numerous examples of the change from *Baal* to *bosheth* or 'shame' in BDB, p. 127. Gaston, 'Beelzebul', p. 252, notes further attempts to avoid attributing the title to Satan. He rejects the translation 'lord of dung' which can be made only by emending the text to βεελζιββουλ. D. Wenham lists the various views in 'Abomination of Desolation', *ABD*, I, p. 639.

Antiochus' god. Many have noted that in Daniel 12.11 שֶׁקּוּץ שֹׁמֵם (הַשִּׁקּוּץ מְשׁוֹמֵם in Dan 11.31) the 'abomination of desolation' is probably a distortion of the name בעל שמים (*Baal Shamayim*) and an example of the Jewish practice of 'substituting a cacophemistic name for that of a heathen god'.[62] It is now commonly held that '"abomination of desolation" is…a derogatory reference to the deity to whom Antiochus rededicated the Jerusalem temple'.[63] Ford has shown that in every instance τὸ βδέλυγμα τῆς ἐρημώσεως (abomination of desolation, Dan. 9.27; 11.31; 12.11, [cf. 8.13], Mk 13.14 par Mt. 24.15) is 'ever linked with the temple'.[64]

Considering the above, a few conclusions are in order. First, although such an honorific title was a problematic attribution for Satan, *Beelzebul* could be identified as Satan because Jews and early Christians considered pagan deities to be demons.[65] Zeus, the chief of the Greek gods,[66] was the perfect fit as the Jewish 'chief of the demons'. In a first-century Jewish context the names *Beelzebul, Baal Shamayim,* and *Satan* could easily be considered synonyms. Second, although the word ζεβούλ, *Zebuîl* could mean either 'temple' or 'heaven' depending on the context,[67] *Beelzebul* was chosen because of its link to the temple. The name had historical significance specifically with regard to Antiochus IV's defiling of the Jerusalem Temple; it also had present significance for just as Antiochus IV acted against the Temple as the representative of *Beelzebul/Baal Shamayim,*

---

62. Gaston, 'Beelzebul', p. 252, notes that this was first recognized by E. Nestle, 'Der Greuel der Verwüstung, Dan. 9.27, 11.31, 12.11': *ZAW*, 4 (1884), p. 246. See too G.R. Beasley-Murray, *Jesus and the Last Days: An Interpretation of the Olivet Discourse* (Peabody: Hendrickson, 1993), pp. 408-12; D. Ford, *The Abomination of Desolation in Biblical Eschatology* (Washington: University Press of America, 1979), pp. 50f.

63. D. Wenham, 'Abomination of Desolation', p. 29. Note 2 Macc. 6.1-2.

64. Ford, *Abomination of Desolation*, p. 2.

65. Fitzmyer, *Luke*, p. 920. E.C.B. MaClaurin, 'Beelzeboul', p. 158. W.E.M. Aitken, 'Beelzebul', *JBL* 31 (1912), pp. 34-53. Note how the LXX of Ps. 95.5 (96.5) substitutes 'idols' for 'demons' (כִּי כָּל־אֱלֹהֵי הָעַמִּים אֱלִילִים) compare ὅτι πάντες οἱ θεοὶ τῶν ἐθνῶν δαιμόνια; Note also 1 Cor. 10.20; cf. LXX Deut. 32.17; Ps. 105.37; Bar. 4.7; Rev. 9.20.

66. Note the ascription in Aeschylus, Fragment 70 (Heliades [Daughters of Helios]) 'Zeus is the fiery upper air, Zeus is the earth, Zeus is the heaven; Zeus is all things, and whatever transcends them'.

67. Aitken, 'Beelzebul', p. 50, lists a number of possible Hebrew terms with similar meanings to זבול that might have been chosen ערבות, מכון, מעון, שחקים, רקיע, ולון, concluding 'one, *zebul,* was chosen; why this particular one we do not know'.

so too Jesus' threats against the Temple made him suspect of the same actions.[68] By using this title, Jesus' opponents, were drawing on Jewish Endtyrant tradition.

Gaston notes that *Zebuîl* may have been chosen because of its link to the Tosephta *Sanhedrin* 13.5, which speaks of certain Minim who will remain in *Sheol* forever because they acted against the Temple. To those who 'stretched out their hands against the Temple' it is said

> *Sheol* wastes away, but they do not waste away, for it is written: 'and their form shall cause *sheol* to pass away'. What brought this upon them? Because they stretched out their hands against the Temple, as it is written: 'because of his temple'; and '*zebul*' means nothing else than 'Temple', for it is written: 'I have surely built thee a *beth zebul*, a place for thee to dwell in forever'.[69]

Jesus' opponents may have viewed him as a Minim, who like Antiochus IV was a threat to the Temple. Jesus spoke against the Temple and even predicted its destruction.[70] It is very possible that Jesus' opponents thought of his statements regarding the temple as an indication that he fit the pattern of Antiochus Epiphanies whose allegiance to Zeus-*Beelzebul*, the 'lord of the temple' threatened the very existence of the nation.

Jesus' predictions of the Temple's destruction are numerous: 'See, your house is left to you' (Lk. 13.34-35a); 'Indeed, the days will come upon you, when your enemies will set up ramparts around you and surround you, and hem you in on every side. They will crush you to the ground, you and your children within you, and they will not leave within you one stone upon another' (Lk. 19.41-44); 'Not one stone will be left

---

68. The Endtyrant theme is in Dan. 7–12; 4QTest 22-30; 1QH 6.29-35; Q246; *T.Mos.* 8. See Jenks, *Origins*, pp. 175-85 for a discussion of the themes involved and texts.

69. Gaston, 'Beelzebul', p. 254. This understanding of Ps. 49.15b is reflected in the later Targum: 'Their bodies will be destroyed in Gehinnom because they stretched out their hands and destroyed the house of dwelling (בֵּית מְדוֹר) of His Shekinah' (*Rosh Hashanah* 17a; *Seder'Olam Rabbah* 3).

70. Craig Evans, 'Predictions of the Destruction of the Herodian Temple in the Pseudepigrapha, Qumran Scrolls, and Related Texts', *JSP* 10 (1992), pp. 89-147. Although admitting to redactional editing, Evans argues for the authenticity of the destruction predictions. He concludes that Jesus not only predicted the Temple's destruction, he also (1) used the language of the prophets (esp. Jeremiah and Ezekiel) transferring their concern for the Babylonian destruction of Solomon's Temple to the destruction of the Herodian Temple; (2) considered the Herodian temple establishment corrupt; and (3) may have held that the Temple's construction by Herod made its destruction inevitable.

here upon another; all will be thrown down' (Mk 13.1-2 and pars); 'When you see Jerusalem surrounded by armies, then know that its desolation has come near' (Lk. 21.20-24). Jesus' 'cleansing' of the Temple appears to have been a symbolic demonstration of its impending destruction. Rather than a call for 'pure' temple worship, his 'overturning' of the tables symbolized its complete destruction and eventual rebuilding. Sanders asserts that Jesus' statement, 'Destroy this temple, and in three days I will raise it up', probably implied his own involvement in its destruction.[71] Jesus was known to have placed himself above the Temple, and some believed he hinted to his own involvement in its destruction. 'I tell you, something greater than the temple is here' (Mt. 12.6). At his trial witnesses stated 'We heard him say, "I will destroy this temple that is made with hands, and in three days I will build another, not made with hands"' (Mk 14.58 par Mt. 26.61).[72] While on the cross Jesus is mocked by his own words, 'Aha! You who would destroy the temple and build it in three days' (Mk 15.29 par. Mt. 27.40).

An objection could be raised that Jesus' threat to the Temple, though serious, does not constitute the monstrous figure seen in the Endtyrant tradition. According to the tradition from Daniel as well as other Jewish Hellenistic sources,[73] this figure was an historicized human manifestation of the ancient chaos monster of combat myths. He was a lawless blasphemer, whose pride and divine claims brought great evils upon Israel. How can Jesus be said to have fulfilled these traditions? It is not beyond reason to posit that Jesus' preaching of the kingdom of God, combined with *any* threat to the Temple, could easily be adapted to Endtyrant tradition. Contrary to earlier beliefs, these traditions proved to be highly malleable to the situation in which the author or community saw itself.[74] Moreover,

71. E.P. Sanders, 'Jesus and the Temple', in *The Historical Jesus in Recent Research* (eds J. Dunn and S. McKnight) from the series *Sources for Biblical and Theological Study* (ed. D.W. Baker; Winona Lake, IN: Eisenbrauns, 2005), p. 374; Similarly in Evans, 'Predictions', pp. 116-17.

72. E.P. Sanders, 'Jesus and the Temple', p. 374. The existence of the threat form 'I will destroy' (Mk 14.58) 'makes it virtually incredible that the entire saying could be *vaticinium ex eventu*...[for] the temple was in fact destroyed by the Romans in the year 70'.

73. *A. Moses* 8.1-2; *4 Ezra* 5.6; 11.29-35; 12.23-31; *2 Apoc. Bar.* 36.7-11; 40.1-3; *Sib. Or.* 3.75-92.611-15; *1 Enoch* 85-90; *Jub.* 23.16-32; 1 Macc. 1; 2 Macc. 4–9.

74. A point often seen with regard to the earliest church's development of the tradition, but also true within Judaism. P. Veilhauer and G. Strecker, 'Apocalypses and Related Subjects', in *New Testament Apocrypha*. II. *Writings Relating to the Apostles; Apocalypses and Related Subjects* (ed. W. Schneemelcher; trans. R. McL. Wilson; Louisville: John Knox: Westminster, 1992), p. 579. Peerbolte, *Antedecents*,

some of Jesus' acts and words, though not of the gravity seen in Endtyrant tradition, could easily be used to cast him in that light.[75] Jesus, therefore, like Antiochus IV may have been seen as an Endtyrant figure who with *Beelzebul* wished to be 'lord of the temple'.

The Beelzebul *Controversy and the False Prophet Tradition*

A second tradition drawn upon in the development of the Antichrist figure was the concept of the false prophet. It seems likely that Jesus was considered a prophet during his lifetime.[76] Morna Hooker notes, 'the fact that Matthew and Luke use prophet-typology of Jesus...even though belief in him as a prophet was in their view inadequate, shows how firmly rooted in the tradition this belief was'.[77] A number of scholars have explored the question regarding Jesus' status as a prophet. Scot McKnight proposes that the eschatological nature of Jesus' ministry and actions had numerous parallels to the first-century Jewish sign prophets, particularly in those elements that align with the actions of Moses and Joshua.[78] He suggests

p. 343, notes the how different antecedent traditions were emphasized between Jewish and early Christian communities based upon their expectations and experiences. Jenks, *Origins*, p. 159, notes that not every aspect of Endtyrant tradition was 'susceptible of transfer for a later time'. This is clear in his study of the differing pictures of the Endtyrant in Jewish literature before and after Daniel (pp. 161-70). Even the more fully developed ideas of earliest church do not present a uniform Antichrist tradition. Various themes were emphasized depending upon community and situation: committing blasphemy and/or declaring himself to be divine (Dan. 7.25; 8.11-12, 25; 11.36-37; 2 Thess. 2.4; *Asc. Isa.* 4.6; Mk 13.6, 22; Lk. 21.8; *Did.* 16.4); deceiving and leading people astray (Mt. 24.10, 24; Mk 13.22; *Asc. Isa.* 2.7; 2 Thess. 2.10-12); performing miraculous signs (Mt. 24.24; Mk 13.22; *Asc. Isa.* 4.4-5, 10; 2 Thess. 2.9; *Did.* 16.4; *Sib. Or.* 2.167-68; *Apoc. Pet.* 2.13; *Apoc. El.* 3.7); setting up an image to himself and/or being worshipped (*Asc. Isa.* 4.11; 2 Thess. 2.4; cf. Dan. 3.4).

75. Blasphemy (Mt. 9.3 par Mk 2.7, Lk. 5.21; Mt. 26.65 par Mk 14.64; Jn 10.33, 36), setting aside the law or setting himself above it (Sabbath [harvesting] Mt. 12.8 par Mk 2.28, Lk. 6.5; [healing] Mt. 12.9-13 par Mk 3.1-5, food laws, Mt. 15.11 par Mk 7.20; parental laws, Mt. 10.34-26; 12.46-50; Lk. 14.26); defying authority (Mt. 23.13-39, Jn 8.44-45).

76. Jesus indicates this of himself (Mt. 10.41; 12.39 [as Jonah?]; Lk. 4.24ff.; 13.33), as well as others (Mt. 21.11, 46; Mk 6.15; Lk. 7.16 [39?]; 24.19; Jn. 4.19; 6.14; 7.40; 9.17).

77. Morna Hooker, *The Signs of a Prophet: The Prophetic Actions of Jesus* (London: SCM Press, 1997), p. 77.

78. Scot McKnight, 'Jesus and Prophetic Actions', *BBR* 10.2 (2000), pp. 197-232. See too Dale Allison, Jr, *The New Moses: A Matthean Typology* (Minneapolis:

the evidence points to the possibility that early Jewish Christologies included the belief in a coming Eschatological prophet like Moses based on Deuteronomy 18.15-18 and Malachi 4.5. These prophets were apocalyptic in nature promising miraculous acts of redemption.[79] Josephus refers to one 'Egyptian' as a 'false prophet' (*War.* 2.261) but thinks no higher of those who do not receive the title. In his discussion of the Passion Narrative, Raymond Brown notes, 'that Jesus acted like a prophet, and thus caused some to think he was one could also have caused others to think that he was a false prophet'.[80] Whether or not Jesus was put on trial as a false prophet is certainly debatable. It is interesting that the charges – blasphemy, threats to the Temple, and possible kingly and divine claims – all have parallels in antecedent Antichrist traditions.

Although an eschatological false prophet is not widely attested in Jewish sources before the time of Jesus,[81] W. Meeks asserts that there is ample

Fortress Press, 1993); J.J. Collins, *The Scepter and the Star: The Messiahs of the Dead Sea Scrolls and Other Ancient Literature* (New York: Doubleday, 1995), pp. 112-22, suggests the presence of a messianic eschatological prophet in 4Q521 who fits the *Elijah redivivus* motif.

79. B. Ehrman, *Jesus: Apocalyptic Prophet of the New Millennium* (New York: Oxford, 1999), concludes something similar of Jesus. A discussion of first-century prophets is in R. Gray, *Prophetic Figures in Late Second Temple Jewish Palestine: The Evidence from Josephus* (New York: Oxford, 1993); see too the discussion of the prophetic types in R. Horsley and J. Hanson, *Bandits, Prophets, and Messiahs: Popular Movements in the Time of Jesus* (Harrisburg, PA: Trinity International Press, 1985), pp. 161-89.

80. Raymond Brown, *The Death of the Messiah, from Gethsemane to the Grave: A Commentary on the Passion Narratives in the Four Gospels* (New York: Doubleday, 1994), I, p. 543.

81. Although E. Lohmeyer ('Antichrist', *RAC* I, p. 453) believes this to be possible; 'Zu solchen Vorstellungen hat vielleicht die Erwartung beigetragen, daß der eschatologische Vollender als 'der Prophet' kommen werde...vielleicht ist auch ein Hauptthema der atl. Religionsgeschichte, der Kampf zwischen wahrem u. falschem Prophetismus, eschatologisiert worden...oder es spiegeln sich darin innere Lehrstreitigkeiten'. It is also suggested by G. Strecker, 'Der Antichrist: Zum religionsgeschichtlichen Hintergrund von 1 Joh 2,18.22; 4,3 und 2 Joh 7', in *Text and Testimony: Essays on the New Testament and Apocryphal Literature in Honour of A. F. J. Klijn* (Kampen: Uitgeversmaatschappij J.H. Kok, 1988), p. 249. 'Möglicherweise liegt dieser Vorstellung eine jüdische Tradition über den endzeitlichen falschen Propheten als Gegenspieler des wahren Propheten zugrunde; jedoch ist für diese Vermutung ein eindeutiger Beleg bisher nicht vorhanden. Immerhin ist denkbar, daß Dtn 13,2-6 schon im Judentum eschatologisiert wurde und – wie es die Erwartung des endzeitlichen Propheten nach Dtn 18,15.18 gab – sich auch eine Vorstellung vom apokalyptischen Lügenpropheten gebildet hatte.'

evidence that 'a fairly firm tradition existed in first century Judaism about "false prophets" who would arise to "lead people astray" by performing "signs and wonders" '.[82] The foundation for this theme is seen in Deuteronomy 13.1-6 and 18.18-22. He notes especially Deuteronomy 13.1-3a, 'If prophets or those who divine by dreams appear among you and promise you omens or portents, and the omens or the portents declared by them take place, and they say, "Let us follow other gods" (whom you have not known) "and let us serve them," you must not heed the words of those prophets or those who divine by dreams'. Meeks believes that the plot to kill Jesus is linked to the false prophet theme in these passages. Meeks goes even further, however, by positing that the Deuteronomy passages provide the basis for Jewish traditions of the false prophet in the Jewish Antichrist legend. 'The New Testament provides several clues to traditions about the false prophet tradition which evidently had developed in apocalyptic circles of Judaism.'[83] In Matthew 24.11 and Mark 13.22, the woes of the last days will include the appearance of 'false prophets' (ψευδοπροφῆται) who will 'lead astray' (πλανάω or ἀποπλανάω).[84] The false prophet will do 'signs and wonders' (σημεῖα καὶ τέρατα). Both of these themes are applied to the Antichrist in later New Testament texts (Rev. 13.11-18; 16.12-16, 19-20; 2 Thess. 2.8-12). In these texts the false prophets is an enemy of God and works under the power of Satan leading people astray and performing miraculous acts. Meeks proposes that this motif comes directly from the Hebrew text[85] and points to similar earlier traditions from Qumran texts that speak of the ' "man of lies" (איש הכוב, 1QpHab 2.2; 5.11; CD 20.15) or "preacher of lies" (מטיף הכוב, 1QpHab 10.9; CD 8.13; 19.26) or (איש הלצון, CD 1.14) "man of scoffing".'[86]

Meek's argument can be augmented by noting the false prophet themes in CD 9.2-3 ('everyman over whom the spirit of Beliar dominates, and he preaches apostasy, will be judged according to the regulation of the necromancer or diviner'), and the similar and strikingly developed language in *Sib. Or* 2.165-69 ('the gathering together is near when some of the

---

82. W. Meeks, *The Prophet-King: Moses Traditions and the Johannine Christology* (Leiden: Brill, 1967), p. 55.

83. Meeks, *Prophet-King*, p. 48.

84. Meeks, *Prophet-King*, p. 48, believes that Mark goes back to a Jewish *Vorlage*.

85. Meeks, *Prophet-King*, p. 50, rejects Bousset's supposition that the works of the false prophet may be explained solely in terms of chaos-dragon mythology (*Der Antichrist*, p. 307).

86. Meeks, *Prophet-King*, p. 51.

deceivers in place of the prophets [ἀντὶ προφητῶν] approach, speaking on the earth. Beliar also will come and will do many signs (σήματα) for men. Then indeed there will be confusion of the holy chosen and faithful men').

G. Stanton further shows that the false prophet accusation is commonly linked to 'some form of demon possession'.[87] By working backwards from later texts he suggests that during his lifetime Jesus was accused of being a false prophet and proposes a connection between this and the *Beelzebul* accusation. By way of argument Stanton notes that in several second-century writings Jesus is said to have 'practiced sorcery and enticed and led Israel astray'.[88] The same charges are found in other false prophet accusations in both the New Testament and other first-century texts.[89] Moreover, accusations of this sort outside of the gospels also include the belief that the success of the false prophet's 'signs and wonders' is due to his 'close relationship to the devil or to demons'.[90] The evangelists include redactional accounts of the accusation that Jesus led people astray and was possessed,[91] but it can also be argued that at least some of the accusations go back to Jesus' lifetime. Stanton argues this primarily of the

87. G. Stanton, *Jesus and Gospel* (Cambridge: Cambridge University Press, 2004), p. 129; see also the earlier 'Early Christian-Jewish Polemic and Apologetic', *NTS* 31 (1985), pp. 377-92.

88. Note *b. Sanh.* 43a; *b. Sanh.*107b; Stanton, *Jesus and Gospel*, pp. 129-32, suggests that these rabbinic accusations are early, independent, and were probably prevalent. He believes that it is to such an accusation that Justin (*Dialogue* 69.7) is responding. Stanton posits that Justin believed the accusation to have been prevalent at the time of Jesus (Twelftree [*Exorcist*, pp. 190-207], vigorously rejects the idea that Jesus was accused of bring a magician/sorcerer during his lifetime). Stanton also points out that a further accusation may be found in Josephus *Antiquities* 18.63, which he believes even with Christian interpolations retains elements of Josephus' hostile account of Jesus. He holds that Josephus' statement that Jesus, καὶ πολλοὺς μὲν Ἰουδαίους πολλοὺς δὲ καὶ τοῦ Ἑλληνικοῦ ἐπηγάγετο, 'drew over to him both many of the Jews, and many of the Gentiles,' to be better worded '*led astray* (ἐπηγάγετο) both many of the Jews, and many of the Gentiles' (pp. 133-34).

89. Stanton, *Jesus and Gospel*, pp. 135-37, notes Acts 13.6-12; Philo, *Spec. Leg.* 1.315; Josephus *Ant.* 20.169-72; 20.97; *Bell.* 2.261-63; Philostratus, *Life* 5.12.

90. Stanton, *Jesus and Gospel*, pp. 137-39, notes Justin, *Dialogue* 69, Origen, *Contra Celsum*, Epiphanius, *Panarion*, 48.1-13, and New Testament examples in Mt. 11.7-19 par Lk. 7.24-35; Acts 13.6-12; 1 Jn 4.1; Rev. 2.20-25; 13.11; 16.13; 19.20; 20.10.

91. Stanton, *Jesus and Gospel*, pp. 139-44, notes Jn 7.12, 25-27, 40; 8.48; 10.19-21; Lk. 23.1-5; Mt. 9.34; 10.25; 27.63-64, and redactional elements of Mk 3.19b-35.

Beelzebul accounts. The fact that each of the synoptic accusations comes from three different groups points to the probability that this was a well-known taunt 'thrown at Jesus by more than one group of opponents'.[92] The false prophet theme appears in each account; Jesus' miraculous works are attributed to a demonic source because he is perceived to be leading the people astray.[93]

In sum, the belief in a demon-possessed false prophet who would lead Israel astray is an independent strand of tradition that would be used by the earliest church in the development of Antichrist tradition. Our study suggests that Jesus' opponents also used the tradition during his lifetime because in their own crisis they saw him as an opponent of God and his people in a way possibly similar to the way Jesus' followers would see the Antichrist only a few decades into the future.

Conclusion

(1) It has been proposed that a purely sociological explanation does not fully answer the question as to why Jesus was accused of casting out demons by *Beelzebul*. That Jesus appeared and ministered among a 'witchcraft society' tells us only in what settings these types of accusations occur. It does not answer the question of *why* this particular accusation was made. The developing traditions within Judaism of the eschatological adversary have been suggested as a more unifying factor for explaining the demon-possession accusations.

(2) Although recent studies have shown that a fully developed Antichrist tradition did not exist in the time of Jesus – that 'The Antichrist' is a Christian construction – the antecedents of that tradition did exist and were developing within Second-Temple Judaism. The similarity of the content of the accusations against Jesus with the antagonist traditions may imply that Jesus' opponents appealed to them in the crisis of dealing with Jesus the miracle worker in much the same way as the earliest church did in confronting its adversaries decades later.

(3) Following Gaston it was proposed that the use of the name *Beelzebul* was intentional by Jesus' opponents. This name linked Jesus to Satan and at the same time to Antiochus IV Epiphanes who dedicated the temple

92. Stanton, *Jesus and Gospel*, p. 144. The accusation comes from the Pharisees (Mt. 12.24), the scribes (Mk 3.22), and the crowd (Lk. 11.15).

93. Mt. 9.33, 'Never has anything like this been seen in Israel'; Mt. 12.23, 'Can this be the Son of David?'; Mk 3.20, 'and the crowd came together again, so that they could not even eat…'; Lk. 11.14, 'and the crowds were amazed'.

to Zeus, served as his representative, and brought great harm to the people. Like Antiochus, Jesus made threats against the Temple, and at the very least, some believed that he would be involved in its destruction. Thus, Jesus' threats fit what is known about an Endtyrant tradition that existed at that time.

(4) It was posited that the charge of demon possession against Jesus suggests the belief that he was a false prophet. The tradition of the miracle-working false prophet is found as early as Deuteronomy and developed in Jewish tradition, especially in the Qumran literature. Beliar possesses the false prophets, and his deceptive signs operate through them. Jesus' opponents interpreted his exorcisms as standing within this tradition. Jesus' rebuttal to his opponents is not to the charge that he was a magician or witch, but to the charge that he was an eschatological antagonist figure like that in the false prophet tradition. His appeal to the kingdom of God makes this clear.

(5) This study does not set aside the work of Malina and Neyrey but rather moves beyond it by positing the actual reasoning behind the accusations. The goal has been to look through the theological eyes of Jesus' opponents and thus truly give a Christology 'from the side'.

JESUS AS GLUTTON AND DRUNKARD: THE 'EXCESSES' OF JESUS*

Joseph B. Modica

Introduction[1]

This essay will explore the accusation against Jesus as 'a glutton and a drunkard' found in Matthew 11.16-19, Luke 7.31-35 and Q 7.31-35. The guiding question will be: What can we further understand about the historical Jesus by understanding this accusation? As Malina and Neyrey have aptly observed, the social labels ('names') affixed to Jesus in the gospels can offer what they cite as a Christology 'from the side'.[2] This approach to Christology differs from the traditional ones: namely, one 'from above' (early church council debates) and one 'from below' (i.e., descriptions of Jesus focused on his humanity) in that it involves more of the 'human perspective and social arrangement marked by the relation of inside and outside, center and periphery'.[3] This Christology 'from the side' is creatively crafted, according to Malina and Neyrey, by a reframing of the following questions: (1) How does reading occur in first-century Palestine?[4] (2) What is the nature and function of language? Furthermore, how does one derive meaning from a text? and (3) How does one recover the social

---

* I borrow this title from J. Koenig, *New Testament Hospitality* (repr. Wipf & Stock, 2001; original Augsburg Fortress, 1985), p. 20ff. This essay is dedicated to Professor William V. Crockett, Professor of New Testament at Alliance Theological Seminary (Nyack, NY) on the celebration of his 28th year of teaching. *Ad multos annos!*

1. I would like to thank the generosity of my colleague at Eastern University, Professor Carl Mosser for offering his insights to my paper. Any deficiencies of course belong exclusively to the author.

2. B.J. Malina and J.H. Neyrey, *Calling Jesus Names: The Social Value of Labels in Matthew* (Sonoma, CA: Polebridge Press, 1988), p. ix.

3. Malina and Neyrey, *Calling Jesus Names*, p. x.

4. Malina and Neyrey adopt what they call the 'scenario model' – that is, each reader has a firm grasp of how the world functions, viz., an awareness of the world.

systems of the original audience of, say, Matthew's gospel (namely, the social-scientific method)?[5]

The Use of 'Labels' in First-Century Palestine

What are roles of 'name-calling' or 'labels' in first-century Palestine? What does 'name-calling' or 'labels' tell us about the alleged accusers? First, according to Malina and Neyrey, 'labeling people and things is an essential feature presumably of every culture'.[6] Labels function as boundary markers, as 'a system of lines to tell where things are in place, where they are clean'.[7]

Second, Malina and Neyrey situate the specific name-calling or labeling pertinent to our study as 'deviance', which 'refers to behavior or conditions that result in a person's being out of normal place. Behavior is deviant when it violates *lines*...(my emphasis).'[8] This is key to understanding labels in general and 'a glutton and a drunkard' in particular – a behavior is labeled deviant when it challenges established boundaries, that is to say 'lines'. Furthermore, a 'deviant', according to Malina and Neyrey, 'is a person perceived to be out of place to such an extent or in such a way as to be redefined in a new, negative place – the redefinition, of course, deriving from the labelers... 'Deviant' is thus a status assumed by persons identified as rule-breakers, that is, those who negatively step or stand out of place in some irrevocable way.'[9]

Moreover, Jerome Neyrey's insightful essay 'The Symbolic Universe of Luke-Acts' develops our understanding of the clash that Jesus had with his accusers: it was a clash of 'worldviews' or 'a symbolic view of the way the universe should be structured and ordered'.[10] He observes that people typically 'draw lines which define and give meaning to their world in

---

5.   Malina's and Neyrey's contribution to Christology is that they address gospel interpretation from a social-scientific perspective. Certainly any perspective, including the social-scientific one, is not without its critics (see F.W. Burnett's review in *CBQ* 52 [Jan. 1990], pp. 165-66, which, although generally laudatory, does question the use of a modern 'Labeling theory' on a pre-modern culture (vis-à-vis first-century Palestine). Also, see R. Hodgson's review in *BTB* 20 (Winter 1990), pp. 171-72, which also raises some methodological concerns.

6.   Malina and Neyrey, *Calling Jesus Names*, p. 36.

7.   Malina and Neyrey, *Calling Jesus Names*, p. 36.

8.   Malina and Neyrey, *Calling Jesus Names*, p. 36.

9.   Malina and Neyrey, *Calling Jesus Names*, p. 40.

10.   Neyrey, 'The Symbolic Universe', in *The Social World of Luke-Acts* (ed. J.H. Neyrey; Peabody, MA: Hendrickson, 1991) p. 273, following P. Berger and T. Luckmann, *The Social Construction of Reality* (Garden City, NY: Doubleday, 1966).

terms of six basic areas: self, others, nature, time, space and God'.[11] Hence, Jesus challenged (and was inevitably 'labeled' himself) because he challenged the lines drawn by his accusers. 'Nor did Jesus observe the expectations encoded in the map of the body to defend its holiness.'[12] It appears then that Jesus did not just challenge the lines drawn by his accusers; he expanded their group boundaries.[13]

Neyrey also observes that Jesus' meal patterns literally turned the societal system upside down. He places the accusation 'a glutton and a drunkard' under the social category of the 'New Maps of Persons' since Jesus strategically eats 'across the board' with those who are marginalized, outside of specific group members.[14] Neyrey observes that 'Jesus could claim to be a following the pattern of a saintly prophet who shared the table of a foreign woman in a foreign land (Luke 4.25-26). But he gives mixed signals in regards to the map of persons; he is upsetting the accepted norms.'[15]

Third, labels are social constructions formulated by a dominant group. Labels are intrinsically social tools. Labels determine 'insiders' versus 'outsiders'. So to label someone is not an arbitrary individual act, but a 'social act of retaliation for some alleged deviance'.[16] Also, since labeling is essentially a social construct, it results in serious negative social consequences for the one(s) who are labeled. Some of those negative social consequences include, but are not limited to: social distancing, the *decanonization* process (a person becomes a non-saint)[17] and finally the force

11. Neyrey, 'The Symbolic Universe', p. 273.

12. Neyrey, 'The Symbolic Universe', p. 288.

13. J. Breech refers to this as the psychology of a group. 'Neither Jesus nor John rebels *against* Judaism. Each of them acts according to his own standards; neither of them pays any attention to the group. But their contemporaries *perceive* them as *defectors* from the group, since they categorize everyone as either a "member" of the group or as a "non-member"...' (*The Silence of Jesus: The Authentic Voice of the Historical Man* [Philadelphia: Fortress Press, 1983], p. 28).

14. Neyrey, 'The Symbolic Universe', p. 378.

15. Neyrey, 'Ceremonies in Luke-Acts', in *The Social World of Luke-Acts* (ed. J.H. Neyrey; Peabody, MA: Hendrickson, 1991), p. 378. M. Douglas uses the term 'grid' rather than 'map'. See *Natural Symbols: Explorations in Cosmology* (New York: Pantheon Books, 1982), especially ch. 7 'Sin and Society'. 'The relation of self to society varies with the constraints of grid and group: the stronger these are, the more developed the idea of formal transgression and its dangerous consequences, and the less regard is felt for the right of the inner self to be freely expressed' (p. 102).

16. Malina and Neyrey, *Calling Jesus Names*, p. 37.

17. An obvious example would be Judas Iscariot, who is often labeled by the evangelists (post-betrayal) as Judas, 'the one who betrayed Him [Jesus]' (see Mt. 26.25; 27.3; Mk 3.19; Lk. 6.16; Jn 12.4; 18.2). Yet there are those who overcome

of stigma.[18]

Bruce J. Malina also suggests that the label 'a glutton and a drunkard' was a dishonoring one. In his essay, 'Honor and Shame: Pivotal Values of the First-Century Mediterranean World', Malina elucidates that honor

> is the value of a person in his or her own eyes plus the value of that person in the eyes of his or her social group. Honor is a claim to worth along with the social acknowledgement of worth. The purpose of honor is to serve as a sort of social rating which entitles a person to interact in specific ways with his or her equals, superiors and subordinates, according to the prescribed cultural cues of society.[19]

Malina then unpacks the societal values of honor and shame in the first-century Mediterranean context.[20] Labels/norms/values inevitably have positive and negative connotations. Honor then is not simply the attribution of a title; rather it also involves a group's evaluation (i.e., social rating) of a particular action or attitude.

The following 'Challenge and Response' model proposed by Malina is valuable when investigating and evaluating these 'accusatory labels' found in the gospels.[21] It involves three separate but interrelated sequences:

(1) *Challenge.* A claim to enter the social space of another, whether positive or negative.

(2) *Perception.* This is the necessary bridge, so to speak, between the challenge and response (*see below*). It involves individual awareness about the challenge and what available responses there are.

(3) *Response.* There are three available responses for the individual being challenged: (a) *Positive Rejection* – scorn, disdain, contempt – which requires vengeance on the part of the original challenger; (b) *Acceptance* – a response which entails a counter-challenge, which allows for the exchange to continue and (c) *Negative Refusal* – which involves no response, simply interpreted as a dishonor. Malina summarizes the challenge-response model:

---

such labels, namely, Rahab 'the prostitute' (Heb. 11.31; Jas 2.25). My thanks to Professor Mosser for this latter observation.

18. Malina and Neyrey, *Calling Jesus Names*, p. 38.

19. B.J. Malina, *The New Testament World: Insights from Cultural Anthropology* (Louisville: John Knox Press, 1981), p. 47.

20. Malina acknowledges that this is only a hypothetical model. It is nonetheless helpful in examining these 'accusations'.

21. See Malina, *New Testament World*, p. 31. The seven accusations are listed in S. McKnight's 'Calling Jesus *Mamzer*', *JSHJ* 1.1 (2003), 73-103, esp. 73-76.

'Now in the first-century Mediterranean world, every social interaction that takes place outside one's family or outside one's circle of friends is perceived as a challenge to honor, a mutual attempt to acquire honor from one's social equal. Thus gift-giving, invitations to dinner, debates over issues of law, buying and selling, arranging marriages, arranging what we might call cooperative ventures for farming, business, fishing, mutual help, and the like – all these sorts of interaction take place according to the patterns of honor called challenge-response'.[22]

By examining the pericopes in both Matthew and Luke, is the above model valuable in beginning to understand the alleged accusation against Jesus? Let us briefly examine the model in light of Matthew's and Luke's contexts:

(1) *Challenge.* Both John and Jesus are challenged by the implied audience initially due to their external behaviors. (a) John 'came neither eating (*no bread*) and drinking (*no wine*)' – the challenge of asceticism. John is also accused of having a 'demon'. (b) Jesus, on the other hand, came 'eating and drinking' – the challenge of excessiveness – being 'a glutton and drunkard'. Jesus is also accused of being 'a friend of tax collectors and sinners'. Both divine messengers are ultimately rejected by their constituencies.

'John and Jesus, central figures in the salvation being effected by God, are nevertheless rejected by the populace. The mystery becomes even greater when, as the Gospel proceeds, each is killed. Those who oppose God will always seem to have reasons to resist'.[23]

(2) *Perception.* This of course rests on the mindset and motivation of each evangelist (i.e., Matthew and Luke). Why do they include their passages where they do? How did they perceive the actions of Jesus? How did they understand their audiences? These questions will be addressed when investigating the actual accusation. Especially pertinent are the evangelists' emphases on the identity of Jesus: Matthew notes in 11.3b 'Are you he who is to come, or shall we look for another?'; Luke follows almost identically (Luke uses ἄλλον; whereas Matthew uses ἕτερον) in 7.19b and 20.[24] The importance here is that each evangelist is concerned about Jesus' identity and what impact that identity will have on the readers.

---

22. Malina, *New Testament World*, p. 32.
23. D.A. Hagner, *Matthew 1-13* (33A; Dallas: Word Books, 1993), p. 311.
24. The preferred reading is ἄλλον because of manuscript evidence; however, *BDF* notes that these two words were used indiscriminately during this period (See J.A. Fitzmyer, *The Gospel According to Luke* I-IX [AB, 28; New York: Doubleday], p. 667; *BDF* §306).

(3) *Response*. Initially, there is no specific response by Jesus to the challenge, since an independent wisdom aphorism concludes both the Matthean and Lukan passages.[25] However, in Matthew's next section, Jesus immediately begins to chastise the unrepentant cities of Chorazin and Bethsaida (Mt. 11.20-24) in what amounts to an eschatological day of judgment (ἡμέρα κρίσεως, see v. 22). Matthew's transitional verse (v. 20), not found in Luke's rendition, certainly supports that time has elapsed, especially with the adverb τότε.

Luke's account also confirms no specific response to the accusation; however, Luke follows it with his own special story of Jesus' pardon of a sinful woman during a dinner in the house of Simon the Pharisee (7.36-50). Luke positions a meal to immediately reinforce the accusation of Jesus as the consummate party animal (to borrow Blomberg's catchy title)[26] – namely, a 'glutton and a drunkard'. Furthermore, what is more preposterous is that during this meal – as it will be shown – 'this stubborn and rebellious' son (Jesus) forgives a woman ('a sinner') her sins.

So one can conclude that Malina's challenge-response model offers a beginning analysis to the purpose and function of the accusation 'a glutton and a drunkard'.

The Accusation: An Examination of 'A Glutton and a Drunkard'
(Matthew 11.19; Luke 7.34; Q 7.31-35)

To my knowledge, the authenticity of this pericope appears to be the majority opinion in New Testament scholarship.[27] Breech, commenting

---

25. One could argue that this is the evangelists' response.

26. See C.L. Blomberg, *Contagious Holiness: Jesus' Meals with Sinners* (NSBT; ed. D.A. Carson; Downers Grove, IL: InterVarsity Press, 2005), ch. 4.

27. See N. Perrin, *Rediscovering the Teaching of Jesus*, 'The arguments for the authenticity of both this simile and its application are very strong indeed' (p. 120). Also J. Breech, *The Silence of Jesus*, who lists the parable as one of the eight authentic core sayings of the historical Jesus. On the other hand, The Jesus Seminar finally rejects its authenticity, offering a 'gray' ('Well, maybe') evaluation, determined mostly because the gospel writers understood the phrase 'Son of Man' in the messianic sense. The Jesus Seminar concludes that this phrase then cannot be attributed to Jesus. But this is tenuous at best, since those who voted on this passage detect that 'The difference between a pink ("Sure sounds like Jesus") and a gray designation hangs on the thread of this single expression' (see *The Five Gospels: The Search for the Authentic Words of Jesus* [trans. and commentary by R.W. Funk, R.W. Hoover and The Jesus

specifically on the accusation of 'a glutton and drunkard', notes: 'It is virtually impossible to imagine anyone in the Christian tradition fabricating a saying that pictures Jesus in this way; hence, with the highest degree of probability, we can accept the saying as authentic'.[28] John Meier concurs: 'It strains credulity to think that the early church would create such a pungent, hostile saying [i.e., 'a glutton and a drunkard'] about Jesus when none existed'.[29]

The genre in which the accusation is embedded appears to be a parable in three organized parts with a wisdom saying (*aphorism*) attached to the end.[30]

We will now examine the slight differences in each account.[31]

Matthew 11	Luke 7
[18] ἦλθεν γὰρ ᾽Ιωάννης μήτε ἐσθίων μήτε πίνων, καὶ λέγουσιν· δαιμόνιον ἔχει.	[33] ἐλήλυθεν γὰρ ᾽Ιωάννης [ὁ βαπτιστὴς] μὴ ἐσθίων [ἄρτον] μήτε πίνων [οἶνον], καὶ λέγετε· δαιμόνιον ἔχει.
[19] ἦλθεν ὁ υἱὸς τοῦ ἀνθρώπου ἐσθίων καὶ πίνων, καὶ λέγουσιν· ἰδοὺ ἄνθρωπος φάγος καὶ οἰνοπότης, τελωνῶν φίλος καὶ ἁμαρτωλῶν. καὶ ἐδικαιώθη ἡ σοφία ἀπὸ τῶν ἔργων αὐτῆς.	[34] ἐλήλυθεν ὁ υἱὸς τοῦ ἀνθρώπου ἐσθίων καὶ πίνων, καὶ λέγετε· ἰδοὺ ἄνθρωπος φάγος καὶ οἰνοπότης, φίλος τελωνῶν καὶ ἁμαρτωλῶν. [35] καὶ ἐδικαιώθη ἡ σοφία ἀπὸ [πάντων] τῶν [τέκνων] αὐτῆς.

There are at least four slight emendations between Matthew's and Luke's account (see above synoptic diagram). Both accounts are nearly identical

Seminar; New York: Macmillan, 1993], p. 303). Contrary, Sanders argues that the pericope 'has the ring of authenticity' (*Jesus and Judaism* [Philadelphia: Fortress Press, 1985], p. 179). A.J. Hultgren also affirms the historicity of the particular accusation (see *Jesus and His Adversaries: The Form and Function of the Conflict Stories in the Synoptic Tradition* [Minneapolis, MN: Augsburg, 1979], pp. 110-11.

28. J. Breech, *Silence of Jesus*, p. 23.

29. J.P. Meier, *A Marginal Jew: Mentor, Message, and Miracles* (New York: Doubleday, 1994), II, p. 150.

30. See C.L. Blomberg, *Interpreting the Parables* (Downers Grove: InterVarsity Press, 1990), pp. 208-10.

31. My investigation assumes the Two Source Hypothesis popularized by B.H. Streeter (*The Four Gospels*, 1924) at the beginning of the twentieth century. There has been a recent wave in NT scholarship questioning the veracity of the Quelle ('Q') source document (see footnote 32 below).

with Q. The first involves verb tenses: Matthew uses the aorist tense; whereas Luke uses the perfect. The second involves minor Lukan additions for clarification and emphasis (the additions are [bracketed] above): Luke adds 'the Baptist' (ὁ βαπτιστὴς) to signify John's role; 'bread' (ἄρτον), 'wine' (οἶνον) and finally 'all' (πάντων) to emphasize the inclusivity of the wisdom saying. Third, there is a reverse word order involving the phrase 'a friend of tax/toll collectors'; Matthew 11.19 has τελωνῶν φίλος; Luke 7.31 φίλος τελωνῶν. Last, and most significant is the textual variant in the concluding wisdom saying: Matthew's rendition reads 'her deeds' (τῶν ἔργων αὐτῆς); whereas Luke reads 'her children' (τῶν τέκνων αὐτῆς).

Scholars have debated the Sayings Source (= Q) *ad infinitum*.[32] This essay will concur with the scholarly consensus that Q did exist in some form and was used by both Matthew and Luke. We will briefly make a few observations of Matthew's and Luke's use of Q and how their emendations assist us in understanding the accusation.

First, the composition of Q 7.31-35 is simple to outline in two (2) parts: (1) Q 7.31-34, which elucidates the traditions of John the Baptist and Jesus and (2) Q 7.35, which includes a wisdom saying, one that was independently appended at the end.[33] 'Q 7.31-35 look in retrospect at the careers of John and Jesus and at their lack of success with "this generation". ... John represents the old aeon and Jesus the new'.[34]

Second, it appears that logion Q 7.34 is identically used by both Matthew and Luke, except for slight verb changes by Luke. Luke uses the perfect ἐλήλυθεν ('he has come') in 7.34; whereas Matthew 11.19 uses the aorist ἦλθεν ('he came'). Both employ the present tense λέγω ('saying'): Luke uses the second person plural λέγετε ('you'); whereas Matthew uses the third person plural λέγουσιν ('they said'). To account for these slight changes, Bock notes that each evangelist keeps the parallelism with John the Baptist (see Luke's use of ἐλήλυθεν in 7.33 and Matthew's ἦλθεν in

32. One need only to digest the massive tome by J.S. Kloppenborg Verbin, *Excavating Q: The History and Setting of the Sayings Gospel* (Philadelphia: Fortress Press, 2000) and the opposing view by M. Goodacre and N. Perrin, *Questioning Q: A Multidimensional Critique* (Downers Grove, IL: InterVarsity Press, 2004). Also see M. Goodacre, *The Case against Q: Studies in Markan Priority and the Synoptic Problem* (Harrisburg, PA: Trinity Press International, 2002).

33. Comments drawn here are from J.S. Kloppenborg, *The Formation of Q* (Philadelphia: Fortress Press, 1987), pp. 110-12.

34. Kloppenborg, *Formation*, p. 112.

11.18).[35] Other than the position of φίλος ('friend') before (Luke) or after (Matthew) τελωνῶν; these passages are identical.

Third, and perhaps most important, the accusatory label φάγος καὶ οἰνοπότης ('a glutton and a drunkard') is identical in each gospel and in Q 7.34. This perhaps suggests a fixed label, which may have been preserved in the early recession of Q (Q^2) and was, interestingly, not tampered with by each evangelist.[36] Why is this? Why tinker with, say, verb tenses and the independent wisdom aphorism, but not the trenchant accusation hailed against the Son of Man? Perhaps, and this is a hypothesis, the expression φάγος καὶ οἰνοπότης functions for each evangelist similarly like the title/label designations 'Son of Man' or 'a friend of tax collectors and sinners'. In other words, structurally and literarily 'Son of Man', 'a glutton and a drunkard' and 'friend of tax/toll

---

35. D.L. Bock, *Luke Volume 1: 1.1–9.50* (BECNT; Grand Rapids: Baker Books, 1994), p. 683.

36. This is the thrust of my argument assuming we can rely on Kloppenborg Verbin's reconstruction of Q and the Q hypothesis in general. Kloppenborg Verbin offers the following explanation about the different stratum of Q. Essentially, there are three: 'Q^1 provides a good example of instructional literature, offering topically organized instructions on several themes' (p. 197). The main redaction of Q occurs in Q^2, which 'has to do with the increased density of chriae – that is, sayings furnished with a brief setting' (p. 201). Kloppenborg Verbin places Q 7.34, and the label 'a glutton and a drunkard', in Q^2. 'Chriae are in fact ideally suited to the display of ethos for they place the speaker in situations requiring decisive pronouncements and clever repartee' (p. 202). The final stratum (Q^3) is, what Kloppenborg Verbin calls the final form of Q, which demonstrates a positive posture towards the Torah and Temple (see *Excavating Q*, pp. 212-13). See also B.L. Mack's informative discussion on the formation of the Q community in *The Lost Gospel: The Book of Q and Christian Origins* (NY: HarperSanFranciso, 1993), pp. 44-49. V.K. Robbins 'The Chreia', in *Greco-Roman Literature and the New Testament* (ed. D.E. Aune; Atlanta: Scholars Press, 1988) is very helpful in defining and describing chreia. Robbins argues that chreia, these maxims or sayings, have a specific aim or target, even if the aim or target might be elusive at times. 'It would be hard to overemphasize the attribution of the chreia to a particular person, because this is *the* aspect which distinguishes it from other forms... But the attribution of a saying or act to a particular person displays aspects of life, thought, action in a mode which integrates attitudes, values, and concepts with personal, social, and cultural realities. The people features in chreiai become authoritative media of positive and negative truths about life. These 'authorities' transmit social, cultural, religious, and philosophical heritage into later historical epochs' (p. 4). Also see D.E. Smith, *From Symposium to Eucharist: The Banquet in the Early Christian World* (Minneapolis: Fortress Press, 2003), who notes that 'a *chreia* was normally utilized to characterize a famous person or hero' (p. 228).

collectors' *all* function as 'titles' – albeit the last two disparagingly – as each offers Christologically and theologically insights that would epitomize Jesus' ministry.

As noted above, there appear to exist literary parallelisms with these 'titles' (viz., 'labels'). In all renditions of the passage, the following three titles ('Son of Man', 'a glutton and a drunkard' and 'a friend of tax collectors and sinners') all share a common grammatical linkage: the nominative of appellation.[37] 'A title appears in the nominative and functions as though it were a proper name. Another case would normally be more appropriate, but the nominative is used because of the special character of the individual described'.[38] Simply, each 'title' (label) is grammatically positioned to be read as such by the reader. This offers credence to the fact that all three, but especially for our examination 'a glutton and a drunkard', functioned as a specific delimiting label.

Finally, the wisdom saying in Q 7.35 is used by both evangelists for their theological agendas.

Excursus: Textual Variant in Matthew 11.19 and Luke 7.31
There is striking difference between the versions of the wisdom saying that concludes the passage (i.e., Mt. 11.19; Lk. 7.31). Does this difference assist to explain the meaning of the label 'a glutton and a drunkard'? Why then does Matthew employ 'deeds' (ἔργων)?[39]

It is often noted that Matthew identifies Jesus with wisdom.[40] Scholars

37. See H.E. Dana and J.R. Mantey, *A Manual Grammar of the Greek New Testament* (Toronto, Ontario: Macmillan, 1955) §83.3.

38. D. Wallace, *Greek Grammar beyond the Basics* (Grand Rapids: Zondervan, 1996), p. 61.

39. Metzger notes: 'The Committee regarded the reading τέκνων (widely supported by B² C D K L X Δ Θ Π and most minuscules) as having originated in scribal harmonization with the Lukan parallel (Luke 7.35). The readings with πάντων represent further assimilation to the passage in Luke' (*A Textual Commentary on The Greek New Testament* [Deutsche Bibelgesellschaft/German Bible Society, Stuttgart, 2nd edn, 1994], p. 24).

40. According to Schweizer *et al.*, Matthew is the only gospel writer among the synoptics to identify Jesus with Wisdom. Also see C.S. Keener, *A Commentary on the Gospel of Matthew* (Grand Rapids: Wm. B. Eerdmans, 1999), p. 343. Also see F.T. Gench, *Wisdom in the Christology of Matthew* (Lanham, MD: University Press of America, 1997); M. Jack Suggs, *Wisdom, Christology, and Law in Matthew's Gospel* (Cambridge: Harvard University Press, 1970); J.D.G. Dunn, *Christology in the Making* (Grand Rapids: Wm. B. Eerdmans, 2nd edn, 2005), pp. 197-206. Also B. Witherington III, *Jesus the Sage: The Pilgrimage of Wisdom* (Minneapolis, MN: Fortress Press, 1994), esp. ch. 4.

have acknowledged that wisdom is a central feature of Christology in both Q and Matthew.[41]

Thus Matthew 11.19 appears to be a wisdom saying with its own independent meaning, since the aorist verb tense is gnomic or timeless.[42] As noted above, this wisdom saying seems to have been adhered independently to the end of the pericope. Hagner seems to summarize this saying correctly: 'In the present context, applied to Jesus the saying means that the deeds of Jesus – including the very ones criticized by the opponents – will ultimately vindicate him'.[43]

Matthew interprets this verse in light of 11.2 with the catchword 'deeds': 'When John heard in prison what the Messiah was doing (τὰ ἔργα), he sent word by his disciples'.[44] Schweizer notes: 'He [i.e., Matthew] thus equates the works of God's Wisdom with the works of Jesus'.[45] Fitzmyer furthermore observes '"Deeds" is almost certainly a Matthean modification, since it picks up the "deeds of the Messiah" in 11.2'.[46]

Here the personification of Wisdom, which has its foundation in the OT (cf. Prov. 8.22ff; 9.1ff; 9.3),[47] seems to connect the title 'Sophia' with the 'Son of Man' (thus Jesus himself).

On the other hand 'children' (τέκνων) in Luke 7.35 appears to have the original saying, except for the addition of 'all', which seems to be a Lukan characteristic.[48] Here 'children' has been added perhaps for the mention of 'children' in verse 32 (the Greek words however are different). There is also precedence about Wisdom's children in the OT.[49]

---

41. E. Schweizer, *The Good News According to Matthew* (trans. D.E. Green; Atlanta: John Knox Press, 1975), pp. 446-47; J.M. Robinson, 'LOGOI SOPHON: On the Gattung of Q' in *Trajectories Through Early Christianity* (Philadelphia: Fortress Press, 1971), pp. 71-113; esp. 112-13; E. Schüssler Fiorenza, *In Memory of Her: A Feminist Theological Reconstruction of Christian Origins* (New York: Crossroad, 1989) pp. 130-40.

42. Wallace describes the gnomic aorist as '…it does not refer to a particular event that *did* happen, but to a generic event that *does* happen' (*Greek Grammar*, p. 562).

43. Hagner, *Matthew*, p. 311.

44. Others too have made this connection: see R.H. Gundry, *Matthew: A Commentary on his Literary and Theological Art* (Grand Rapids: Eerdmans, 1982), p. 213.

45. Schweizer, *Matthew*, p. 265.

46. Fitzmyer, *Luke*, p. 681.

47. Cf. Sirach 24.4-17, where Wisdom speaks in the assembly of the Most High to tell of her glories. Also note the personification of Wisdom in Sirach 51.

48. See Fitzmyer, *Luke*, p. 681. He also notes that Luke has a 'generic predilection for the adjective "all"' (πᾶς, ἄπας). See Fitzmyer, *Luke*, p. 524.

49. Fitzmyer references Sir. 4.11 'Wisdom teaches her children and gives help to

Thus 'children' appears to have been the original rendition. Matthew redacts the aphorism to enhance a personal wisdom Christology in the passage; one that specifically identifies Jesus with wisdom and that his deeds will vindicate him.[50]

Schweizer insightfully compares and contrasts the purposes of John the Baptist and Jesus, with wisdom personified as 'deeds' (Jesus) or as 'children' (John the Baptist):

> In retrospect what stands out is the cryptic saying about the presence of God's Kingdom as an object of violence, hatred and attack... Anyone looking for a trendie or weather vane to guide him, in order to be left in peace with all wishes gratified, has certainly found the wrong man in the Baptist. But anyone who allows the call of Jesus to take hold of him will discover that John is indeed greater than all the prophets, because in him the new world of God commences, and that the least in the Kingdom – attacked, resisted, and suppressed by men – will be even greater than John.[51]

The Contexts of the Accusations: Matthew 11.19 and Luke 7.34

Matthew 11.16-19

This parable (Mt. 11.16-19) fits nicely into Matthew's overall theological plan: John is presented as the *Elijah redivivus* contrasted to the 'Son of Man' (ὁ υἱὸς τοῦ ἀνθρώπου) – a designation that refers to both Jesus himself (= 'I') and perhaps to an apocalyptic messianic allusion in Daniel 7, especially in verse 13.[52] Fitzmyer observes that the NT usage of ὁ υἱὸς

---

those who seek her'. and Prov. 8.32 'And now, my children, listen to me: happy are those who keep my ways' (see *Luke*, p. 681).

50. Leivestad begs to differ and argues that σοφια in Matthew's text is used ironically, not as a Christological theme. This is difficult of course to argue since, Leivestad himself notes, 'We have no other example in the gospels where is σοφια used ironically...' ('An Interpretation of Matt 11.19' *JBL* 71.3 [1952], pp. 179-81, 181).

51. Schweizer, *Matthew*, p. 265.

52. See J.A. Fitzmyer, *A Wandering Aramean* in *The Semitic Background of the New Testament: Combined Edition of Essays on the Semitic Background of the New Testament* and *A Wandering Aramean: Collected Aramaic Essays* (The Biblical Resource Series; Grand Rapids: Wm. B. Eerdmans, 1997), who recognizes the complicated origin of the phrase (pp. 143-55; esp. 155). He notes that 'the Son of Man' in Daniel 7.13 is not used in the titular sense. Also see D.M. Sweetland, *Our Journey with Jesus: Discipleship According to Luke-Acts* (Collegeville, MN: Liturgical Press, 1990), who argues more decisively for a dual meaning of this title in

τοῦ ἀνθρώπου is unique because it is found in the arthrous (with the definite article) form.[53] The parallelism with John is also striking: 'For John came neither eating nor drinking, and they said: "He has a demon"' (v. 18).[54] Matthew is determined to reveal the different identities of each main character in the narrative: John is an obedient son of Elizabeth and Zechariah – at least by Jewish standards; whereas Jesus is, because of his actions, a disobedient son of Mary and Joseph. The paradox for Matthew here is that both John and Jesus are ultimately rejected by the audience (vis-à-vis 'this generation'), since John, although not 'eating and drinking' is said to be demon-possessed (v. 18) and Jesus, because he came 'eating and drinking', is 'a glutton and a drunkard' (v. 19).

Luke 7.31-35

Luke's rendition of this parable (as noted above) shares many of the same characteristics as Matthew's. The key comparison is of John the Baptist and Jesus: both are rejected though both behave differently. Luke's parenthetical verses in 7.29-30, as noted by Blomberg, imply that Luke's

Luke's gospel: both to Jesus' earthly ministry and to his future coming in glory/ judgment (p. 98). R.L. Brawley also agrees with the connection of the 'Son of Man' with the referent 'I' (see 'Table Fellowship: Bane and Blessings for the Historical Jesus', *PRSt* 22 (1995), pp. 13-31.

53. '...the arthrous form must be understood as a *title* for Jesus' (Fitzmyer, *Wandering Aramean*, p. 154; my emphasis). There is considerable and ongoing debate on whether 'Son of Man' is a title, what its origins are, and its subsequent implications for understanding the historical Jesus. See the recent major article by P. Owen and D. Shepherd, which affirms the specialness of this expression, 'Speaking Up for Qumran, Dalman and the Son of Man: Was *Bar Enasha* a Common Term for "Man" in the Time of Jesus?' *JSNT* 81 (2001), pp. 81-122; the rebuttal by M. Casey ('Aramaic Idiom and the Son of Man Problem: A Response to Owen and Shepherd', *JSNT* 25.1 [2002], pp. 3-32) and further reflections by L.W. Hurtado (who affirms Owen and Shepherd's thesis) in *Lord Jesus Christ: Devotion to Jesus in Earliest Christianity* (Grand Rapids: Wm. B. Eerdmans, 2003), esp. pp. 301-306. Hurtado's view, which is also maintained in this essay, is noted as 'The function of the expression is further indicated in the fact that Jesus is not only the sole referent of its eighty-one uses in the Gospels, he is also the only one who uses it. "The son of man" is Jesus' own special way of referring to himself' (p. 304).

54. There is also considerable debate on whether the phrase 'Son of Man' is actually an allusion to Daniel 7. See D. Juel, *Messianic Exegesis: Christological Interpretation of the Old Testament in Early Christianity* (Philadelphia: Fortress Press, 1988), especially ch. 7 (pp. 151-70) for the nuances of the debate.

audience for the parable was more inclusive; rather than Matthew's Pharisees and scribes.[55]

The Content of the Accusations: Matthew 11.19 and Luke 7.34

We will now examine the three basic couplets found both in Matthew and Luke followed by an independent wisdom aphorism. We identify each couplet by use of the conjunction και ('and'). We will also examine any similarities/differences between the Matthean and Lukan accounts.

There are three couplets that both passages share in common. Here I am defining a 'couplet' as two nouns or verbs connected by the use of και. Each couplet assists the structure for each passage found in Matthew and Luke. I will briefly examine each one, noting similarities and differences.

(1) *'Eating and drinking'* (ἐσθίων καὶ πίνων). This exact couplet is found both in Matthew 11.19 and Luke 7.34. It has its origins in Q 7.34. Simply, this caricature bodes well with the following accusation of Jesus as 'a glutton and a drunkard'. Hagner observes 'This caricature was perhaps caused by Jesus' frequent attendance at banquets'.[56] It is also an antithesis, according to Nolland, to John the Baptist's behavior: 'Jesus seemed to behave as though there was continually something to celebrate (cf. 5.33-34), and drew into this celebration tax collectors and sinners – people known to be unsavory types who lived beyond the edge of respectable society (cf. 5.30).[57] As both Matthew 11.18 and Luke 7.33 note, John the Baptist came neither eating nor drinking. Jesus showed no restraint 'as a token of the freedom of the kingdom that he was proclaiming'.[58]

(2) *'A glutton and a drunkard'* (φάγος καὶ οἰνοπότης). This is the main couplet/label under investigation. This phrase is found Matthew 11.19, Luke 7.34 and Q 7.34. It is nowhere else found in the NT. This phrase has allusions to the Jewish Scriptures, particularly to Deuteronomy 21.20: 'They shall say to the elders of his town, "This son of ours is stubborn and rebellious. He will not obey us. He is a glutton and a drunkard."'

Robert J. Karris observes that Deuteronomy 21.20, along with Proverbs 23.20-21, sheds some light on the origin and purpose of the label.[59]

---

55. See Blomberg, *Contagious Holiness*, p. 117.
56. Hagner, *Matthew*, p. 310.
57. Nolland, *Luke*, pp. 345-46.
58. Fitzmyer, *Luke*, p. 681.
59. See Robert J. Karris, *Eating your Way through Luke's Gospel* (Collegeville, MN: Liturgical Press, 2006), pp. 26-27.

Proverbs 23.20-21 reads 'Do not be among winebibbers, or among gluttonous eaters of meat; [21] for the drunkard and the glutton will come to
poverty, and drowsiness will clothe them with rags'.[60] The LXX rendition
of the phrase 'a glutton and a drunkard' in Deuteronomy is συμβολοκο-
πῶν οἰνοφλυγεῖ, which is not identical to Matthew's or Luke's rendition
(φάγος καὶ οἰνοπότης). This is also true for Proverbs (οἰνοπότης = 'winebibbers'; συμβολαῖς = 'gluttonous eaters'). Thus, some have suggested
then that the gospel writers are not associating the label 'a glutton and a
drunkard' with 'a stubborn and rebellious' son. One example is U. Luz
who contends that Deuteronomy 21.20 does not play a role, since Matthew 11.19 and the LXX rendering is too different.[61]

Perhaps the best approach to understanding Deuteronomy 21.20 and to
appraise whether or not there is a valid connection between 'a glutton and
drunkard' and 'a stubborn and rebellious' son, is to grapple with the original context. Deuteronomy 21.18-21 is situated within a larger context
concerning things that defile the covenant relationship with Yahweh, what
Cairns suitably describes as 'threats to the covenant'.[62] The topics
addressed in this chapter stem from how to handle unsolved murders
(21.1-9), to women prisoners of war (21.10-14), to the inheritance of the
firstborn (21.15-17) and finally to how to bury persons after their execution (21.22-24). Thus the description of 'a stubborn and rebellious son'
is viewed as a threat to the covenantal relationship with Yahweh. Why?
Because this description and the subsequent indictment of stoning,
although extremely harsh, is a direct affront to the fifth commandment:
'Honor your mother and father' (Deut. 5.16; cf. Exod. 20.12).[63] Wright

---

60. The phrase 'ἐκτείνου συμβολαῖς κρεῶν τε ἀγορασμοῖς' rendered as 'gluttonous
eaters of meat' (NRSV) is a difficult one to translate. Karris suggests the parallel 'a
glutton and a drunkard' between Prov. 23, Mt. 11.19 and Lk. 7.34, might be more
ambiguous, since the following verse (Prov. 23.21) should be more accurately translated 'a drunkard and fornicator' (πορνοκόπος), although many English translations
continue the parallel from v. 20 and render it 'for the drunkard and the glutton will
come to poverty…'. So the parallel between verses 20 and 21 may inevitably break
down (see Karris, *Eating your Way through Luke's Gospel*, p. 27).

61. U. Luz, *Matthew 8–20* (Hermeneia; trans. J.E. Crouch; Minneapolis: Augsburg
Fortress, 2001), p. 149 n. 37.

62. I. Cairns, *Deuteronomy: Word and Presence* (ITC; Grand Rapids: Wm B.
Eerdmans, 1992), p. 187.

63. Interestingly, scholars are in agreement that there is no specific evidence that
this law was ever invoked in Israel (see commentaries by Wright, p. 236; Cairns,
p. 192; Miller, p. 166). Callaway also notes that Prov. 23.21 – another text which highlights the consequences of gluttony and drunkardness – knows no death penalty.

concurs: 'The young man is not be to executed for gluttony and drunkenness in themselves, but for incorrigible flouting of the fifth commandment in ways that were squandering and endangering the family's substance'.[64]

Why then the seriousness of such an accusation? Why is the accusation so damaging?

The seriousness rests on a twofold indictment. 'A stubborn and rebellious son' is firstly disobedient to his parents, who are in essence representatives of God. Thus to disobey one's parents is to disobey God. Second, and perhaps not immediately evident, 'a stubborn and rebellious son' is disobedient (i.e., disruptive) to the Israelite community. This son causes disharmony, discord and distraction within the community – an impediment to discerning the Lord's way. Miller observes that

> ...rebellion is clearly regarded as resistance to divine direction as mediated through parental authority and teaching. That behavior is not simply a bad thing but is representation of a festering sore in the midst of the people, a corruption that can undo the community's devotion to its Lord and its continued attention to the Lord's way.[65]

Bellefontaine makes a compelling case that Deuteronomy 21.18-21 does indeed embody not one condemnation (which is typically argued), but actually two.[66] She unpacks the legal implications depicted in Deuteronomy 21.18-21a which entails (1) the procedure of how family members rid themselves of a obstinate child with (2) how a clan or tribe would rid itself of an 'irreformable' (Bellafontaine's word) deviant. Hence, a 'legal' shift from the indictment of the individual within the family, to the community-at-large. Bellafontaine argues that the accusation 'He is a glutton and a drunkard' is perhaps an added and independent tradition – based on Proverbs 23.21.[67] This addition strengthens the legal case. Callaway also observes the inherent connection between Deuteronomy 21.20 and Proverbs 23.21a. – a seamless combination of law and wisdom.[68]

Proverbs 23 then seems to tackle the moral implications of such actions – one should avoid being a 'winebibber' and 'gluttonous eaters of meat';

---

64. C.J.H. Wright, *Deuteronomy* (NIBC; Peabody, MA: Hendrickson, 1996), p. 238.

65. Miller, *Deuteronomy*, pp. 167-68.

66. See E. Bellafontaine, 'Deuteronomy 21.18-21: Reviewing the Case of the Rebellious Son', *JSOT* 13 (July 1979), pp. 13-31.

67. Also see P.R. Callaway, 'Deut. 21.18-21: Proverbial Wisdom and Law', *JBL* 103.3 (1984), pp. 341-52, esp. p. 343.

68. See Callaway, 'Deut. 21:18-21', p. 346.

whereas Deuteronomy 21 addresses the specific accusation (i.e., 'label') with its unambiguous legal consequences.[69] Bellafontaine observes that although Proverbs offers wisdom on how to handle these situations; Deuteronomy 21 is the legal authority for such an indictment, not the other way around. 'The wisdom admonitions in Israel never attained the level of law. They remain no more than words of advice and caution even when spoken by father or teacher.'[70]

Bellafontaine maintains that the indictment may be broader than what is often argued as a direct violation of Exodus 20.12. She notes the dual accusation brought forth by the parents: the son is *both* (1) stubborn (sôrēr) and rebellious (mōreh) and (2) a glutton (zôlēl) and drunkard (sōbē'). C. Wright agrees that this is not a case of a 'difficult' child.

> The law is not talking about naughty young children but about seriously delinquent young adults. If the law intentionally balances the preceding one, then it may envisage a firstborn son who is proving totally unworthy of his inheritance... If this is how the son behaves while still a minor, then what will he do with the family's substance when he inherits it?[71]

Bellafontaine observes that outside this narrative there is no specific biblical law demanding the death of a 'stubborn and rebellious son'.[72] Nevertheless, it is a serious accusation, since the focus 'is not a particular action or omission of the son but his direct relationship to his parents... Whatever the specific issues involved in the family controversy, it is evident that the authority of the parents has been rejected by the son'.[73]

Secondly, after examining ANE parallels, particularly the Code of Hammurabi, Bellafontaine remarks that the penalty for disobeying parents is not death, but the cutting out of the boy's tongue.[74] Thus, the seriousness of the Deuteronomy passage is inexorably heightened; the indictment of a 'stubborn and rebellious' son is more devastating and ultimately is rooted in the covenant relationship between Yahweh and his people. After surveying other variations of the phrase 'stubborn and rebellious' in the Hebrew Bible,[75] Bellafontaine concludes:

---

69. Prov. 28.7 warns 'Those who keep the law are wise children, but companions of gluttons shame their parents'.

70. Bellafontaine, 'Deuteronomy 21:18-21', p. 22.

71. Wright, *Deuteronomy*, p. 235.

72. See pp. 16ff. 'According to *b. Sanh* 71, the "rebellious son" was never stoned to death. The goal of such laws was to reward those [i.e., rabbis] who studied them' (Callaway, 'Deut 21.18-21', p. 348 n. 30).

73. Bellafontaine, 'Deuteronomy 21:18-21', p. 17.

74. Bellafontaine, 'Deuteronomy 21:18-21', p. 17.

75. See Ps. 78.8; Isa. 65.2; Neh. 9.29; Jer. 5.23 among others.

The thrust of these judgments upon Israel is her persistent infidelity. Israel has consistently failed to conduct itself in accordance with the covenant relationship which binds it to Yahweh. It is not by one act or on one occasion that she has displayed her defiance. Her whole character is portrayed as rebellious and disobedient.[76]

Hence, 'the stubborn and rebellious son' reflects a larger reality, since parents are often viewed as Yahweh's representatives to their children;[77] it reflects the totality of the relationship between Yahweh and his people. 'Thus, "stubbornness" and "rebelliousness" bear meaning of persistent disobedience to one who, by reason of a binding relationship, has the right to demand obedience. Rebelliousness denies that authority and rejects the relationship.'[78]

So what specifically then can be said of this 'stubborn and rebellious son'? This behavior had both communal and familial implications: 'Thus, the son's deviant behaviour not only corrupted himself but may have meant serious negative consequences for this neighbours'.[79] Bellafontaine continues 'The son's persistent excesses [i.e., gluttony and drunkenness] despite his parents' efforts marked him as "stubborn and rebellious" as well'.[80]

Finally, as Karris notes, although the LXX version of Deuteronomy 21.20 does not have the exact couplet (φάγος καὶ οἰνοπότης) found in Matthew 11.19 and Luke 7.34,[81] the indication appears unambiguous: there are social (vis-à-vis familial) and religious implications for those who are perceived as 'gluttons'[82] and 'drunkards'.

76. Bellafontaine, 'Deuteronomy 21:18-21', p. 18.

77. 'The parents are the first rank of persons whose authority must be acknowledged in order for human community to work in behalf of goodness and peace' (Miller, *Deuteronomy*, p. 167).

78. Bellafontaine, 'Deuteronomy 21:18-21', p. 19.

79. Bellafontaine, 'Deuteronomy 21:18-21', p. 21. Miller also notes the combination of individual-communal consequences: 'While the sin or crime takes place in the context of the family and the parents are given the responsibility for initiating actions as the ones who know of and are the recipients of the child's rebellion, the community is clearly the context and vehicle for all the judicial action that takes place ... Punishment is not determined by how much explicit harm has been done to individuals but by the depth of the wound to the body politic and religious when the fundamental directions of the Lord's way are violated' (*Deuteronomy*, p. 168).

80. Bellafontaine, 'Deuteronomy 21:18-21', p. 23.

81. The order is reversed in the initial couplet: The LXX has μέθυσος καὶ πορνοκόπος ('the drunkard and glutton') in Prov. 23.21; whereas v. 20 uses οἰνοπότης for 'drunkard' and συμβολαῖς for 'glutton'.

82. '... a figurative extension of meaning of γαστήρ "belly", φάγος (derivative of

The inference is compelling and word-to-word correlation is not needed to suggest a parallel or intertextual echo.[83]

There is also a revealing extra-canonical source for equating the designation of 'the stubborn and rebellious son' with 'a glutton and a drunkard'. In an extended passage from *Tractate Sanhedrin* 8.1ff., which also cites Proverbs 23.20, one sees the logic of the argument:

> 'A stubborn and rebellious son' – when can he be condemned as a stubborn and rebellious son? From the time that he can produce two hairs until he grows a beard... for it is written, 'If a man have a son – a son and not a daughter, a son and not a man'; a minor is exempt since he has not yet come within the scope of the commandments.
>
> When is he culpable? After he has eaten a *tritimor* [50 zuz = ⅓ lb.] of flesh and drunk a half-log [~ 1 liter] of Italian wine. R. Jose says: A mina of flesh and a log of wine. If he consumed it at a gathering that was a religious duty, or at the intercalation of the month, or if he consumed it as Second Title in Jerusalem, or if he ate carrion or flesh that was *terefah* [= torn, especially by wild beasts] or forbidden beasts or creeping things, if by consuming it he had fulfilled a command or had committed a transgression, if he ate any foodstuff but did not eat flesh and drinks wine, for it is written, *A glutton and a drunkard.* And though there is no proof for this, there is an indication, for it is written, *Be not among winebibbers; among gluttonous eaters of flesh* (insertions of weights and measures by author).[84]

the stem φαγ "to eat", the aorist of ἐσθίω): a person who habitually eats excessively... A glutton is often spoken of idiomatically, for example, "a large belly" or "a person who is only a stomach" or "a professional eater"' (Greek-English Lexicon of the New Testament Based on Semantic Domains. Volumes 1-2; NY.UBS, 1988, 1989, §23.19 under the rubric 'Physiological Processes and States').

83. See R.B. Hays' groundbreaking *The Echoes of Scripture in the Letters of Paul* (New Haven: Yale University Press, 1998) which lists seven tests, albeit for Paul's letters, to determine intertexual echoes from the OT (see pp. 29-32). The tests that 'a glutton and a drunkard' seems to pass are (1) *Availability* – the source of the echo was available to the evangelists through the importance of the Deuteronomic tradition (2) *Thematic Coherence* – the source of the echo fits the theme or line of argument of the passage (3) *Historical Plausibility* –the historical veracity of the passage and specifically the credibility of the accusation is deemed unwavering by the academy and finally (4) *Satisfaction* – the reading of 'a glutton and a drunkard' as a caricature, a slur, a derogatory label against the historical Jesus does 'satisfy' this proposed reading of the account.

84. *Tractate Sanhedrin* 8.1-2 from H. Danby, *The Mishnah* (Oxford, UK: Oxford University Press, 1933). It is quite obvious from the gospels that Jesus passed the litmus test to be 'a stubborn and rebellious son'.

A couple of observations are in order. First, as noted here and also in
m. Nid 6.11-12, the implications of this law are specific to a time period
between when 'he [that is, the 'stubborn and rebellious son'] can produce
two hairs until he grows a beard...' Those who are younger are not liable.
This depiction strongly suggests that the historical Jesus, although not yet
forty years old, indeed had more than two hairs and probably a beard. He
would indeed qualify under this stipulation. Second, Sanders notes the
oddity of first-century Palestinian Jews eating large quantities of meat,
except during the festivals, or if they were wealthy.[85] Hence the accusation of 'glutton' may also carry a socio-economic slander: Jesus congre-
gated often with the wealthy.

(3) *'A friend of tax collectors and sinners'* (φίλος τελωνῶν καὶ
ἁμαρτωλῶν). This phrase is found in both Matthew 11.19 and Luke 7.34.
However, the words φίλος τελωνῶν are reversed in Matthew's version.
Kloppenborg observes that the original arrangement (Q 7.34) was probably Matthew's τελωνῶν φίλος, due to the awkward construction of
τελωνῶν φίλος.[86] It may also result because of a Matthean emphasis,
since Matthew's gospel has an expressed interest in tax collectors, so that
'τελωνῶν advances to the first position...'[87] Even so, it appears that this
phrase also functions as a 'label' for Jesus' accusers – one that expounds
the prior one of 'a glutton and a drunkard'. 'The accusation points up to
the impression left by Jesus in his dealings with social groups of his day,
especially the impression made on the "establishment" of his generation'.[88]

We will now briefly examine certain details of this 'label':

(A) *'Friend'* (φίλος).[89] Karris notes that the concept of φίλος has at least
two appropriate parallels for this passage: OT Wisdom literature and
the Greco-Roman world. There are numerous passages in the Wisdom

---

85. 'Most people ate red meat only a few times a year...and fowl or fish only on
holy days...' (E.P. Sanders, *Judaism: Practice and Belief: 63 BCE-66 CE* [Philadel-
phia: Trinity Press International, 1992], p. 129).

86. It appears more syntactically logical to connect two plural genitives together,
using the conjunctive καὶ. However, grammatical logic is not always how languages
function.

87. 'Because of Matthew's interest in publicans...τελωνῶν advances to the first
position (contrast Luke)' (Gundry, *Matthew*, p. 213).

88. Fitzmyer, *Luke*, p. 681.

89. An exhaustive discussion of 'friend' and 'tax collectors and sinners' is beyond
the scope of the present study. The point here is to simply demonstrate that both terms
are used by the accusers as further 'labels' to complement and reinforce the accusation
'a glutton and a drunkard'.

literature; Karris cites Sirach 13.13-18 as cogent advice about choosing one's friends:

> Be on your guard and very careful, for you are walking about with your own downfall. Every creature loves its like, and every person the neighbor.[16] All living beings associate with their own kind, and people stick close to those like themselves. What does a wolf have in common with a lamb? No more has a sinner with the devout. What peace is there between a hyena and a dog? And what peace between the rich and the poor?

Second, Karris observes that Luke's concept of friendship embodies the Greco-Roman notion of sharing one's life and possessions communally. Hence, the oft quoted passage in Acts 2.44: 'All who believed were together and had all things in common'. Here Jesus is critiqued not just because he is a 'friend' of 'tax collectors and sinners' and subsequently eats with them; the catch here is reciprocity – Jesus is also befriended by these outcasts. Doubly scandalous.

Interestingly, Koenig notes that 'friend' nowhere else appears in the NT as a self-designation on the lips of Jesus or as a charge leveled against him.[90] This suggests that it is very early material and was used differently than the other labels/titles usually ascribed to Jesus.[91]

Hence, Jesus is labeled a 'friend' clearly here for derogatory reasons.

(B) *'Tax collectors and sinners'* (τελωνῶν καὶ ἁμαρτωλῶν). We will examine this phrase collectively because of the use of the couplet with καὶ, which intentionally parallels, as we have noted: 'eating and drinking', and 'a glutton and a drunkard'. The use of καὶ here, not to overstretch the point, stylistically connects these three couplets together. There are many other instances where Jesus befriends tax collectors and sinners (see Mt. 9.10-13; Mk 2.14-17; Lk. 15.2; 19.7). Corley rightly notes that this practice by Jesus advocates, what she calls, an 'Open Table Practice'. Additionally, Corley skillfully expands the label 'tax collector' to include those who associated with promiscuous women; likewise with the label 'sinner'. It is also argued by Corley and others that the designation 'tax collectors and sinners' is best understood as a boundary-marker, namely, a slanderous label to denounce Israelite 'outsiders' from those who are seen as 'insiders'.[92] Hence a division along sectarian lines. Dunn notes 'that

---

90. See Koenig, *New Testament Hospitality*, p. 24.

91. Not surprisingly, the other titles mentioned by Koenig (i.e., shepherd, physician, master, teacher) are generally used positively in the gospels (*New Testament Hospitality*, p. 24).

92. See Kathleen Corley, 'Jesus' Table Practice: Dining with Tax Collectors and

boundaries could also be drawn *within* the people of Israel, with "sinners" used to describe those of whom a particular faction disapproved'.[93] He continues to argue that the Gospel usage of "sinner" is a 'factional term, describing those whose conduct was regarded as unacceptable to a sectarian mentality – that is, not just the blatantly wicked but those who did not accept the sect's interpretation of the law or love in sufficient accord with that interpretation'.[94] Hence, a cogent argument to view this phrase as a label, a boundary-marker, one that offers insight into a 'Christology from the side'. Corley aptly recaps: 'Thus, the entire phrase, "tax collectors and sinners" should be categorized as a *topos* in the Greco-Roman Jewish polemic'.[95]

Conclusion

We have arrived at the conclusion of our examination. We now refer back to our initial question: What can we further understand about the historical Jesus by understanding this accusation? There are several points that we can derive from our study:

(1) The accusation 'a glutton and a drunkard' serves an ecclesiological and a theological (i.e., Christological) purpose for the evangelists. These different purposes cannot easily be separated, since they are inevitably embedded in the evangelists' interpretative framework. Daniel Harrington notes well the interconnectedness of these purposes for Matthew's gospel:

> While Matt 11.1-19 served sociological and ecclesiological functions in helping the Matthean community to locate itself vis-à-vis the Pharisees and the Baptist movement, it also fulfilled a Christological function. It tells us that Jesus did 'the deeds of the Christ' and therefore he is the

Sinners, Including Women' (SBL 1993 Seminar Papers; ed. Eugene H. Lovering; Atlanta, GA: Scholars Press, 1993), pp. 444-59 (447). Also see D.E. Smith, 'The Historical Jesus at Table', SBL Seminar Papers 28 (Atlanta, GA: Scholars Press, 1989): pp. 466-86, esp. p. 482, where Smith observes that 'the category "tax collectors and sinners" has to be taken as symbolic from the outset, as representative of a *type*, for the motif that Jesus associates/dines with them is taken to represent a *pattern* for him, not a one-time individual activity'.

93. See J.D.G. Dunn, 'Pharisees, Sinners, and Jesus', in *The Social World of Formative Christianity and Judaism: Essays in Tribute to Howard Clark Kee* (eds J. Neusner, P. Borgen, E.S. Frerichs, and R. Horsley; Philadelphia: Fortress Press, 1988), p. 277. *Contra* Perrin who suggests that 'tax collectors and sinners' are those Jews who had made themselves as Gentiles (*Rediscovering*, p. 120).

94. Dunn, 'Pharisees, Sinners, and Jesus', p. 279.

95. Corley, 'Jesus' Table Practice', p. 447.

Christ… The ecclesiological function…can also help Christian community today deal with the phenomenon of rejection.[96]

(2) The accusation 'a glutton and a drunkard' is best understood as one couplet (i.e., 'label') sandwiched between the one that *precedes* it: 'the Son of Man came eating and drinking' and the one that *follows* it: 'a friend of tax collectors and sinners'. The couplets were intentionally designed (borrowed) by the evangelists to offer a perspective to the identity of the historical Jesus. One who inevitably would follow and be compared with, but not be confused with John the Baptist. 'The figure of Jesus – accused of enjoying himself too much with the wrong kinds of people – balances off the picture of John'.[97]

(3) The accusation 'a glutton and a drunkard' is best understood as steeped in the Deuteronomic tradition of legal codes and familial relations.[98] What does this then say about the function of Deuteronomy for the gospel writers in the formulation of these accusations?

First, E. Achtemeier has observed 'that there is no book more basic for understanding the New Testament than Deuteronomy'.[99] The book of Deuteronomy cast a long shadow upon the evangelists as they interpret the historical Jesus.

Additionally, C. Wright notes the utmost importance of Deuteronomy for the NT writers. '[I]f we add the influence of the book [Deuteronomy] on Jesus, Paul, and the early NT church, it is a profoundly significant book in the whole Christian canon of scripture.'[100] Much more can be said about the importance of Deuteronomy; nevertheless, it appears that Deuteronomy is a significant backdrop for understanding these accusations. Carmichael

---

96. Harrington, *Matthew*, p. 162. Similar purposes can also be offered for the Lukan community. See L.T. Johnson, *The Gospel of Luke* (Sacra Pagina, 3; Collegeville, MN: The Liturgical Press, 1991), pp. 124-25.

97. Harrington, *Matthew*, p. 162.

98. Are there Deuteronomic textual echoes with each alleged accusation? Are the gospel writers cognizant of the connections? Possibly. We have already noted that S. McKnight has observed seven accusations against Jesus in 'Calling Jesus *Mamzer*'. McKnight recognizes that the allegation of Jesus as an illegitimate son has its underpinnings in Deut. 22.13-21, 23-27, 28-29 (see p. 79 n. 22).

One can begin to see the parallel of the gospel accusations with an indictment in Deuteronomy. A further study would be needed to confirm or deny these parallels. See Appendix at the end of this chapter.

99. E. Achtemeier, *Deuteronomy, Jeremiah* (Proclamation Commentaries; Philadelphia: Fortress Press, 1978), p. 9.

100. See Wright, *Deuteronomy*, p. 1.

argues that a major source of Mosaic Law is embedded in Deuteronomy 21.15–22.5 and that there is a special link between the laws and the narrative traditions, so much so that Carmichael postulates that perhaps the Deuteronomist views Esau as exemplifying some of the traits of the 'stubborn and rebellious' son.[101] Although Esau is not specifically represented in Deuteronomy 21.20, 'it is a hypothetical Esau that is depicted in the law'.[102]

So as the evangelists preserved the accusations against Jesus, they appeared to intentionally connect these accusations with the legal stipulations of Deuteronomy.

(4) The accusation 'a glutton and a drunkard' personifies Jesus as 'the stubborn and rebellious son' of Deuteronomy 21. This indictment is twofold: familial (inside) and societal (outside). Interestingly, 'Christology from the side' ought to encapsulate both dimensions, since it appraises, according to Malina and Neyrey, both Jesus' followers ('insiders') and enemies ('outsiders').[103]

Although there is no specific evidence that the 'stubborn and rebellious son' indictment was ever implemented in Judaism, Karris' insight is telling: 'Jesus shows a faithful God's universal love and mercy. To the religious leaders Jesus' promiscuous table fellowship is apostasy and an act of perverting the people... Jesus, a glutton and a drunkard, will die for the way he eats.'[104]

---

101. See C.M. Carmichael, 'Uncovering a Major Source of Mosaic Law: The Evidence of Deut 21.15–22.5', *JBL* 101.4 (1982), pp. 505-20, esp. 508-11.

102. Carmichael, 'Uncovering', p. 511.

103. See Malina and Neyrey, p. x.

104. Robert J. Karris, *Luke: Artist and Theologian* (New York: Paulist Press, 1985), p. 60.

APPENDIX

*The Gospel Accusations paralleled with the Indictment in
Deuteronomy*

Accusation	Deuteronomic 'Echo'
'Lawbreaker' (e.g., Sabbath: Mk 2.24; Lk. 13.14; 14.1-6; food customs: Mk 7.1-4; *et al.*)	Deut. 27.12-26 (twelve curses as a result for breaking the Law)
'Allegiance with Satan' (Mt. 9.34; 10.25; Mk 3.22)	Deut. 18.9-14; esp. vv. 10-11 'No one shall be found among you who makes a son or daughter pass through fire, or who practices divination, or is a soothsayer, or an augur, or a sorcerer, [11] or one who casts spells, or who consults ghosts or spirits, or who seeks oracles from the dead.'
'A Glutton and a Drunkard' (Mt. 11.19; Lk. 7.34)	Deut. 21.20 'They shall say to the elders of his town, "This son of ours is stubborn and rebellious. He will not obey us. He is a glutton and a drunkard."'
'Blasphemous' (Mk 2.7; 11.11-18; 14.6; Lk. 19.39	Deut. 8.14-17 'then do not exalt yourself, forgetting the LORD your God, who brought you out of the land of Egypt, out of the house of slavery, [15] who led you through the great and terrible wilderness, an arid wasteland with poisonous snakes and scorpions. He made water flow for you from flint rock, [16] and fed you in the wilderness with manna that your ancestors did not know, to humble you and to test you, and in the end to do you good. [17] Do not say to yourself, "My power and the might of my own hand have gotten me this wealth."'
'False Prophet' (Mt. 27.62-64; Mk 8.11-13; 14.65; Lk. 7.39; 23.2, 5, 14)	Deut. 18.20 'But any prophet who speaks in the name of other gods, or who presumes to speak in my name a word that I have not commanded the prophet to speak-- that prophet shall die.'
'King of the Jews' (Mk 15.2, 9, 12, 16-20, 26, 32)	Deut. 17.14-20 'When you have come into the land that the LORD your God is giving you, and have taken possession of it and settled in it, and you say, "I will

Accusation	Deuteronomic 'Echo'
	set a king over me, like all the nations that are around me", [15] you may indeed set over you a king whom the LORD your God will choose. One of your own community you may set as king over you; you are not permitted to put a foreigner over you, who is not of your own community. [16] Even so, he must not acquire many horses for himself, or return the people to Egypt in order to acquire more horses, since the LORD has said to you, "You must never return that way again". [17] And he must not acquire many wives for himself, or else his heart will turn away; also silver and gold he must not acquire in great quantity for himself. [18] When he has taken the throne of his kingdom, he shall have a copy of this law written for him in the presence of the levitical priests. [19] It shall remain with him and he shall read in it all the days of his life, so that he may learn to fear the LORD his God, diligently observing all the words of this law and these statutes, [20] neither exalting himself above other members of the community nor turning aside from the commandment, either to the right or to the left, so that he and his descendants may reign long over his kingdom in Israel.'
'Illegitimate Son' (see Mt. 1.18-25; Lk. 1.26-38 – passages that depict Jesus' miraculous birth)	Deut. 23.2 'Those born of an illicit union shall not be admitted to the assembly of the LORD. Even to the tenth generation, none of their descendants shall be admitted to the assembly of the LORD.'

JESUS AS BLASPHEMER

Darrell L. Bock

The charge of Jesus as 'blasphemer' is certainly one of the more serious charges raised against Jesus. It appears at his trial and in a couple of scenes where Jesus forgives sins in a very direct manner. The charge requires a look at four questions: (1) What constitutes blasphemy in Judaism? (2) Does the claim to forgive sins relate to this theme? (3) How do claims associated with being able to sit with God relate to this theme? and (4) Which New Testament passages raise this theme? We shall take each idea in turn.

Blasphemy in Judaism

This idea I have covered thoroughly in a monograph on the topic, the key elements of which I summarize here.[1] There are two kinds of blasphemy, verbal and blasphemy of action. Verbal blasphemy was legally limited to a pronunciation of the divine Name in an inappropriate way as *m. Sanh.* 7.5 taught. However, this was not all there was to the charge culturally.

There is little discussion of formal judicial examples of blasphemy in the Jewish literature. Trials for blasphemy are not present in these texts, though *m. Sanh.* 7.5 does define a procedure for examining a charge and limits the offence to speaking the very Name of God. Leviticus 24.10-16 is the one passage that many of the texts discuss where blasphemy is presented (note Josephus, *Ant.* 4.202). It possessed ambiguities that made defining blasphemy, especially where euphemisms were used, a subject of some rabbinic debate. Numbers 15.30-31 is often cited as a similar situation to blasphemy with its Sabbath violation followed by a death penalty. To use the divine Name in an inappropriate way is certainly blasphemy and is punishable by death (Lev. 24.10-16; *m. Sanh.* 6.4 and 7.5; Philo, *On the Life of Moses* 2.203-206). At the base of these ideas about blasphemy

---

1.   Darrell L. Bock, *Blasphemy and Exaltation in Judaism and the Final Examination of Jesus* (WUNT II/106; Tübingen: Mohr/Siebeck, 1998).

lies the command of Exodus 22.27 not to revile God nor the leaders he appointed for the nation.

Debate exists whether use of an alternative name for such an utterance is blasphemy, though some sentiment exists for including these examples (*m. Sch^eb.* 4.13; *b. Sch^eb.* 35a; *b. Sanh.* 55b-57a, 60a). Warnings were certainly issued in such cases where a range of euphemisms was used for utterances, but it does not appear, at least in the rabbinic period, to have carried an automatic death sentence.

What happened if a warning was ignored seems easy to determine, given the parallel with another warning involving the incorrigible son in *m. Sanh.* 8.4. An unheeded warning would lead to potential liability on the second offence. The official rabbinic position is that the use of the divine Name constitutes the only clear case of capital blasphemy (*m. Sanh.* 7.5). One is even to avoid blaspheming foreign deities as a sign of respect for the Name of God, texts that certainly reflect an apologetic stance taken with outsiders (Josephus, *Ant.* 4.207; Philo, *On the Life of Moses* 2.205; *Special Laws* 1.53).

Yet beyond utterances of blasphemy involving the Name, there is also a whole category of acts of blasphemy. These examples move beyond mere utterance of the Name, though often including it. Here one can start with of the use of a range of substitute titles. But beyond these offensive utterances one can see discussed a whole range of actions offensive to God. Almost any religiously sensitive Jew would have seen such actions as blasphemous, even if they were not specifically addressed by any formal, ideal legal statute. Their existence suggests a category of cultural blasphemy that all would recognize as representing an offence against God.

Acts of blasphemy seem to concentrate on idolatry (as a violation of the first commandment), a show of arrogant disrespect toward God, or the insulting of his chosen leaders. Often those who blasphemed verbally went further and acted on their feelings as well. God manages to judge such offences one way or another. Examples in Jewish exposition are Sisera (Judg. 4.3 and *NumR* 10.2; disrespect toward God's people), Goliath (1 Sam. 17 and Josephus, *Ant.* 6.183; disrespect towards God's people and worship of Dagon), Sennacherib (2 Kgs 18–19 = Isa. 37.6, 23; disrespect for God's power), Belshazzar (Dan. 3.29 Q [96] and Josephus, *Ant.* 10.233, 242; disrespect for God's presence in the use of temple utensils at a party), Manasseh (acting against the Torah; *Sifre* § 112) and Titus (*b. Gitt.* 56 and *ARN B* 7; entering, defaming the Temple, slicing open the curtain and taking the utensils away). Acting against the Temple is also blasphemous (1 Macc. 2.6; Josephus, *Ant.* 12.406). Significantly, comparing oneself to

God is also blasphemous according to Philo and reflects an arrogance like that seen in other acts of blasphemy just noted above (*On Dreams* 2.130-31; *Decalogue* 13-14, 61-64). At Qumran, unfaithfulness in moral action by those who pretend to lead the people (CD 5.12) or the act of speaking against God's people (1QpHab 10.13) are blasphemous. In the Mishnah and Talmud, idolatry and blasphemy are seen as very similar, while in a few texts they are said to be virtually the same (*y. Sanh.* 7.25a). Still other examples treated more briefly in this rabbinic material are: Adam, the generation of the flood, Sodomites, Pharaoh, Naboth, Korah, Amalek, Nebuchadnezzar, and Rome, as well as Tabor and Carmel as false locales of worship. Within Israel, the outstanding example is the golden calf incident, where idolatry is offensive to the holiness of Israel's God (Philo, *On the Life of Moses* 2.159-66).

Blasphemy represents an offence against God and a violation of a fundamental principle of the faith. Sometimes God alone punishes the blasphemer (e.g., Pharaoh, Korah, Titus), while at other times judgment is to be carried out by the community (the Israelite woman's son). But a second important level of blasphemy is attacking God's people verbally, as Sennacherib or Goliath did. Here Exodus 22.27 has a special role to play. Those who challenge the leadership God has put in place for his people are also seen as attacking God himself. So blasphemy operates in a rather wide range of insulting speech or activity.

How this view of blasphemy in Judaism relates to the leadership's examination of Jesus requires careful consideration of one other important topic, namely, the highest Jewish forms of exaltation. By 'high' exaltation is meant a very specific kind of activity, going directly into God's presence in heaven. The question does not involve merely the ability to go into heaven as a righteous one. The possibility of a heavenly abode offended no Jew who believed in an afterlife for the righteous. Rather the crucial question concerns the possibility of going directly into God's presence to be or serve at his side. Did Jews consider God's holiness to be so unique that such a place would be inappropriate for anyone, human or angelic? Thus, the next section considers the issue of who gets to go into the presence of God and labours at his side. It is only when the themes of blasphemy and exaltation within Judaism are carefully understood that one can then ask about the basis for the charge that Jesus was a 'blasphemer'.

Exaltation in Judaism

Early Jewish views of heavenly access to God show just how respected and unique the deity was. His presence radiates with a brilliant glory and his honour is protected by an elaborate structure of restricted access, which only his sovereign direction breaks.[2] Though heaven is full of inhabitants who serve and praise him, only a few even get an intimate glimpse of his presence. Those who get to sit in his presence are directed to do so.

The list of those who sit in heaven is a select one, consisting either of the great luminaries of the past or of anticipated eschatological luminaries of the future who sometimes represent a mixing of transcendent-human qualities. When it comes to the angels, only Gabriel is said to sit next to God's presence, and that is merely as Enoch's escort (*2 En.* 24.1-3). But even this text is not entirely free of suspicion as a Christian interpolation.[3] Those angels who share in the heavenly council appear to function as a 'first among equals' and are sent to carry out a judgement that God has authorized (11QMelch 2.9-11, 13-14). When it comes to angels, getting into God's presence relates to service and worship, not sitting.

But what can be said of human figures? Adam, Abel, Enoch, Abraham, Moses, David, Job, the Messiah, Enoch-Son of Man, Enoch-Metatron are said to sit. Enoch sits to receive revelation about the end (*Jub.* 4.20; *T. Abr* 11.3-8[B]; *2 En.* 24.1-3). Adam and Abraham serve as witnesses to the judgment (*T. Abr* 10–12). Adam is reinstated to the authority he had before the Fall (*Life of Adam and Eve* 47.3; *Apoc. Mos.* 39.2-3). Job, whose seating is disputed, argues he gets a seat as one of the righteous (*T. Job* 34–38). In another text, Abraham also accompanies Messiah for his seating, with Abraham on the left and Messiah on the right (*Midrash Ps.* 18.29). It is a seating representing honour and reward. Messianic seating is also probably

---

2. Access to God was also restricted by various barriers put in the way of getting to heaven. Not only is there fire, but some texts discuss a variety of obstacles, including a curtain, a host of avenging angels, as well as intense cold and heat. A famous talmudic text on how difficult it is to get access to God appears in *b. Hag.* 14b, 15b, where four rabbis attempt to see God and only one barely survives to tell the story. It discusses the obstacles to getting close to God. The account has several parallels (*t. Hag.* 2.3; *y. Hag.* 77b). These traditions have not been treated because they appear in later materials. They serve to underscore how rare such access is and that the ascents associated with such visits were only temporary.

3. Bock, *Blasphemy*, pp. 164-65, nn. 146-47. In fact, Jewish tradition is divided on the question of whether angels can sit in heaven and the idea that they can is, at best, a minority position, if this text is Jewish and not Christian.

noted at Qumran, as the Messiah is given honour worthy of the deliverer who is seated as the first of kings among the righteous in heaven (4Q491 1.13-17). Another Qumranian text has David seated before God on Israel's throne, as an expression of honour to the head of the dynasty and as leader of the righteous (4Q504 frag. 2.4.6). Here is great honor, but it seems to fall short of a vice regency, looking more like a reward for faithfulness. Still another Davidic text comes from a suggestion by Akiba that David sits by God in heaven. This is strongly rejected by another rabbi as a major offence against God (*b. Hag.* 14a; *b. Sanh.* 38b). Abel exercises a temporary role as a judge in the end (*T. Abr.* 13.2).

The most significant exaltation scenes involve Moses and the transformed Enoch figures (Son of Man and Metatron). Moses is enthroned with great authority, but his exalted role is merely a metaphorical picture of his authority in establishing the nation (*Ezek. Trag.* 68-89). The references to his 'deification' appear to be explained by his function as God's powerful agent, so he is 'like a god before Pharoah' (Exod. 7.1; Philo, *Life of Moses* 1.155-62; *The Worse Attacks the Better* 160-62; *Sacrifices of Abel and Cain* 9–10). Thus, the Moses imagery turns out on closer examination to be less exceptional than it first appears.

Enoch-Metatron is given great authority over heavenly affairs, but he also is disciplined when that authority is misused in a way that might confuse him with God (*3 En.* 3–16). This late text tells us how comprehensive the high exaltation texts could be, especially in some of the later texts. It also indicates the intense fear and reaction such exaltation texts produced when they were seen as giving too exalted a position to someone other than God.

Only Enoch-Son of Man is portrayed as the great eschatological judge of the end, seated next to God (*1 En.* 45.3; 51.3; 61.8; 62.2-6; 70.27, especially 46.1-3 and 71.1-17). It is a remarkably unique picture.

As noted, these final two portraits of Enoch-Metatron and Enoch-Son of Man produced controversy. These figures appear in other passages in ways that show great nervousness about the extent of exaltation attributed to them (*T. Abr.* 11.3-8 [B]- for Enoch; *3 En.* 16; *b. Hag.* 15a; *b. Sanh.* 38b; and *b. AZ 3b*- for Metatron). God's honour is unique and is not to be confused with anyone else's status. To equate anyone else with God is to risk thinking blasphemously.

In sum, it is clear that for some within Judaism, being seated by God was possible, but it was limited to very few and usually involved very limited circumstances. With the one exception of Gabriel, all those who sit are human luminaries or humans transformed into a new, glorious heavenly form and role. The highest forms of exaltation apparently also met with some strong opposition or clear qualification of such claims by other Jews, showing it was not a universal opinion that such a thing was to be tolerated. When one places these few examples of seating around the numerous references to a wide array of other types of heavenly activity and the few texts disputing such claims, it is evident just how rare and privileged the honour is. It takes God's direct intervention and invitation to permit it, and all such authority is still derived authority. Some get close to God at his direction and as an expression of their significance in some key phase in God's plan. But candidates do not apply for the role nor do they claim it for themselves. Only God can direct such a seating.

This Jewish backdrop on blasphemy and exaltation sets the context and provides the cultural script to understand the reaction to Jesus and his claims. Now a set of questions remains. How do the background study of blasphemy and the views surrounding access to God impact the under-standing of the Jewish examination of Jesus and his claims to forgive sin? How would the Jewish leadership have received his self-claim to be given a seat at the right hand of God? For these questions we need to turn to the New Testament texts where Jesus offers forgiveness of sins and where he is examined by the Jewish leadership.

The First Basis of the Charge of Blasphemy: Jesus' Claim to Forgive Sins

In Mark 2.1-2 and parallels, as well as in Luke 7.36-50, Jesus directly offers forgiveness of sins in a way that the theologically rooted Jews in the audience claim is blasphemy. Now this concept of Jesus forgiving sins is multiply attested in terms of the criteria of authenticity with its appearance in a tradition reflected in Mark and one that Luke alone uses (so Mark and Luke). In both places the instant reaction is the same by the Jewish theologians present. They object, 'Who can forgive sins but God?'

The best we can tell there are only two parallels to this kind of an act in Judaism. One is in 2 Samuel 12.13, where Nathan as a prophet declares to David, 'The Lord has taken away your sin'. The second is a text found at Qumran known as 4QPrNab (=4Q242) 1.4. In this work, known as the *Prayer of Nabonidus*, an exorcist is said to have forgiven sin. No rabbinic texts make such an association. Forgiveness is seen as God's business.

What can be made of these parallels? Nathan merely announces what God has done. It is the Lord who forgives the sin. So in this text, Nathan merely functions as a prophet, declaring what God alone has clearly done. The *Nabonidus* text simply summarizes the impact of what the exorcist helps to facilitate on the basis of a principle expressed in the Jewish

Talmud of the fifth Century AD, 'No one gets up from his sickbed until all his sins are forgiven'. (*Nedarim* 41a).

In fact, there is discussion and debate about this Qumran text as well. Eric Eve has traced this discussion in some detail.[4] He begins by noting how fragmentary this text is. Many lacunae have to be filled in order to make sense of the text. The key line here is, 'I was afflicted [...] for seven years...and an exorcist pardoned my sins'.[5] He notes that frequent attempt to connect the text with Daniel 4 is possible but not certain. He goes on to question whether a translation of sin pardoned is also appropriate. One rendering is '[when I had confessed my sins and]my faults, [God] granted me a soothsayer'. Others note that the assumption against an orthodox Jewish background is that God does the forgiving and that the exorcist's role is little different than that of Nathan with David. In other words, the text presents a kind of shorthand view of forgiveness where the exorcist simply bears the message of God. Finally, Eve goes on to note that the term translated 'exorcist' can also mean 'seer', as usage in Daniel 2.26; 4.7; 5.7, 11 shows, which puts it in a more prophetic mode. When one adds to all of this the fact that one has to supply what took place before (the king's possible prayer for help or other such possibilities), then one has a text whose exact import as a parallel is less than certain.

Even without this caveat about the *Nabonidus* text, these two examples are different than the text involving Jesus, where he declares sins forgiven directly. Now he does say, 'your sins are forgiven' with a passive verb, suggesting God does the forgiving, but in Mark 2.10 he says far more, 'That you might know that the Son of Man has authority on earth to forgive sins, I say to you get up and walk'.

Here Jesus links an act that cannot be seen (forgiveness) with an act that can and that requires God's work (healing a paralytic), so that God can be seen to act in response to Jesus' initiative in a text where the authority Jesus claims is his own as Son of Man. This is precisely the reverse of what one would expect in terms of the declaration of authority for the action. Yes, God has given authority to forgive sins, but when it comes to the Son of Man, Jesus' favourite name for himself; he will ultimately associate the imagery of judgement and ruling authority with Daniel 7.[6] So Jesus has

4. Eric Eve, *The Jewish Context of Jesus' Miracles* (JSNTS, 231; Sheffield; Sheffield Academic Press, 2002), pp. 182-89.

5. The citation is from Eve, *Jewish Context*, p. 183, with the breaks in the text provided and the discussion that follows is indebted to him.

6. The debate over the authenticity of the Son of Man title is almost endless. I

authority to forgive sin, an authority closely linking him to God and the divine work. The charge seems to revolve around Jesus' taking up an exclusively divine prerogative with such directness based on his own authority. The offence appears to revolve around the fact that forgiveness comes outside any cultic requirements in a mere declaration, an approach that also points to Jesus' own authority.[7]

Now Eve makes another point about the miracle tradition tied to Jesus that is relevant to this scene. It is that Jesus claims a miraculous authority in a manner distinct from almost all other parallels. So not only is the way Jesus declares forgiveness of sins unique, but also the way he healed in this context. Eve makes an important distinction between different kinds of healer-exorcists that in turn is dependent on work by Werner Kahl.[8] There are three types of approaches to healing. There are those who are (1) 'bearers of numinous power' (BNP), (2) those who are 'petitioners of numinous power' (PNP) and (3) those who are 'mediators of numinous power' (MNP). Mediators use formulae or some other means as an aid in their work, Petitioners simply pray for the healing. Bearers of numinous power act directly with no intermediary elements. They 'incorporate healing power in themselves'.[9] What is crucial to see is that Jesus is a bearer of such power, while Jewish examples like Eleazar, noted by Josephus in his *Ant.* 8.45-49, is a mediator of such power. Eve also notes a parallel in Greco-Roman works with a later figure Apollonius of Tyana (he is a figure from 150 years later). Otherwise Eve says that Jesus is 'virtually unique in being an immanent BNP'.[10]

In his conclusion, Eve sees that Jesus as unique in the surviving Jewish literature of his time in being portrayed as performing a large number of healings and exorcisms. Kahl is correct that he is virtually unique in

---

have defended its authenticity in my *Jesus according to Scripture* (Grand Rapids: Baker, 2002), pp. 601-605.

7. For this reading of Mk 2, see J.D.G. Dunn, *The Parting of the Ways* (London: SCM Press, 1991), pp. 46-47. Forgiveness was possible without recourse to priests or rabbis. The implications for religious authority structures are huge, since these authorities would believe that the way they bestowed forgiveness was in line with divine instruction. See also B. Chilton, *The Temple of Jesus* (University Park: Pennsylvania State University, 1992), pp. 130-33, on Jesus and forgiveness.

8. W. Kahl, *New Testament Miracle Stories in their Religious-Historical Setting: A Religionsgeschichtliche Comparison from a Structuralist Perspective* (Forschungen zur Religion und Literatur des Alten und Neuen Testaments, 163; Göttingen: Vandenhoeck & Ruprecht, 1994).

9. Kahl, *Miracle Stories*, p. 76.

10. Eve, *Jewish Context*, pp. 15-16. Citation is on p. 16.

Jewish literature in being portrayed as an immanent BNP in these acts of power, with two provisos. First, some Jewish texts can appear to make human figures act as immanent BNPs where the context suggests they are really only mediators of God's numinous power. Secondly, whatever may be true of individual miracles stories, the gospels show some tendency to indicate it is God's power at work in Jesus, not merely his own (e.g., Mt. 12.28/Lk. 11.20; Lk. 5.17). If Jesus is a BNP, it is because he is a bearer of God's Spirit, which is the source of Jesus' power. Indeed, if God were not in some sense behind Jesus' acts of power, they would not count as miracles.[11] Still the consistency of the presentation of Jesus' authority here is worth noting. If Jesus repeatedly claimed such direct authority in the manner he chose to forgive sin, this would have caused offence to the Jewish leadership and helped to strengthen their sense of reaction. The fact that Jesus repeats such a claim in the anointing scene of Luke 7.36-50, mentioned almost in passing as a text that is highlighting Jesus' acceptance of the woman, would do nothing to help alleviate the leadership's concerns about Jesus' claim.

Thus, the claim to forgive sins would set the stage for concern about Jesus performing acts of blasphemy and making claims that indicate, in the leadership's view, a lack of respect for the unique authority of God.

The Second Basis of the Charge and the Key Scene: The Jewish Examination of Jesus and Blasphemy

The examination before the Jewish leadership appears to have extended from the evening into the early morning. It proceeded in two stages: (1) the attempt to see if a charge could be gathered around the Temple incident with its seeming implication of reform or destruction of the Temple without consent of the leadership, and (2) the examination of Jesus' self-understanding. The goal of the examination was to determine if a charge related to some form of sedition could be brought before Pilate. In terms of historical credibility, there is a pattern in the sequence of arrest, appearances before the Jewish leadership and Pilate, Peter's denials, crucifixion and empty tomb that is so deeply imbedded in all versions of these events that this basic outline appears to be historically credible.

The attempt to see if a charge worthy to take to Pilate could be connected to the Temple appears only in Mark 14.53-56 and Matthew 26.59-63a. It fits the cultural backdrop for the examination to begin here. Jesus'

11. Eve, *Jewish Context*, pp. 378-79.

act in the Temple was public and would have been controversial. The act coheres with remarks in John 2.19 about Jesus rebuilding a destroyed temple. Mark 14.58 has a similar remark that parallels other Marcan texts (13.2; 15.29; 11.17-18). The act also coheres with the idea that the eschaton would bring a cleansing and restoration of Jerusalem (Tob. 14.5-7; *Ps. Sol.* 17–18).

However, the charge is dismissed on two basic grounds. First, the testimony is called false, because the witnesses are not able to agree (Mk 14.59). Matthew strengthens this to say the council sought such testimony (Mt. 26.59). So, this effort goes nowhere. Apparently the leadership had a sense that this charge would not be convincing to Pilate. The gospels are circumspect enough to note that they sensed this. The key here may be the attribution of these witnesses that Jesus claimed he would destroy the Temple. The remark as it is tied to Jesus in the tradition appears to be that the Temple will be destroyed by someone other than Jesus. In remarks about the Temple's or Jerusalem's fate that do go back to Jesus, it appears Jesus anticipates a judgement on the nation for covenant unfaithfulness (Lk. 13.34-35; 19.41-44; Mk 13.2 and parallels). The fact that this charge became a dead-end meant that it was not related in Luke's account of this scene. John skips this interrogation completely, probably because it was well known in the church's oral tradition.

This led to by far the most important portion of this account for the emergence of the charge of blasphemy. It is the examination by the high priest and Jesus' response (Mk 14.60-65). Mark juxtaposes this scene with Peter's denials (14.66-72). The most common objection to the historicity of this scene is the juxtaposition of christological titles (Messiah, Son, Son of Man) and texts (Ps. 110.1; Dan. 7.13-14) in Jesus' reply.[12]

Some question whether the transition from temple charge to a question about being Messiah is a natural one. They argue that the transition is too abrupt and the topics are too unrelated. However, the work of Betz and the association of renewal of Jerusalem with the end shows that the sequence is a natural one, especially given the range of claims associated with Jesus that are made upon his entry into the city.[13] The high priest's question about Jesus being the Son of the Blessed has the ring of respect for God about it that fits such a solemn setting about such grave issues.

12. The debate here and several key related issues are treated in detail in Raymond E. Brown, *The Death of the Messiah* (ABRL; New York: Doubleday, 1994), I, pp. 461-547.

13. 'Probleme des Prozesses Jeus', in *ANRW* 2.25.1, pp. 565-647.

The 'Blessed' is an indirect reference to God rooted in language that ties God to acts of blessing. It is neither a common expression in Judaism nor in Christianity, so it does not have the feel of being a created title by Mark (*m. Ber.* 7.3; *1 En.* 77.2; 4Q209). Jesus' reply in Mark keeps the tone of respect by speaking of the right hand of power (*1 En.* 62.7; numerous texts in *Mekilta* where the power exercised at the Exodus is the point: *Mek-Beshallah* 2 [26a] on Exod. 14.2; *Mek-Amalek* 1 [54b] on Exod. 17.3; *Mek-Amalek* 4 [59b] on Exod. 18.19; *Mek-Bahodesh* 9 [71a] on Exod. 20.18; *Sifre* Num § 112; *ARN*). Such exceptional usage is against a Marcan creation, especially when Mark is comfortable referring to the 'Son of God' (Mk 1.1; 3.11; 5.7; 15.37).

The most crucial element within this scene is Jesus' reply. Two basic views exist about Jesus' reply: (1) This reply was placed on Jesus' lips as a christological summary of the confession of the early church.[14] In this reading, Jesus is the model of how one responds to persecution for the communities to which the gospels are written. (2) In my monograph, I have defended in detail the position that this is a faithful summary of what Jesus said.[15] The most discussed part of the reply is the juxtaposition of Psalm 110.1 with Daniel 7.13-14, given that all the Synoptics appear to affirm the association with the Christ, in at least a qualified manner. Mark has an unqualified 'yes' to open the reply, while Matthew and Luke speak in terms of 'you have said so', an idiomatic response that means, 'Yes, but not entirely in the sense in which it has been asked'. This is not a complete rejection of the category, but more a qualification on it. The remainder of the response makes that qualification clear, so that the force of the three Synoptics is in agreement as to the thrust of Jesus' response. It is hard to understand how the term Christ became so completely attached to Jesus in the early church, if he in fact absolutely rejected the title.

Since it is this portion of the scene that is the most crucial, it is important to walk through the issues of historicity pro and con a step at a time. Against the scriptural connection going back to Jesus are two key arguments. (1) The christological reflection here looks advanced, even post-Easter. (2) Jesus did not normally link such texts together in such a midrashic manner.

---

14. Argued for most persuasively by N. Perrin, 'Mark XIV.62: The End Product of a Christian Pesher?', *NTS* 12 (1965–66), pp. 150-55, and his 'The High Priest's Question and Jesus' Answer (Mark 14.61-62)', in *The Passion in Mark: Studies on Mark 14–16* (ed. Werner Kelber; Philadelphia: Fortress Press, 1976), pp. 80-95.

15. Bock, *Blasphemy*, pp. 209-33.

However, these objections are not as strong as they initially seem. (On 1) The key to Jesus' reply is his reference to the Son of Man, while the priest's messianic question is basically what the Temple action was likely to have suggested, especially if the concern is to consider a political charge to raise with Pilate. The availability of Son of Man speculation to Jesus (*11QMel* 2.18; *Ezek. Trag.* 76; *1 En.* 46.2-4; 48.2; 62.5-14; 63;11; 69.27-29; 70.1, 14-17; *4 Ezra* 13) and Jesus' exclusive use of this title speak to its likely role as a self-reference by Jesus.[16] The multiple attestation that belongs to the apocalyptic Son of Man sayings also speaks for its availability versus being a creation in a gospel that is aimed at a predominantly Greek audience (Mark [Mk 8.38 par; Mk 13.26 par; Mk 14.62 par], Q

16. John J. Collins, 'The Son of Man in First-Century Judaism', *NTS* 38 (1992), pp. 448-66 and William Horbury, 'The Messianic Associations of "The Son of Man"', *JTS* 36 (1985), pp. 34-55. Whether there was *a* Son of Man concept might be debated, but there certainly was speculation about an exalted figure whose roots lie in Daniel 7. The summary evidence involves a wide array of sources from Judaism of varying strength. For example, in 11QMel 2.18, there is reference to the bearer of good tidings who is 'the messiah of the spirit of whom Dan[iel] spoke'. Now the allusion in the context is probably to Daniel 9.25 as seven weeks are mentioned, but Horbury notes that this text was often associated with Daniel 2 and 7 in Jewish thinking, so that the same figure may be in view. In *Ezek. Trag.*, a text where in a dream Moses gets to sit on God's throne, it can be noted how the throne of exaltation on which Moses sat was associated with the plural expression 'thrones', language from Daniel 7.9. Other slightly later texts have even clearer points of contact. *1 Enoch* is filled with Son of Man references (46.2-4; 48.2; 62.5, 7, 9, 14; 63.11; 69.27, 29 [2×]; 70.1; 71.14, 17). His enthronement in 62.2-14 is clearly connected to Daniel 7, with its reference to a seat on the 'throne of glory'. *1 Enoch* 46.1 and 47.3 also seem to allude to Daniel 7, as do 63.11; 69.27, 29. The three variations in the way Son of Man is referred to here do not alter the point that it is Daniel 7 that is the point of departure for the imagery here. *4 Ezra* 13 is another, later text that also reflects speculation about the figure of Daniel. A rabbinic dispute attributed to the late first century involves Akiba's claim that the 'thrones' are reserved for David. It suggests an interesting regal, Daniel 7 connection (*b. Hag.* 14a; *b. Sanh.* 38b). Some have compared the Melchizedek figure to aspects of Son of Man speculation (P.J. Kobelski, *Melchizedek and Melchiresha* [CBQMS, 10; Washington: Catholic Biblical Association, 1981], p. 136). Finally, there is the image of the exalted figure in 4Q491, who also echoes themes of Daniel 7. The variety of passages indicates that Daniel 7 imagery was a part of first-century Jewish eschatological and apocalyptic speculation, apart from the question of the presence of a defined Son of Man figure. This means that Daniel 7 was a text that was present in the theologically reflective thinking of Judaism and was quite available to Jesus once he started thinking in eschatological-vindication terms. There is nothing here that requires a post-Easter scenario. So the availability of Daniel 7 for reflection about the end seems clear enough.

[Mt. 24.27-Lk. 17.24; 24.37-L. 17.26; 24.39–Lk. 17.30], M [Mt. 10.23; 13.41; 24.44; 25.31], L [Lk. 17.22]). (On 2) There is evidence that Jesus did link texts together in a midrashic style (Mk 7.6-10=Mt. 15.4-9; Mt. 22.33-39 like Mk 12.29-31). More important is a point Raymond Brown makes with emphasis in his work about Jesus' death: 'The perception that OT passages were interpreted to give a christological insight does not date the process'. He goes on to add: 'Hidden behind the attribution to the early church is often the assumption that Jesus had no Christology even by way of reading the Scriptures to discern in what anticipated way he fitted into God's plan. Can one really think that credible?'[17] The issue of who Jesus was is just as live an issue in the thirties as it was in the sixties. There is nothing in these objections that requires a church creation and several factors argue against it. So the likelihood is that when we confront this charge, we are dealing with the situation as it was at the trial and have walked into a central scene in Jesus' life.[18]

What would have been Jesus' point in such a qualified reply? Jesus answers somewhat affirmatively to the messianic query of the high priest but then adds to it to make it clear that the question really misses the point. Jesus does not merely affirm the query; he goes beyond it. The remark about the Son of Man coming on the clouds and being seated at God's right hand, whether it was heard as a reception into heaven or a return to earth to rule (and that is debated), affirms a divine vindication of Jesus that assumes (1) a session by God's side and (2) the right to judge one day. In other words, Jesus may be on trial now, but one day he would be vindi-cated so that rejecting him meant being a defendant before God and his chosen representative at a decisive final judgement. To a leadership that did not accept that Jesus was a candidate for such vindication, this claim and the intimacy and authority it implied was blasphemous. For them blas-phemy would have included making oneself too close to God (Josephus, *Ant.* 6.183; 10.233, 242; Philo, *On Dreams* 2.130-31; *Decalogue* 13-14, 61-64). In claiming to be their future judge one day, he may well have also tripped over, in their view, Exodus 22.27 and its remarks on blas-phemy. Luke's failure to mention blasphemy at this point of the examina-tion means little, as he tells his story for an audience that only needed to understand that what Jesus said led him to Pilate. Matthew and Mark do

---

17. Brown, *Death*, pp. 513-15.

18. I have updated my discussion of this scene in 'Blasphemy and the Jewish Exami-nation of Jesus', *BBR* 17.1 (2007), pp. 61-122, especially by interacting with alternative views since my original work in 1998.

record the reception of the claims as being blasphemous (Mk 14.64; Mt. 26.65). Neither is there a need to have pronounced the divine name to get to such a verdict, although this has been argued by Gundry.[19] This view is possible, but by itself it cannot explain the reaction of the leadership, since the divine Name would have come in the context of the citing of Scripture, something in itself that would not be offensive. Other contextually noted elements, namely the extent of Jesus' claim of vindication, must have triggered the negative reaction to Jesus' response.

One more key objection to authenticity remains. It has been claimed that the stacking up of titles like that in this text is an argument against authenticity.[20] But on formal and conceptual grounds, this claim can be rejected as going beyond the evidence. In discussing the Son of Man it was noted that development is not the private domain of the early church and that combining allusions does not date when such combinations took place. Jesus was capable of formulating an association between Psalm 110.1 and Daniel 7.13. But this response only deals with the nature of Jesus' reply. What about the way the high priest forms his question with multiple titles? Is the stacking up of titles in his question necessarily artificial?

That the high priest would be concerned about Jesus as Messiah is natural, since a charge is being considered that the leadership feels makes Jesus a candidate to be taken to the Roman authorities. As also was noted, the Temple incident and sayings might suggest that Jesus had associated himself with events tied to the return of the Messiah. The Son of Man title is Jesus' way to refer to himself, so both of these elements fit. The only potentially extraneous element is the allusion to Son of the Blessed.

But on formal grounds it is not unusual in Judaism for titles to be piled on one another when one is emphasizing a point. I already noted in an earlier discussion how two names were given for God in *1 Enoch* 77.2, namely 'Most High' and 'eternally Blessed'. One can point to *1 Enoch* 48.2 with its reference to 'the Lord of Spirits, the Before-time', a construction much like the one seen in Mark 14. Similar is *Psalms of Solomon*

---

19. Robert Gundry, *Mark: A Commentary on His Apology for the Cross* (Grand Rapids: Eerdmans, 1993), pp. 883-922. Updated and developed in his *The Old Is Better: New Testament Essays in Support of Traditional Interpretations* (WUNT, 1.178; Tübingen: Mohr/Siebeck, 2005), pp. 98-110.

20. As Donald Juel states about the Mark 14 combination, 'The combination of allusions presumes a developed stage of reflection'. This is similar to the midrashic argument in another form, only here titles not texts are in view. See his *Messianic Exegesis: Christological Interpretation of the Old Testament in Early Christianity* (Philadelphia: Fortress Press, 1988), p. 146.

17.21 with its reference to 'their king, the son of David'. Of course, the outstanding biblical example of the piling up of names is *Isaiah* 9.6 [Eng], and here also it is a regal figure being named. When this takes place there is something solemn about what is being said. So there is nothing formally odd about the high priest questioning Jesus and doing so with a combined set of titles that suggests the moment's seriousness.

So was Jesus crucified because he claimed to be Messiah? Was that the core of the blasphemy charge? This is how some challenge the scene's historical value, but that is not what is going on, even though it is the political charge that is highlighted before Pilate. Read in this light, it appears that the high priest is asking Jesus to confirm his messianic status. If that is the case, then the scene has been challenged in the past because it is not a capital crime in Judaism to claim to be Messiah, that is, a messianic claim is not blasphemous.[21] The point that messianic confession is not inherently blasphemous is a correct one as the examination of blasphemy within Judaism shows.

However, this objection makes an assumption about the question sequence that should be critiqued. The incorrect assumption is that what the examination was seeking and what resulted from the examination were exactly the same thing. It assumes that Jesus' affirmative reply to the high priest's messianic question makes the blasphemous remark revolve around messiahship. But the contention of this study is that this is not the relationship between the priest's question and Jesus' answer. The examination was about messiahship, so that a socio-political issue could be taken to Rome. The threat that Jesus represented to the people in the leadership's view, in a view much like 11QTemple 64.6-13 expresses, meant that he should be stopped and brought before Rome as a political-social threat. If a messianic claim and danger could be proven, then Jesus could be taken to Rome as a challenger ruler whom Rome did not appoint. The charge would be sedition, a crime capable of a death penalty. The Jewish leadership could have developed real concern about this threat when Jesus uttered the parable of the wicked tenants, which was clearly an attack on the leadership and suggested that Jesus was a 'son', whose rejection would be vindicated by God.[22] His act in the Temple could be seen as a political

---

21. See the remarks in Joel Marcus, 'Mark 14.61: "Are you the Messiah-Son-of-God?"', *NovT* 31 (1989), pp. 127-29.

22. This is perceptively noted by Jack Kingsbury, *The Christology of Mark's Gospel* (Philadelphia: Fortress Press, 1983), pp. 118-19. On this parable see Klyne Snodgrass, *The Parable of the Wicked Tenants* (WUNT, 27; Tübingen: Mohr/Siebeck, 1983).

challenge not only to the Jewish leadership but to the Romans who allowed such political authority to exist there. Thus, the threat to Jewish leadership could be translated into a threat to Rome's leadership as well. Jesus believed that he represented God and had authority from above. This could be represented as possessing a claim to independent authority, a risk to all current socio-political structures and a potential source of public instability. This is what the priest's question sought to determine.

But Jesus' reply responds to this messianic query *and yet does even more*. It represents a severe assault on the sensibilities of the Jewish leaders at two levels. First, the reply speaks of an exalted Jesus who sees himself as too close to God in the leadership's view. Second, he makes claims as a ruler or judge who one day will render a verdict and/or experience a vindication against the very leadership that sees itself as appointed by God. In the first element of Jesus' affirmation, the leadership sees a dangerous claim to independent authority that they can take to Rome. In both aspects of Jesus' reply there is, in their view, cause for seeing the highest of religious offenses possible, namely, blasphemy. The high priest's ripping of his garments says as much (Num. 14.6; Judg. 11.35; 2 Sam. 1.11; 1 Macc. 2.14; *y. Mo'ed Katan* 3.83b [= Neusner 3.7]; *b. Sanh.* 60a). What started out as an investigation about Messiah becomes more than that because of the way Psalm 110.1 and Daniel 7.13 are woven together. This does not mean that the messianic charge is wrong or even that it is 'corrected'. It means that Jesus defines who the Messiah is in terms of the totality of the authority he possesses. This figure is so close to God that he possesses authority even over the nation's highest religious authorities. That is Jesus' claim. It parallels the claim he made earlier in the parable, except that now God's vindication is to be carried out by and/or on behalf of the very person they are trying to condemn. Jesus claims total independence from the authorities of the day. He can be taken to Pilate.

This point has a corollary for those who try to argue that Mark's concern is strictly pastoral and not historical. In this narrative theological view, Jesus is a model in how to face charges of blasphemy for the early church that is facing similar charges.[23] Mark's pastoral lesson is that in suffering as Jesus did, they follow his way and example. The point is true enough about Mark's goal, but in separating history and pastoral theology the significance of the uniqueness of Jesus' reply about himself is understated. Jesus is an example in how he faces the charge, but the reply he gives is unique to him and is not in its content an example to be followed. In fact, the reply explains the unique vindication Jesus receives at God's right hand. Now the question begs, if Jesus is only an example in how he faces the charge of blasphemy and the scene is Mark's or the early church's creation, why have an exemplary reply that does not help Mark's members with how they should reply? The difference suggests that both teaching Jesus' example and making a point about the historical Christology that lies at the core of the tension are addressed.

In sum, this event has a stronger claim to authenticity than suggestions that Mark or the early church created the scene. With some form of a regal claim for divine vindication into heaven, Jesus ironically supplies the testimony that led to his being taken on to Pilate so that Rome could now make the decisive judgment.

Summary

Now we can pull all the strands of background and text together. The charge that Jesus was a 'blasphemer' fits very well into the historical background in which it appears in the biblical materials. Here Jesus' claims of exaltation ran headlong into Jewish views of the unique glory of God and resulted in the leadership concluding, because of their rejection of his claims, that he had blasphemed.

In sum, Jesus' reply is what leads to his conviction on a blasphemy charge. This reply had socio-political elements in it, as well as a religious dimension that constituted blasphemy. None of the objections to the historicity of this scene have persuasive substance. Though one cannot prove absolutely that the dialogue goes back to Jesus and the high priest, the evidence makes it likely that the Marcan summary is reflective of what took place or is a reasonable representation of the fundamental conflict of views. It has great historical plausibility with the background that would apply to such a scene. Moreover, the scene possesses clear indications that make it more likely that it goes back to the trial scene and not to Mark.

Jesus' blasphemy operated at two levels.

(1) There was a claim to possess comprehensive authority from God, something his earlier claims to forgive sins also affirmed. Though Judaism might contemplate such a comprehensively authoritative position for a few, this teacher from Galilee was not among the luminaries for whom such a role might be considered. As a result, his remark would have been seen as a self-claim that was an affront to God. To claim to be able to share God's glory in a Jewish context would mean pointing to an exalted status that is even more than a prophet or any typical view of the Jewish

Messiah. That is how the Jewish leadership would have seen the claim. What Jesus' statement means is that he saw his mission in terms of messianic kingdom work that also involved his inseparable association and intimacy with God. His coming vindication by God would indicate all of this. Psalm 110.1 and Daniel 7.13-14 taken together explain it. Jesus was Christ, Son of the Blessed One, and Son of Man in one package and the right hand of God awaited him after his unjust death. That coming vindication and the position it reveals him to possess at God's right hand helps all to see and the church to explain who Jesus was and is.

(2) Jesus also attacked the leadership, by implicitly claiming to be their future judge and/or by claiming a vindication by God for the leadership's anticipated act. This would be seen by the Jewish leadership as a violation of Exodus 22.27, where God's leaders are not to be cursed. A claim that their authority was non-existent and that they would be accounted among the wicked is a total rejection of their authority. To the leadership, this was an affront to God as they were, in their own view, God's established chosen leadership.

Jesus' claim to possess comprehensive independent authority would serve as the basis of taking Jesus before Rome on a socio-political charge, as well as constituting a religious offence of blasphemy that would be seen as worthy of the pursuit of the death penalty. In the leadership's view, the socio-political threat to the stability of the Jewish people is an underlying reason why this claim had to be dealt with so comprehensively. Jesus' reply, in his own view, simply grew out of the implications of who he saw himself to be.

The scene as a summary of trial events has a strong claim to authenticity, a stronger claim to it than to the alternative that the scene was created by Mark or by the early church. This means that this examination is a core event for understanding the historical Jesus. The charge of Jesus as a 'blasphemer' is one of the most significant charges his opponents ever leveled at him. It is a hub from which one can work to some degree backwards into the significance of his earthly ministry or forwards into how these events were the catalyst for the more developed expressions and explanations of who Jesus was.

The conflict between Jesus and the Jewish leadership two millennia ago was grounded in fundamentally different perceptions of who he was and the authority he possessed for what he was doing. Either he was a blasphemer or the agent of God destined for a unique exaltation/vindication. Either he was a deceiver of the people or the Son of the Blessed One. The claims Jesus apparently made were so significant and the following he gathered was so great that a judgement about him could not be avoided.

This essay has tried to understand how those who examined Jesus saw his claims in light of their legal-theological categories. A study of Jewish views of blasphemy and exaltation illumines the ways in which the Jewish leadership perceived Jesus' claims. They saw in Jesus' claim of exaltation an affront to God's unique honour and to their position as representatives of God's people. Jesus saw in his anticipated exaltation a vindication of his calling, ministry and claims, so that one day he would be seen by all as Son of Man seated at God's right hand. In other words, the ancient sources and their cultural scripts reveal how blasphemy and exaltation clashed during this examination in ways that changed the course of history. What this essay has argued is that the historical case for the ultimate clash between Jesus and his opponents rotating around the charge of blasphemy is strong and historically quite credible.

JESUS AS FALSE PROPHET

James F. McGrath

Introduction

The present study will differ from many others in the present volume by virtue of the fact that, whereas we have explicit accusations of Jesus having been demon-possessed, a blasphemer, or a glutton and drunkard within the Gospels, we do not have a similarly explicit accusation of Jesus having been a false prophet.[1] It may, of course, be implicit at certain points, and most previous studies of this topic have concluded that this is indeed the case.[2] But in addition to attempting to ascertain whether such accusations are implicit in the Gospel tradition, it is also important to ask why they do not feature as prominently and/or explicitly as others do. One possible answer to this question has to do with the tendency in the developing trajectories of early Christianity to downplay the understanding of Jesus as prophet as at best inadequate, and to focus more on other themes and titles, such as Messiah and Son of God.[3] This being the case, it is not surprising that there is little direct focus on the accusation that Jesus was a false prophet in the New Testament – after all, what point was there for opponents of the early Christians to contest claims that the Christians themselves were not emphasizing? Yet although Christians came to prefer other

---

1. Graham Stanton, 'Jesus of Nazareth: A Magician and a False Prophet Who Deceived God's People?', in *Jesus and Gospel* (Cambridge: Cambridge University Press, 2004), pp. 127-61 (here 146). An earlier version of his study was published in *Jesus of Nazareth: Lord and Christ* (ed. Joel B. Green and Max Turner; Grand Rapids: Eerdmans, 1994), pp. 164-80.

2. Stanton, 'Jesus of Nazareth', pp. 127-61.

3. Cf. N.T. Wright, *Jesus and the Victory of God* (Minneapolis: Fortress Press, 1996), pp. 162-71. The tendency to downplay prophetic aspects of Jesus' words and actions may have been a response to the many other prophetic figures who appeared in the decades after him, who may have been felt to discredit the whole category. On the points of contrast see William R. Herzog, *Prophet and Teacher* (Louisville: Westminster/John Knox, 2005), pp. 106-108.

perspectives on Jesus, the traditions they passed on were still in many cases shaped by precisely the view of Jesus as prophet. Nevertheless, those who sought to counter early Christian preaching in later decades and even centuries tended to focus their attention on claims Christians continued not only to make but to emphasize. And so it is that in later literature we encounter polemical inversions of the virgin birth, that he bore the divine Name, and that he was himself divine.

The tendency to speak less and less of Jesus as 'prophet' within Christian circles was by no means universal, however. The later Jewish Christian Pseudo-Clementine literature still considered prophet a key Christological term, as does the special material in Luke's Gospel.[4] Was it in response to such views that the theme of Jesus as false prophet became part of the Rabbinic corpus? The specific features of the relevant Rabbinic passages suggest the primary concern may well have lain elsewhere. The focus in the texts in question is on the basis in Deuteronomy 13 for a formal charge against and the legal condemnation of Jesus. In the period in which the Rabbinic literature was produced, Christianity had come to a position of dominance, and the accusation that the Jewish leaders had falsely accused and unjustly condemned Jesus was a common one. Although the Rabbinic literature may have been drawing on earlier accusations, its reason for doing so seems to be the more specific desire to present a legitimate basis for Jesus' execution according to Jewish law, as a response to Christian polemics.[5] Whether this concern was already present in New Testament times or even earlier remains to be seen.[6]

Within Luke's Gospel, at one point doubt is expressed by a Pharisee as to whether Jesus is a prophet (7.39). But is doubting whether someone is a prophet the same as claiming that the person in question is a *false* prophet? This would seem to depend on whether or not the person in question was *claiming* to be a prophet. Indeed, many accusations (such as being in cahoots with Beelzebub) may, in fact, be at least in part accusations that Jesus was a false prophet, if he was in fact claiming to speak for God.[7]

---

4. Cf. Lk. 7.16, 39-50; 13.33; 24.19; Acts 3.22. See also Mt. 21.11, 46.

5. Cf. Stanton, 'Jesus of Nazareth', p. 129.

6. Scot McKnight finds evidence of precisely these concerns in several NT passages. See his 'Calling Jesus *Mamzer*', *JSHJ* 1 (2003), pp. 73-103 (here 75-76). On the problems with using Rabbinic sources for historical research about Jesus see Robert E. Van Voorst, *Jesus Outside the New Testament* (Grand Rapids: Eerdmans, 2000), pp. 104-106.

7. Cf. Stanton, 'Jesus of Nazareth', p. 129 on the close connection.

And so, whereas other studies of this subject have often taken the approach of searching for implicit accusations that Jesus was a false prophet, the approach taken here will be to establish the probability that Jesus was not only viewed in prophetic terms by some of his contemporaries, but also spoke or acted so as to give this impression.[8] It will then be possible to evaluate on that basis the relevance of a wide range of traditions which may (at least in part) have been responses to Jesus' prophetic claims.

Prophecy in the Time of Jesus

It has often been maintained that many or all of Jesus' contemporaries would have dismissed *a priori* any claim that he was a prophet, because they believed that prophecy had ceased. One source usually dated c. 300 CE, namely *Tosephta Sotah* 13.2, claims that after the last of the canonical prophets died, the Holy Spirit ceased to be active in Israel. This statement is qualified by an acknowledgment that revelation could still be received via a heavenly voice (bat qol). It is thus important to observe that this statement does not suggest there was a complete disappearance either of revelation, or of people who claimed that God spoke to or through them. On the contrary, if anything this Rabbinic source *confirms* that such claims continued to be made. What is being asserted here is rather that any such ongoing revelation differed in kind from that received by the canonical prophets, and thus must be judged against the standard of Scripture. If anything, therefore, such affirmations seem to be responses precisely to ongoing claims to revelation and something akin to prophetic experiences. The relevance of such late texts for our understanding of views in the time of Jesus is of course far from clear, but it is worth mentioning them nonetheless, precisely because of their use to suggest a widespread consensus that prophecy had ceased, and as we have just seen, this passage does not support such a conclusion.

Although 1 Maccabees seems to presuppose that prophecy is not a current reality, this is not necessarily implied in the relevant passages (1 Macc. 4.45-46; 14.41), and the author at the very least expects a time to come

---

8. For a survey of recent scholarship that also raises important methodological and terminological points, see Markus Öhler, 'Jesus as Prophet: Remarks on Terminology', in *Jesus, Mark and Q* (ed. Michael Labahn and Andreas Schmidt; Sheffield Academic Press, 2001), pp. 125-42. On Josephus' view of Jesus in relation to this topic see especially Geza Vermes, *Jesus in his Jewish Context* (Minneapolis: Fortress Press, 2003), pp. 91-98.

when prophets will be found once more. 1 Maccabees 14.41 may perhaps even hint that there continued to be some who claimed prophetic inspiration, since it specifies that it is not a prophet per se but a *trustworthy* one that is being awaited. Furthermore, many even among those who believed prophecy had ceased may have been willing to espouse that a future eschatological 'prophet like Moses' would appear, as predicted in Deuteronomy.[9] For them, perhaps, a claim to be a prophet would have had eschatological implications, and not merely revelatory ones. Josephus, however, with his claims to prophetic inspiration both for himself and for John Hyrcanus, provides evidence that not everyone treated prophecy as a thing of the distant past.[10] Josephus also refers to individuals he deems false prophets (*War* 2.259-62; *Antiquities* 20.169-71), but it is their claims and the ends that they meet that place them in this category, rather than any presupposition on his part that prophetic inspiration no longer existed in this period in history.[11]

In short, there is no reason to think that most people in Jesus' time would have regarded a claim to hear from and speak for God as *by definition suspect*, based on a belief that prophecy had ceased.[12] Some may

---

9.   Richard A. Horsley and John S. Hanson, *Bandits, Prophets, and Messiahs* (San Francisco: Harper & Row, 1985), pp. 148-49, 160, argue that there is little evidence of a living tradition of expectation that such a figure would come; here, however, we are simply suggesting that the possibility of such a figure, made on the basis of the relevant texts, would not necessarily have seemed out of the question. At any rate, absence of evidence for this expectation is not evidence of its absence.

10.   Rebecca Gray, *Prophetic Figures in Late Second Temple Jewish Palestine: The Evidence from Josephus* (New York: Oxford University Press, 1993), pp. 7-34.

11.   In *Against Apion* 1.41, Josephus seems to make a similar distinction to the Rabbinic sources, in setting apart Scriptural prophecy from later examples, without denying the reality of the latter. Cf. Louis H. Feldman, 'Prophets and Prophecy in Josephus' in *Prophets, Prophecy, and Prophetic Texts in Second Temple Judaism* (ed. Michael H. Floyd and Robert D. Haak; New York: T&T Clark, 2006), p. 222. On the broader topic of social memory and the way Jesus may have been recalled in a prophetic mold, see Richard A. Horsley, 'A Prophet Like Moses and Elijah: Popular Memory and Cultural Patterns in Mark' in *Performing the Gospel: Orality, Memory, and Mark* (ed. Richard A. Horsley, Jonathan A. Draper, and John Miles Foley; Minneapolis: Fortress Press, 2006), pp. 166-90; also John P. Meier, 'From Elijah-like Prophet to Royal Davidic Messiah' in *Jesus: A Colloquium in the Holy Land* (ed. Doris Donnelly; New York: Continuum, 2001), pp. 45-83.

12.   On this topic see further John R. Levison, 'Philo's Personal Experience and the Persistence of Prophecy' in *Prophets, Prophecy, and Prophetic Texts in Second Temple Judaism* (ed. Michael H. Floyd and Robert D. Haak; New York: T&T Clark, 2006), pp. 194-209; Horsley and Hanson, *Bandits, Prophets, and Messiahs*, p. 151; Morna Hooker, *The Signs of a Prophet* (Harrisburg: Trinity Press International, 1997), pp. 6-7.

have held this view, but most of our evidence points to a belief that inspiration (even if of a sort that somehow differed from that of the canonical prophets) was an ongoing reality, or at the very least something with the potential to reappear. But what did being a prophet imply to those living in Jesus' historical and social context? Although we hesitate to generalize in the way Joachim Jeremias did (on the basis of Strack-Billerbeck) that 'To possess the Spirit of God was to be a prophet', nevertheless it does seem that there is significant agreement among our sources that possession of (or by) the Spirit led to someone being understood in prophetic terms – leaving as the real question whether one was a true prophet or a false one, which might be phrased in other words as the question of *by what sort of spirit* one was possessed.[13] This may be one reason why Josephus describes those he views as false prophets as being in the category of goēs, which has the broader sense of 'charlatan' but more strictly means a *sorcerer*.[14] One potential characteristic was that of odd behavior. That the effects of prophetic inspiration or possession by God could resemble the characteristics of insanity can be seen in the fact that the same verb, existēmi, is used in reference to both.[15] The labelling of Jesus as demon-possessed and 'out of his mind' may well relate to this.[16] In a sense, one might be able to say that there were three options with regard to such individuals, comparable to the three options regarding Jesus made famous by C.S. Lewis: Either an individual was possessed (by some other spirit), a pretender, or a prophet possessed by God's Spirit.[17] It should be added that, in the first century as apparently throughout Israel's history, prophecy was something people sometimes *did*, without this necessarily indicating that the person in question *was* a prophet in the sense of having this as a defined role, vocation or profession. And thus the question of whether Jesus ever spoke prophetically is not exactly the same question as whether he

13. Joachim Jeremias, *New Testament Theology. I. The Proclamation of Jesus* (London: SCM, 1971), p. 78. See also Morton Smith, *Jesus the Magician* (Berkeley: Seastone, 1998), p. 104.

14. Cf. Eric Eve, *The Jewish Context of Jesus' Miracles* (JSNTS, 231; Sheffield Academic Press, 2002), p. 298.

15. See the specific references collected in James D.G. Dunn, *Jesus Remembered* (Grand Rapids: Eerdmans, 2003), pp. 595-96 n. 233.

16. Note the similar views of other prophetic figures recorded by Josephus (*War* 6.300-309; *Ant.* 10.114-19), and the discussion in Gray, *Prophetic Figures*, p. 30.

17. See, e.g., C.S. Lewis, *Mere Christianity* (Fontana: Glasgow, 1955), p. 52. From the famous 'trilemma' (liar, lunatic or Lord) is usually omitted a fourth category, 'legend', which is an important one to include when dealing with ancient sources.

was recognized as someone with what we might call a 'prophetic vocation'. Nevertheless, when there were accusations of false prophecy, these
had to do with specific predictions or other claims that prophets made, and
thus false prophecy could likewise be something someone did, apart from
the question of whether the person in question was (as it were, by profession) a false prophet. Indeed, it might be possible to go so far as to say
that, in the time of Jesus, the *vocation* of prophet (in the sense of someone
who did nothing but prophesy, e.g., as advisor to the king) was largely
unknown, and that those cases we have of prophetic claims are claims to
predict the future or to speak with divine authority, rather than to occupy
a particular social position or function.[18]

Jesus as Prophet

Since the key issue in this period was prophetic speech and actions, rather
than a particular social role, we need not spend much time debating the
issue of whether Jesus understood himself in prophetic terms. If even a few
of the predictions attributed to him in the Gospels are authentic, then we
have evidence that Jesus prophesied – whether truly or falsely.[19] Although
there is significant debate about a number of these sayings, there are
enough instances of Jesus speaking in a prophetic manner found throughout the tradition that it appears all but certain that he understood himself
at times to be prophesying. Yet although there are many sayings and
actions of Jesus that can be interpreted in prophetic terms, there is only
one saying with multiple independent attestation in which Jesus appears

18. It is worth mentioning explicitly that the question of Jesus as prophet did not
automatically exclude the application to him of other perspectives or titles. In other
words, Jesus could be viewed in prophetic terms and yet also as king, as political
leader, as priest – as one who occupied perhaps any sort of societal role, or indeed no
specific one at all. For one individual who (according to Josephus) occupied such
multiple roles, see the discussion in Robert L. Webb, *John the Baptizer and Prophet*
(Sheffield: Sheffield Academic Press, 1991), pp. 317-18.

19. The relevant passages include: the prediction of Jerusalem's destruction (with
or without mention of subsequent rebuilding); the prediction that they will not see
him again until they say 'Blessed is he who comes in the name of the Lord'; the
prediction that the son of man must suffer (three times in Mark and John), assuming
this was not in its original form a general statement about human suffering; the prediction that the son of man will come on a heavenly throne; the prediction that Peter will
deny him; the prediction that he will be betrayed. Others (such as the reference to a
vision of Satan falling like lightning from heaven, if understood to be a vision of an
event still to occur) might be added to the list.

to *refer to himself* as a prophet, namely the famous saying that 'a prophet is not without honor except in his home country'.[20] Is this an authentic saying of Jesus, and is it indicative of a prophetic self-understanding on his part? If the two-line version in Thomas is a secondary reworking of the saying based on Luke's narrative, then it may have little or no value as far as discussions of the historical Jesus are concerned, and multiple attestation between the remaining sources may be enough to settle the matter. On the other hand, scholars who believe the Thomas version can make a serious claim to representing the original form tend to also conclude that Jesus was speaking proverbially and metaphorically about his activity (since Jesus is not known for having claimed to be a 'doctor'), in which case the saying may not provide evidence that Jesus had a prophetic self-understanding. Although we cannot discuss this topic fully here, the arguments for the originality of the Thomas version have been adequately presented elsewhere.[21] Among the relevant evidence is the fact that Mark, after including the saying about a prophet being without honour, goes on to talk about Jesus' activity (or relative lack thereof) with respect to healing.[22] Also noteworthy is that John, immediately after his use of the saying, employs the verb *dechomai* the verb from which the adjective *dektos* (found in the Oxyrhynchus Greek fragment of Thomas) is derived. There is also the additional 'physician' proverb given by Luke in this context. Unless one posits that Thomas intersects with Mark, Luke and John through sheer coincidence, one would have to suppose either that the author of Thomas knows *all* of the canonical Gospels and here is carefully working into his second line allusions to the narrative context in which each of them employed the saying, or that a saying like the one in Thomas, with both its parts, was in the mind of each of the canonical authors who quotes the first half thereof. A strong case thus can be made for the originality of the version found in Thomas.[23] This does not,

20. Versions are found in Mk 6.4; Mt. 13.57; Lk. 4.23-24; Jn 4.44 (see also Jn 1.11); Thom. 31.

21. This was argued already by Rudolf Bultmann, *The History of the Synoptic Tradition* (New York: Harper & Row, 1963), pp. 31-32, building on the earlier insights of Emil Wendling. See also the additional arguments provided by John Dominic Crossan, *In Fragments* (San Francisco: Harper & Row, 1983), pp. 283-84.

22. Robert W. Funk, Roy W. Hoover, *et al.*, *The Five Gospels* (New York: Polebridge, 1993), p. 491.

23. It adds to the argument for authenticity that the assumption underpinning the second half of this proverb is precisely what we find in early layers of the tradition of Jesus' healing activities, namely that he was unable to perform many healings in those places where he was well known. Later authors who made use of such stories found

however, indicate that Jesus is simply quoting proverbial sayings. The Aramaic word for 'doctor' is 'asyan, and it also means *healer*.[24] If the saying goes back to Jesus, therefore, it need not be taken as speaking merely proverbially about 'doctors', but may have used not one but *two* designations that seem appropriate for him in light of our sources. The possibility that he was quoting an already known proverb remains, but given the reference to two categories into which Jesus seems to have been placed by his contemporaries, it seems unlikely that the proverb or proverbs, if these existed, were quoted without any thought to the question of Jesus' identity and activity. In short, a good case can be made for this saying being applied to Jesus by himself because it related to aspects of his activity, and thus quite plausibly of his self-understanding.

The close connection between healings/miracles and prophecy in this particular strand of Gospel tradition is not surprising. In concluding his recent study of Jesus' miracles in the Jewish context of his time, Eric Eve argues that the principle category into which the performance of miracles placed someone was *prophet* – whether a true or false one. Performing miracles depended on being in possession of, or possessed by, a spiritual power.[25] Especially if a person claimed not only to *act* but also to *speak* as a result of this, then some sort of 'prophetic' category was inevitably appropriate. In the case of most exorcists and healers, whatever their popularity, they seem to have garnered relatively little attention when compared to Jesus. A logical explanation for this fact is that Jesus' alleged miraculous activity was combined with a claim to authoritative speech. It is only this that can account for the attention accorded to Jesus by other teachers and various authority figures in his time. Had he simply been a charismatic healer and exorcist, even one that also told interesting stories, he would have been relatively uncontroversial. It is only by assuming (as the Gospel tradition suggests) that his miracles were treated as supporting a claim to inspired *speech*, and thus to *authority*, that one can explain the

this assertion of Jesus' inability uncomfortable and regularly edited it out, and this is usually taken as a strong argument for its authenticity. If the Thomas form is more original, then the narrative of Jesus' failure to perform many miracles/healings may be an expression in story form of what Mark knew as a saying of Jesus.

24. This is the word used in Lk. 4.23 in the Syriac Peshitta. It is the word that is sometimes thought to have given the Essenes their name, and they are sometimes identified with the group called Therapeutoi in Greek sources. Jastrow's Aramaic dictionary gives *thaumaturg* (i.e., miracle worker) as one of the meanings in Rabbinic sources.

25. Eve, *The Jewish Context of Jesus' Miracles*, pp. 384-85.

controversies. We may thus suggest that it was not his exorcisms per se that were the focus of the Beelzebul controversy, but it was the *message* or *teaching* of this exorcist that his opponents were concerned to undermine.

Scholars consistently emphasize that the prophets of ancient Israel were not merely 'foretellers' but were in the first instance 'forth-tellers', or in other words, their activity did not focus primarily on predicting the future, but on challenging social ills in their own time. Be that as it may, the popular understanding of prophets as being first and foremost those who make predictions about the future, whether it be correct or a misconception as far as the classical prophets of ancient Israel are concerned, appears to go back to the time of Jesus.[26] One weakness of some previous studies of whether Jesus fits into the category of a (true or false) prophet is the tendency to focus on whether he fits the mould of the classical prophets of the Jewish Scriptures, rather than focusing on whether he resembles the paradigms of prophetic speech and activity prevalent in his own time.[27]

Predictions about the Temple

According to Eric Eve, one of the features that he believes distinguished Jesus from the 'sign prophets' listed and denounced as false by Josephus is the fact that Jesus did not predict one particular and spectacular miracle would soon occur to confirm his claims.[28] On this point, the evidence from the Gospel tradition suggests rather than Jesus *did* make such a claim, when he predicted that the Temple would be destroyed and then rebuilt in three days. This prediction is attributed to Jesus throughout the Gospel tradition (in some instances as a genuine saying of Jesus, in others as something of which he is falsely accused), and it was certainly a key point of controversy between early Christians and their detractors. Its inclusion in so many early Christian Gospels, and the effort invested in reinterpreting it and otherwise neutralizing its apparent status as a false prophecy

26. This is noted, e.g., by George J. Brooke in his study 'Prophecy and Prophets in the Dead Sea Scrolls' in *Prophets, Prophecy, and Prophetic Texts in Second Temple Judaism* (ed. Michael H. Floyd and Robert D. Haak; New York: T&T Clark, 2006), p. 155.

27. As noted by Gray, *Prophetic Figures*, p. 3. The study of Morton Smith, *Jesus the Magician*, pp. 41, 48-49, 210-29, is particularly susceptible to criticism on this point. His focus on Jesus' failure to preface his words with 'Thus says the Lord' would appear to apply to *all* prophetic figures in this period.

28. Eve, *The Jewish Context of Jesus' Miracles*, p. 385.

uttered by Jesus, suggests it was widely known beyond Christian circles and was cited there as a motive for doubting or denying Jesus' prophetic ability.

This may seem somewhat ironic, given that the simpler prediction that the Temple would be destroyed seems like a good candidate for an *accurate* prediction about the future made by Jesus. In the case of the saying about the Temple's destruction and rebuilding, however, it was the specific time frame specified, as well as the apparent audacity of the claim spoken in the first-person (even though this presumably represented an instance of Jesus speaking prophetically with the divine voice), that caused it to become a focus of controversy. It is in connection with this saying that the wider issue of Jesus' prophetic ability takes on particular prominence in the passion narrative in the Synoptic tradition. In Mark 14.65, closely following a charge relating to the saying about destroying and rebuilding the Temple, Jesus is mocked by guards who explicitly demand that he prophesy. The saying about his accusers seeing the son of man seated at the right hand of Power is also a prediction and ties into this same theme. Whatever one may think of the historical value of the depiction of the trial in Mark's Gospel, it is still noteworthy that he regards the focus of the trial as relating to Jesus' prophetic ability. In a similar way, the perception that Jesus is claiming to be a prophet or have a prophetic ability lies behind the motif of requests for a sign.[29]

How certain can we be that Jesus said something about the Temple being destroyed and rebuilt?[30] Although the evidence from the Gospels is from decades later, and for the most part reflects knowledge of the events of 70 CE, there is reason to think that this saying about the Temple was not only known, but had been reinterpreted along the lines found in Mark and John, as early as the time of Paul.[31] Paul twice uses wording and imagery

29. See Mk 8.11-12; Mt. 16.1-4; Lk. 11.16, 29-30; Jn 2.18; 6.30. See also Scot McKnight, 'Calling Jesus *Mamzer*', pp. 75-76.

30. The question is raised within the Gospel tradition itself: even though Matthew states that two witnesses were found who heard Jesus say something about the destruction and rebuilding of the Temple, Mark suggests there were problems with their testimony (Mk 14.57-59; Mt. 26.60-61).

31. One of the very few studies to discuss the Pauline evidence in relation to the transmission of the Jesus tradition is J.P.M. Sweet, 'A House Not Made With Hands' in *Templum Amicitae* (ed. William Horbury; JSNTS, 48; Sheffield: JSOT Press, 1991), pp. 368-90. See also Frances Young and David F. Ford, *Meaning and Truth in 2 Corinthians* (London: SPCK, 1987), pp. 132-33; Kåre Sigvald Fuglseth, *Johannine Sectarianism in Perspective* (SupNovT, 119; Leiden: E.J. Brill, 2005), p. 174.

that is closely related to this part of the Gospel tradition. In 2 Corinthians 5.1, Paul speaks of a tent or tabernacle being *pulled down*, and the existence of a house *not made with hands*, in both cases using precisely the same word as is found in Mark 14.58. And in 1 Corinthians 3.17, Paul writes that if anyone destroys the temple of God, God will destroy that person. It is thus Paul, our earliest Christian author, who provides our earliest witness to this tradition. The most obvious connections one sees at first glance are of course between Paul's statements and the specifically Marcan form of the saying, with its reference to another dwelling *not made with hands*. However, we will have difficulty making sense of what Paul wrote in relation to the Gospel tradition unless we also bring the evidence from John into the picture. For it certainly seems highly unlikely that Paul could have known the saying in the form in which it is found in the Synoptics and Thomas, with the first person 'I' on the lips of Jesus, and still have claimed that God would destroy the one who destroys God's temple. Likewise, given his positive use of the image of one tent that will be taken down and another not made by hands that will replace it, it seems clear that Paul did not simply regard the saying as inauthentic, as Mark would have had his readers believe.

How is one to account for these elements of the Pauline knowledge and use of this tradition? The most satisfactory explanation is that Paul was familiar with a transformation of the saying along the same lines as would much later find its way into the Gospel of John, in which the saying was applied to death and resurrection, and where the agency for the destruction of the body-temple is attributed to others rather than Jesus himself.[32] The evidence from Paul's correspondence with the Corinthians therefore strongly suggests that a form of this saying resembling *both* the Marcan *and* the Johannine variants was produced sometime before Paul wrote these letters. It nonetheless continues to remain most probable that the form in which the saying is found in John is a secondary transformation of a saying of Jesus, applied with hindsight (as the Fourth Gospel itself suggests) to the death and resurrection of Jesus. Yet the evidence from Paul suggests that this transformation took place not decades later at the time the Fourth Gospel was written, but very early, sometime before Paul wrote his letters to the church in Corinth.[33] At any rate, Paul provides us with our earliest

32. C.H. Dodd has observed that the saying in its Johannine form can be understood as an idiomatic conditional, and thus particularly close in meaning to the Pauline form. See Dodd, *The Interpretation of the Fourth Gospel* (Cambridge: Cambridge University Press, 1953), p. 302 n. 1.

33. The Pauline evidence thus indicates that some elements of the Johannine

evidence for the Temple saying we have been discussing, and also bears witness to the ways in which it was transformed and reinterpreted, thus allowing us to date the debates over the saying to a still earlier period.

On the other hand, even relatively late sources that show signs of dependence on the canonical Gospels may at times contain pieces of information that are of some independent historical value. There is an intriguing reference in the Gospel of Peter to Jesus' original followers having been in hiding because it was suspected that they might set fire to the Temple. Given that there is no obvious reason that a Christian author would invent such an accusation, and that the creation of it by Christians after they had been accused of setting fire to Rome in Nero's time seems absolutely unthinkable, it is best taken as a genuine piece of historical data that made it down to the time of the author of the Gospel of Peter, whether orally or in some writing that is no longer extant. It indicates that Jesus' prediction was a key issue with regard to how he was viewed by his contemporaries, so much so that the Jewish authorities feared that his disciples might try to bring about the fulfillment of his prophecy themselves.

Nevertheless, as in the sayings attributed to Jesus in the Gospels predicting the full dawn of the kingdom within the lifetime of Jesus' hearers, the seeming failure to materialize of any literal fulfillment of these predictions was less than decisive with regard to Jesus' status as prophet. For those familiar with other examples of prophetic literature, this will not be surprising. Prophetic speech, while rarely as vague as Woody Allen's famous parody ('Two nations will go to war, but only one will win'),[34] usually allowed for the possibility either of reinterpretation or of projection further into the future, so that the problem of apparent lack of fulfillment

Gospel are indeed *early*, but we are reminded in the process that an early date alone is insufficient basis for assessing a tradition's historical value. John, at any rate, does not only tell us about two levels, that of the historical Jesus and that of the Christian community in the 80s or 90s, but also about stages in between. Space prohibits us from exploring here the possible evidence from the book of Revelation that the form in Thomas may also be early. On this see further Gilles Quispel, 'The Gospel of Thomas and the Trial of Jesus' in *Text and Testimony* (ed. T. Baarda *et al.*; Kampen: J.H. Kok, 1988), pp. 197-99, although Quispel does not make a convincing case for the *originality* of the form in Thomas. Indeed, the evidence from Revelation could equally be taken to show knowledge of something like the *Johannine* form of the saying, with its identification of *Jesus* as the Temple, just as in Revelation the Lamb is the Temple. Nevertheless, the anti-sacrificial attitude of Jewish Christianity suggests that Thomas too is a strong contender for representing an early, widely known form of the saying.

34. Woody Allen, *Without Feathers* (New York: Random House, 1972), p. 13.

was mitigated.[35] Clearly this was true even in the case of an apparently specific prophecy, with a specific timeline, such as the one we have been considering here.

In the end, therefore, accusations of being a false prophet were unlikely to be effective ways of countering claims by or about someone who was perceived by his followers to be a true prophet. After all, by the rigid standards proposed in Deuteronomy, the canonical prophet Jonah might be deemed a false prophet, since his prediction that Ninevah would be destroyed in forty days failed to come true in the specified time frame. In actual fact, however, prophecy appears never to have been viewed in such inflexible terms. If fulfillment of a prediction of judgment did not materialize, it was at least as likely that an explanation would be offered in terms of God relenting as in terms of the prophet being mistaken, and the book of Jonah once again provides an example of this. Also particularly noteworthy is Josephus' statement that the Essenes' predictions were *rarely* wrong, suggesting that it was overall accuracy rather than 'inerrancy' that was the standard expected from prophets, even those of the highest calibre.[36] The Dead Sea Scrolls, as well as the New Testament writings themselves, attest to a widespread awareness that prophecies were things that not only could but ought to be reinterpreted and reapplied, adapted not only to lack of fulfillment on a literal level, but also to changing needs and circumstances. The classic example within the biblical tradition itself was the reinterpretation of Jeremiah's seventy years of exile in the book of Daniel as seventy *weeks* of years.[37] The focus on the temple saying in the Gospel tradition shows precisely the process we have been discussing: the potential of this saying to be understood as an inaccurate prediction spurred the various adaptations and explanations found in the Gospels. Nevertheless, *after* the destruction of the Temple in the year 70, Jesus' predictions would have borne a close enough resemblance to what actually happened to be evaluated as a *true* prediction – and any details that did not correspond could be reinterpreted, in keeping with the process of interpretation and reinterpretation of this and other sayings that appears to be datable back to at least the time of Paul.[38]

35. On cognitive dissonance see further Robert P. Carroll, *When Prophecy Failed* (New York: Seabury, 1979).

36. Josephus, *War* 2.159.

37. Jer. 25.11; 29.10; Dan. 9.1-2, 24.

38. On the advantage of hindsight in interpreting omens see Josephus, *War* 6.291-96; Hanson and Horsley, *Bandits, Prophets, and Messiahs*, pp. 181-82.

The shortest and simplest (and most likely original) form of the saying is preserved on the lips of opponents of Jesus in the Gospels (Mk 15.29). This may reflect a historical reality: it seems likely that whereas the Christian community either denied that Jesus said such a thing, or (more commonly) radically rewrote and reinterpreted the saying, it was the *opponents* of the early Christian movement who kept alive the memory that Jesus had uttered this particular saying in its earliest and most difficult form. And so, on the one hand, the false prophecy accusation served (as did other accusations and questions by outsiders) to stimulate development in the early Christian tradition, and may through the process of reinterpretation have contributed to the formation of important ideas such as Jesus' body, and the Christian community as a whole, as God's Temple.[39] On the other hand, the fact that there were other voices recalling the words of Jesus, including some inconvenient ones, suggests that historical Jesus research must take seriously as a control on development and alteration of Jesus' teaching not only the presence of eyewitnesses (some of whom must have been involved in the reinterpretation of the sayings they remembered, given the early date at which this process of reworking and transforming appears to have begun), but also the presence of opposing voices who refused to let the followers of Jesus forget that he had said things that, from their point of view, seriously discredited the claims Christians were making about him.[40]

Conclusion

Let us conclude this chapter by asking directly the question that has been in view throughout this article: What can opponents' labelling of Jesus as

39. See further my book *John's Apologetic Christology* (Cambridge: Cambridge University Press, 2001), pp. 34-43, for a discussion of how controversy spurs and contributes to the process of doctrinal development.

40. It is to the credit of authors such as Keith Ward (*What the Bible Really Teaches* [New York: Crossroad, 2005], pp. 42-65) and Ulrich Luz (with Axel Michaels, *Encountering Jesus and Buddha* [Minneapolis: Fortress Press, 2006], pp. 45-46) that they seek to take seriously, and reflect on the theological implications of, sayings such as these. We may briefly mention here two theological implications of this saying of the historical Jesus. First, this saying pushes us to move away from the Apollonarian tendencies in much popular Christology. Second, it perhaps suggests that (once again in contrast with many streams of contemporary Christianity) what the biblical tradition suggests is most valuable in God's eyes is not accurate knowledge, but our attitude and in particular our desire to see God's kingdom replace the injustice of the world we live in.

'false prophet' tell us about the historical figure of Jesus? Because of the lateness of sources that use the explicit label, we are in fact forced to work in the opposite direction – from our information about Jesus' own explicit and implicit claims, to implied (and at times hypothetical) reactions and responses of his contemporaries. Nevertheless, what information we have and what we can reasonably surmise is not insignificant. That it was possible to make the accusation that he was a false prophet at all is in itself noteworthy: the predictions that Jesus made were apparently not of such a public and overwhelming character, and/or were not consistently fulfilled in such a precise and obvious way, that it was impossible to dispute his prophetic ability. Although we have seen that mere fulfillment of a prediction was not the only issue, some fulfillment at least some of the time was presumably essential, and we must posit that there must have been at least some predictive sayings of Jesus that were widely viewed as true prophecies for him to obtain this reputation at all. There are, of course, stories told in the Gospels in which Jesus did make specific predictions – such as that someone that he was asked to heal but was not present would get better – but we are also told of other instances in which he could not accomplish miracles. This problem plagues the evaluation of faith healers in our own time as well: anecdotal evidence is severely problematic, since some people who are prayed for or upon whom hands are laid do indeed get better, while others do not, and demonstrating a causal connection is impossible. For the most part, however, ancient polemicists did not engage in the types of arguments used by modern-day sceptics, who appeal to the possibility of scientific explanation or outright deception. In general, ancient authors tend to grant that something we would call supernatural may be involved, but attribute the source of the power involved to a diabolical rather than a divine source. And so it is that other accusations that appear both in the New Testament and in later sources – of demon possession, sorcery, and so on – are intrinsically connected to the question of Jesus' prophetic status, his claims (and claims made about him by his followers) that he spoke for God and that his miracles confirmed or at least lent plausibility to these claims. And so we have found another reason that the accusation that Jesus was a 'false prophet' may not have been a central focus in the New Testament: not that the prophetic claims made by or about Jesus were not contested, but that they were contested indirectly, by disputing the *source* of his powers rather than his powers *per se*.

The 'false prophet' accusations (both explicit and implicit) suggest that apologists looking for persuasive arguments will find their claims about Jesus' prophetic abilities met with scepticism – if it was possible to doubt these claims during the lifetime of Jesus and/or not long thereafter, on what basis could we possibly hope to offer greater certainty in our time, from our much further removed standpoint in history? From a historian's perspective, however, our study suggests a far more positive conclusion: that debate between Christians and those outside the Christian community about things Jesus was recalled to have said continued in the decades that intervened between Easter and the writing of the Gospels, and that this ongoing conversation helped keep alive the memory of things Jesus said and did (as well as leading to its reinterpretation, presumably by both parties). The accusations against Jesus thus are extremely valuable for the historical study of Jesus, as well as having provided a dynamic driving force behind the development of Christian literature and theology.

JESUS AS KING OF THE JEWS

Lynn H. Cohick

Introduction

'What I have written, I have written', Pilate is said to have declared when challenged about his charge against Jesus. Scholars debate whether Pilate spoke as much, but few doubt that he installed (or had installed) the charge 'King of the Jews' upon Jesus' cross at his death. What would have given rise to this charge: what words and acts by Jesus, what claims by followers and dissenters, what broader political tensions and postures might have created this 'perfect storm' which ultimately led to Jesus' crucifixion under the banner of 'King of the Jews'?

Historical Jesus studies are known for their vastly different portrayals of Jesus, due in no small measure to the sources chosen, the various methods used and the philosophical underpinnings governing assessments of history itself. As Richard Bauckham observes, 'All history – meaning all that historians write, all historiography – is an inextricable combination of fact and interpretation, the empirically observable and the intuited or constructed meaning'.[1] This concern is particularly acute when determining how (or whether) to appropriate the canonical gospels and what facts historical research can yield about Jesus' life. James Dunn's comment reflects the researcher's dilemma: 'the "historical Jesus" is not the man who walked the tracks and hills of Galilee; "the historical Jesus" is what we know about that Jesus, what we can reconstruct of that Jesus by historical means'.[2] Aware of the common complaint that a reconstruction of Jesus' life often reflects more closely the researcher's own convictions, nevertheless, careful use of historical research tools helps mitigate against an idiosyncratic Jesus.

---

1. Richard Bauckham, *Jesus and the Eyewitnesses: The Gospels as Eyewitness Testimony* (Grand Rapids, MI: Eerdmans, 2006), p. 3.

2. James D.G. Dunn, *A New Perspective on Jesus* (Grand Rapids, MI: Baker Academic, 2005), pp. 28-29.

In discussing the historical Jesus, I locate myself within the Third Quest. This group, though quite diverse, shares certain assumptions including the Jewishness of Jesus. This group also attempts to separate the historical Jesus from theological and narrative constructions of his life. As such, the canonical gospels are read with attention to historian's concerns rather than theological (or Christological) questions. For some, the gospels have almost no useful information on the historical Jesus, for the gospel writers have overlaid the historical Jesus with confessional claims almost impossible to scrape off. Others, and I place myself here, look with more generosity at the material, finding useful existential facts which can then be explained in a coherent narrative.

Methodology takes centre stage in historical Jesus studies, for good reason: the goal of historical Jesus studies is to present a credible picture of the first-century CE man named Jesus, quite apart from reliance upon theological assessments of his person, work or message. One method thought to accomplish this goal was the criterion of dissimilarity, wherein a saying of Jesus was judged authentic if it was dissimilar both to its Jewish context and to the later early Christian context. Results failed to produce a credible picture, however, and ironically actually reinforced a theological Jesus who stood above history rather than within it.

Excessive reliance upon the criterion of dissimilarity falls under its own presumptuous weight. The alleged great divide between Jesus and his early followers represents a theological or ideological conviction that strains the credulity of historical criticism. As Sanders notes that while it is possible that Jesus taught one thing, and was killed for something else, and his followers believed yet a different thing about him, thus eliminating any connection between Jesus' life, death and subsequent Christian movement, this analysis, in the end 'is not satisfying historically'.[3]

Used sparingly and with great care, however, the criterion of dissimilarity when used in relation to Early Judaism[4] and the later church is useful.[5] An excellent case in point is the titulus 'King of the Jews' found on

---

3. E.P. Sanders, *Jesus and Judaism* (Philadelphia: Fortress Press, 1985), p. 22.

4. N.T. Wright, notes that used effectively, the criterion can locate Jesus 'firmly within Judaism, though looking at the reasons why he, and then his followers, were rejected by the Jewish authorities', Wright, *Jesus and the Victory of God*, p. 86.

5. James H. Charlesworth, argues 'the two most important criteria for authenticity are the criterion of dissimilarity to the Christology and theology of the members of the Palestinian Jesus movement and the criterion of embarrassment to his followers'. He advocates that a tradition should be considered authentic until data suggests otherwise. *Jesus Two Thousand Years Later* (ed. James H. Charlesworth and Walter P. Weaver; Harrisburg, PA: Trinity Press International, 2000), pp. 101-102.

Jesus' cross. This title was not exploited in a confessional sense by early Christians, making it less likely that the title was manufactured by the gospel writers. Again, modifying the criterion's parameters opens new uses for the tool. N.T. Wright advocates the criterion of double similarity and dissimilarity, wherein the historicity of an event in Jesus' life is judged both by its similarity to Early Judaism and its (sometimes subversive) distinctiveness to the same, as well as its connectedness to, but not strict reproduction in, early Christianity.[6]

Rather than focus solely on the criterion of dissimilarity, scholars in the Third Quest tend to use the criterion of plausibility in examining traditions about Jesus.[7] Of first importance, Jesus' Jewish context is paramount, and his words and deeds must fit plausibly within his first-century Roman Palestine context – its social, political, religious and cultural milieu.[8] A related concern which is not shared equally by all who find a home in the Third Quest is the plausible connection between Jesus and the early church. I find myself resonating with Sanders' sentiment noted above, that a more satisfying history does not detach the life of Jesus' followers after his death from their life with him during his ministry. I am more sympathetic to a view which holds that the disciples were more likely to continue traditions learned from Jesus, rather than create brand new positions about his person and actions.[9]

---

6. Wright, *Jesus and the Victory of God*, p. 132.

7. For a summary and critique of criteria see Gerd Theissen and Dagmar Winter, *The Quest for the Plausible Jesus: The Question of Criteria* (trans. M. Eugene Boring; Louisville: Westminster/John Knox, 2002). See also Craig Evans, *Fabricating Jesus: How Modern Scholars Distort the Gospels* (Downers Grove, IL: InterVarsity Press, 2006), pp. 46-51.

8. Jesus' Jewish context, however, has been used to create vastly different pictures of the historical Jesus, due in part both to our limited knowledge of Early Judaism and its variety. For example, Paula Fredriksen contends that it was '*not* [author's italics] his teaching as such, nor his arguments with other Jews on the meaning of Sabbath, Temple, purity, or some other aspect of Torah, that led directly to Jesus' execution as King of the Jews', Fredriksen, *Jesus of Nazareth King of the Jews* (New York: Alfred A. Knopf, 1999), p. 266, while Sanders concludes, 'A man who spoke of a kingdom, spoke against the temple, and had a following was one marked for execution... Jesus and his followers thought of there being a kingdom in which Jesus was the leader, and he was executed as "king of the Jews",' Sanders, *Jesus and Judaism*, p. 295.

9. Dunn, *A New Perspective on Jesus*, p. 30 writes, 'And as we can tell the shape of the seal from the impression it makes on the page, so we can tell the shape of Jesus' mission from the indelible impression he left on the lives of his first disciples as attested by the teaching and memories of Jesus that they were already formulating

The Third Quest takes seriously the Jewish context of Jesus' life and death. Exploring that context often involves using tools from the social sciences. In our particular case, we will take advantage of research done on colonial experiences, given that Jesus' immediate context was Jewish life lived under Roman occupation. I will not be reading the gospels from a post-colonial perspective, as valuable as that reading can be in answering certain questions. But because we want to develop a picture of the historical Jesus, we will concentrate primarily on interaction between colonial powers and leaders of the dominated group.[10] Two areas need our attention: (1) collaboration and its ramifications,[11] and (2) the political challenges of the disenfranchised as seen by both the oppressors and their collaborators.[12] Specifically, we must explore the relationship between the chief priests and Pilate as it plays out in Jesus' death sentence, and as they both reacted to Jesus' words and acts in the final week of his life. This focus becomes especially acute as most scholars recognize the intense political nature of Jesus' ministry.

Supporting my research is a philosophical conviction variously dubbed critical realism or practical realism.[13] This position presents the medium between modernist confidence in objective science and the post-modernist's confidence in subjectivity, both of which are in a sense absolutist.

during their initial discipleship'. See also Wright, *Jesus and the Victory of God*, p. 90; Sanders, *Jesus and Judaism*, pp. 57-58; Howard Clark Kee, 'Christology in Mark's Gospel', pp. 187-208 in *Judaisms and their Messiahs at the Turn of the Christian Era* (ed. Jacob Neusner, Willliam S. Green and Ernest S. Frerichs; Cambridge: Cambridge University Press, 1987).

10. Warren Carter, *The Roman Empire and the New Testament: An Essential Guide* (Nashville, TN: Abingdon Press, 2006).

11. Richard A. Horsley, *Jesus and Empire* (Minneapolis: Fortress Press), pp. 60-62.

12. Carter, *Roman Empire and the New Testament*, p. 11, notes that 'elites legitimated and expressed their domination with an *ideology or set of convictions*. They asserted it was the will of the gods... They claimed social hierarchy and exploitation were simply the way things were.'

13. Wright, p. 35, explains critical realism as 'a way of describing the process of "knowing" that acknowledges the *reality of the thing known, as something other than the knower* (hence "realism"), while also fully acknowledging that the only access we have to this reality lies along the spiraling path of *appropriate dialogue or conversation between the knower and the thing known* (hence "critical")' [author's italics]. N.T. Wright, *The New Testament and the People of God* (Minneapolis: Fortress Press, 1992), p. 35.

Practical realism allows that an object or thing exists both in an external sense and within a knower's mind. Language is a suitable vehicle to express facts or information about that object without conflating the object with the subject.

Titulus: *Jesus of Nazareth, King of the Jews*

Beginning with the *titulus* keeps our focus on the task at hand: examining Jesus' opponents' views which gave rise to the charge. One might complain that a more secure departure would be gained by beginning with Jesus' triumphal entry or Temple cleansing. Yet in the end, these apparent discrete facts are not understandable apart from their narrative form. So too the *titulus* gains its meaning within its first-century CE Roman Palestine context. A picture emerges of the full impact of the charge by examining events and actions of the recent past from both Roman and Jewish history, as well as noting connections with what developed after Jesus' death. From this larger narrative we gain insight into the possible historical meanings attached to the title, King of the Jews. We cannot rule out irony, misdirection and politicking on Pilate's part with Jesus as a pawn in a larger game. Attention to political tensions rooted in the Roman occupation of the Jewish homeland can shed light on the various meanings this title generated in its various viewers.

Why would Pilate conclude that Jesus required crucifixion under the title 'King of the Jews'? Was his appraisal shared? These questions tantalize, enticing the reader into the story of Jesus' last week. And yet perhaps by starting at the beginning of that fateful week, we grab the wrong end of the stick. I propose to begin with the *titulus* and investigate what sort of person one would expect to find hanging beneath it. By recovering evidence from Pilate's time, we can create a general profile which provides a template for comparison with evidence from Jesus' life. The differences which emerge between our imagined picture of a crucified Jewish king and the one presented by the facts surrounding the historical Jesus lead to a few conclusions. First, we must consider Jesus' words, actions (and ambitions, where discernable) with an eye toward a political reading of those events. Second, we must be open to the possibility of irony behind Pilate's title. Third, we must include the decisive role played by the chief priests in any interpretation of the *titulus*. In assessing each data piece and player, I suggest that Jesus' title as King of the Jews is understandable in relation to his words and deeds if the title's irony is appreciated and Pilate's interplay with the chief priests is adequately accounted for.

In our recreated sketch of a crucified 'King of the Jews', we would find the man hanging beneath[14] the charge first of all to have led a military excursion against Rome. A king needs followers, a military horde to lead, a plot of land to defend and a group to represent. A king is more than a mere leader, he is an implicit owner of the kingdom and its people, and requires supreme allegiance. The king of the Jews hanging on the cross would have battle scars and fresh wounds from his recent defeat, and probably a insolent glint in his eye. His defiance would be part bravado, because to the end he must show himself a fearless king to his soldiers dying with him on their own stakes.

This king of the Jews would also lay claim to royal blood in his veins, though to which royal family he belonged might be an open question. Perhaps this king claimed Hasmonean blood, thereby recalling the halcyon days[15] one hundred years earlier when Jews were free to govern themselves. Or perhaps our king located himself in Herod the Great's line. After all, both Alexander Jannaeus and Herod were called King of the Jews. Finally, the man dying on the cross would have claimed a strong Jewish heritage, an identity with ancient Israel and its descendents.

My fictional king is based on examples presented by Josephus. These descriptions serve as helpful illustrations of what political opposition to Rome looked like in first century CE Palestine. Richard Horsley notes that at the time of Herod the Great and Jesus, Galilee and Judea were boiling over with insurrectionists and anti-Roman sentiment. 'For just at the time of Herod and Jesus, several significant movements emerged among the Judean and Galilean people that were headed by figures acclaimed by their followers as kings or by figures who promised to reenact the deliverance of Israel from foreign rule in Egypt.'[16] In *Antiquities* 18.10.5-7, Josephus develops in detail the destructive deeds of three pretender kings: Judas, son of Ezekias, Simon, Herod's slave, and Athronges. According to Josephus' description, each man was tall and strong, each attacked both Jews and Romans and each had royal ambitions. These warrior-kings led a multitude of men on their rampages, often targeting royal palaces or squaring off directly with the Roman military.

Studying Josephus' description, several interesting points rise to the surface. First, the would-be kings were physically stronger than their

14. I recognize that we do not know where the *titulus* was placed, so I am drawing on typical portrayals of its position relative to the crucified body.

15. That those times were anything but peaceful is not the point. Memory has a way of erasing the unpleasant and magnifying the good.

16. Richard Horsley, 'Messiah, Magi, and Model Imperial King', in *Christmas Unwrapped: Consumerism, Christ, and Culture* (ed. Richard Horsley and James Tracy; Harrisburg, PA: Trinity Press International, 2001), pp. 139-61 (141).

peers. It is, in part, upon this characteristic that their authority rests. Their lack of fear and their ruthlessness – killing both Jew and Roman, intensified the perception of their power. Reading between the lines, in his condemnation of these men Josephus reveals what he considers valid authority for a king: proper heritage, significant wealth, and skill in warfare. Second, Josephus highlights that these men chose political targets, including palaces and Roman military sites. Clearly these fighters were agitated by Roman occupation and political collusion by Jewish leaders. Third, each man is identified as having royal aspirations. Both Simon and Athronges claimed the title king and placed on their heads a diadem. For these men and their followers, the title king implied a military opposition to Rome and its collaborators.

Along with the illegitimate kings described disparagingly by Josephus, we also read of true kings such as Herod the Great, and earlier, Alexander Jannaeus. The Hasmonean and Herodian families continued to be the power brokers in Pilate's day. Herod's son, Herod Antipas, perhaps longed for such a title.[17] His marriage to Herodias, a member of the Hasmonean family, might have been an attempt to further such a goal. Moreover, Josephus reveals that Antipas had armour for 70,000 men, a suspiciously large number for a tetrarch of Galilee (*Ant.* 18.7.2).[18] Luke's gospel suggests that Herod Antipas was in Jerusalem for the Passover (Lk. 23.6-7). Josephus describes him as following Jewish traditions[19] and attending feasts (*Ant.* 18.5.3), so it is plausible that he was in Jerusalem at the time.[20] If so, I wonder if Pilate was thinking of Antipas' unfulfilled aspirations and his father's now divided kingdom when he condemned Jesus as 'King of the Jews'. Was Pilate subtly mocking Antipas, declaring any hope of kingship a forlorn one?

17. Crossan, makes the interesting suggestion that with the rebuilding of Sepphoris and the construction of Tiberias completed about 20 CE, the peasants in the area were further burdened with taxes. 'New cities...are not good news for the local peasantry, at least not as a whole – especially where, in ancient law, the land belongs to God'. J.D. Crossan, *Who Killed Jesus* (New York: HarperSanFrancisco, 1996), p. 42. See also Horsley, *Jesus and Empire*, pp. 37-39.

18. Josephus' insistence that Antipas was content to live quietly as Tetrarch of Galilee, and was driven to pursue kingship by his wife, sounds like special pleading, and follows Josephus' pattern of blaming royal women for their men's downfall.

19. Josephus, *Ant.* 18.37f. also notes that Antipas' building projects were contentious – he built Tiberius on a cemetery, offending Jewish sensibilities concerning cleanness, and he decorated the palace there with animal illustrations, a violation of the commandment against images.

20. If one concludes he was not in Jerusalem, my argument is not weakened substantially. Antipas would learn soon enough about the charge on the cross.

We know that after Pilate's procurator-ship, both Antipas' and his brother-in-law, Agrippa's, fortunes change. According to Josephus, Herodias goaded her husband into applying for the title king after her brother received the same from the new Emperor, Gaius Caligula. Antipas' request is denied after Agrippa accused him before Gaius of sedition. Antipas was exiled to Lyons, Gaul, but Herodias was offered freedom based on her brother's good standing. She declined, and lost her property. Josephus concludes that Herodias received fair punishment for envying her brother's good fortune, and Herod Antipas got his just desserts for listening to his wife's vainglorious pestering. The scandal surrounding the title king, though occurring directly after Pilate left office, presents intriguing possibilities. Might Pilate have mockingly compared Jesus to Herod the Great, with his vast lands, magnificent buildings, and military skill? Could he as well have been ridiculing Antipas, who had but a fraction of that land, only one great city to his name (Tiberius on Lake Galilee) and armour without the men to wear it?

In sum, we can conclude a few solid facts from Josephus' evidence about the tumultuous first-century CE Roman Palestine. Pilate entered a world where Jewish prophets and wanna-be kings whipped up public support, only to be brutally crushed by Rome. The crowds followed men who were strong, tall, brave and brash – who looked the part of a warrior. Those who gained the support of the masses promised freedom from Roman rule and set about destroying and stealing the wealth accumulated by those who sided with Roman occupation. At least some Jews looked eagerly for a king to lead them out from under Roman oppression. In this time of heightened intensity, not a few men chose to wear a diadem, if only for a short time before meeting their death at Rome's hand.

When we turn to the few secure pieces of evidence we can garner from the historical Jesus' life, we search in vain for any insurrectionist call to arms against Rome. We discover that Jesus' teaching and healing in Galilee was confined primarily to Israel and, I would add, understood in light of Israel's scriptures. So far in the investigation, Jesus shares more similarities with John the Baptist than those insurrectionist kings in Josephus who are burning down palaces and threatening Roman soldiers. Surely Pilate knew of John the Baptist, and Herod Antipas' dispatch of the same. A closer look at this story is needed to detect possible connections to Jesus' fate.

According to Josephus (*Ant.* 18.5.4), John the Baptist had great influence among the Jewish people because he taught them to be virtuous to each other and pious before God. Herod Antipas feared John's growing influence, and chose to nip in the bud any potential insurrection. So John was arrested and taken to Macherus, a fortress built by the Hasmoneans and improved by Herod the Great, who built a palace on this Transjordan site. There John was executed. In Josephus' telling, the content of John's message did not alarm Herod Antipas, but rather John's prominent public persona. Thus Herod's move to execute John was preemptive, a precaution against any political aspirations that might tempt John to rebel against Herod and Rome. With his increasing popularity, John was a rising threat to Herod's power.

Most scholars agree that only Rome had the power to execute by crucifixion, and so John's beheading by Antipas reflects the option available to the latter in terms of capital punishment. But Pilate's choice of crucifixion suggests two significant differences between the condemned men. As far as we know, John the Baptist did not publicly denounce the Temple or make any direct symbolic acts within its environs. Moreover, he did not act symbolically as Israel's prophesied king in the manner of Jesus' triumphal entry into Jerusalem suggests.[21] By acting as he did, Jesus invited the critique of the Jewish leadership in Jerusalem; their active participation in his ultimate downfall is a crucial piece of the puzzle that is Jesus' death as King of the Jews.[22] Understanding the implications of the *titulus* requires that we broaden our search to examine two key events in the week preceding Jesus' crucifixion: the triumphal entry and the Temple cleansing.

Triumphal Entry

According to the canonical gospels, Jesus' entry into Jerusalem for what will end up being the last week before his crucifixion is met with great celebration and shouts, 'Hosanna to the son of David' (Mt. 21.9) and 'Blessed is the King who comes in the name of the Lord' (Lk. 19.38) and 'Blessed is he who comes in the name of the Lord, even the King of Israel' (Jn 12.13). The language asserting Jesus as King is prominent, and the connection with David's lineage suggests that the crowd identified Jesus

21. Sanders, *Jesus and Judaism*, p. 235, notes that Jesus 'deliberately demonstrated, by riding on an ass, that the claim to a special role in God's kingdom was being made by one who was "meek and lowly"'. See also Wright, *Jesus and the Victory of God*, p. 521.

22. Sanders *Jesus and Judaism*, p. 289, concludes that the priestly aristocracy were the 'prime movers behind Jesus' execution', and as 'intermediaries between the Jewish people and the Romans...they were thus in a position to represent him to the Romans as dangerous', p. 290. See also Wright, *Jesus and the Victory of God*, pp. 549-50.

as Messiah, or at least as the messenger of God's Kingdom. The label Messiah means God's anointed, and because kings were anointed by God, it was natural for some Jews to speak of the Messiah as the King of Israel. The pilgrims' words reflect hope that God would bring in his just kingdom and rule over Israel. Clearly these exclamations carry political overtones; the crowd is implicitly condemning Roman rule and by implication the collaboration of the chief priests.

Jesus' ride into Jerusalem, however, has been challenged as a creation of the early Church, for some doubt that Jesus would imitate deliberately a messianic prophecy from Zechariah. Yet most of the other Jewish prophets noted by Josephus (and killed by the Romans) had drawn upon Israel's scriptures to explain their actions.[23] It seems more likely that Jesus encouraged such demonstrations based on his own estimate of his ministry and person. John J. Collins contends that this event is the only one in Jesus' life which fits the scriptural paradigm of Messiah. And because no other ancient work connects Zechariah 9.9 with messianic prophecy, it seems less likely that the early Christians created the event. Jesus was an eschatological prophet who in 'the manner of his entry into Jerusalem appears to be an enactment of the coming of the Davidic messiah'.[24]

Collins, however, does not go far enough with his insight. I would argue that the temple action (misleadingly referred to as the cleansing) which happens later in that week (see below) also symbolizes a reference to Messiah/king.[25] Many Jews pinned their hopes on a Messiah who would renew God's covenant, banish the unrighteous, and rebuild the glory of Israel. They might point to scriptures,[26] as did those at Qumran, or they

---

23. Josephus, *War* 2.261-62 and *Ant.* 20.169-70 speaks of an Egyptian 'false prophet' who gathered a following at the Mount of Olives and promised with a word to fell the walls of Jerusalem, much as did Joshua in Israel's history.

24. John J. Collins, *The Scepter and the Star: the Messiahs of the Dead Sea Scrolls and other Ancient Literature* (ABRL; New York: Doubleday, 1995), p. 206. Collins suggests that with this event Jesus shows himself unique, but we should not be surprised that someone who had such an impact in history likely stood out in his own time.

25. E.P. Sanders grounds his discussion of Jesus with the latter's activity at the Temple, which Sanders interprets as symbolic destruction, *Jesus and Judaism*, pp. 61-70.

26. For example, the Targum on Isa. 53.5 reads, 'He [the Messiah] shall build the sanctuary that was polluted because of our transgressions and given up because of our iniquities'. The substitution of 'build the sanctuary that was polluted' for 'pierced/ wounded' suggests a tight connection made by at least some Jews of the Messiah's role vis-à-vis the Temple.

might look to the examples of David and Solomon, who planned and built the Temple. More recent examples of Jewish kings include Judas Maccabeus' restoration of the temple in 164 BCE and Herod the Great's current extensive building project. Jesus' actions in the temple fit expectations that the Messiah/king of Israel would restore or renew (perhaps rebuild) the temple. If, as it seems likely, Jesus taught that he had a role to play in God's Kingdom to come (even as he promised the disciples they would play a part), then it is natural that he or his disciples viewed him as king or God's 'viceroy'.[27] A king in their eyes is God's anointed one, the Messiah.

The crowds' language adds a further dimension to our exploration of Pilate's 'King of the Jews' phrase by introducing concepts taken from Israel's scripture and tradition. Certainly the widespread messianic hope among Jews of a Jewish leader sent by God to free Israel from her oppressors kept Pilate awake at night. Our brief look at Josephus' description of some such figures indicates that Rome was continually on watch for such 'radicals' and quickly snuffed out kingdom aspirations. Is Pilate reacting to this appellation with his title 'King of the Jews'?[28] And why was Jesus not arrested at this time? Why was not the crowd dispersed or killed? We know that Pilate could put down any uprising with speed and brutality. Did he see Jesus' actions as a threat?

It is generally accepted that Pilate did not view Jesus as a direct immediate threat to overthrow Jerusalem or Judea. Rome's delay in arresting Jesus might have been a calculated risk that the event would fizzle into yesterday's news.[29] Jesus' action in the temple stoked the fire, and Rome gave him another hard look. Moreover, because Pilate and Caiaphas worked hand in glove in other operations to maintain the status quo in Jerusalem, perhaps emissaries for both parties worked behind the scenes, juggling for the best position publicly and all the while keeping up the pretense of autonomy. When an agreement over procedure was reached, the temple guards and some of Pilate's own men were sent to seize Jesus quietly, away from the crowds.

---

27. Sanders, *Jesus and Judaism*, p. 308.

28. E.P. Sanders, *The Historical Figure of Jesus* (London: Penguin Books, 1993), p. 254, postulates that Jesus purposefully enacted the Zech. 9.9 prophecy, declaring himself a king.

29. Sanders, *The Historical Figure of Jesus*, p. 254, suggests that Jesus' demonstration was likely 'quite modest: he performed a symbolic gesture of insiders' and thus avoided arrest. Paula Fredriksen agrees, *Jesus of Nazareth, King of the Jews* (New York: Alfred A. Knopf, 1999), p. 242.

This conclusion leads to speculation about the crowd size and nature of the event. Many rightly advocate that the crowd size was large enough to be noticed, but small enough to warrant a wait-and-see posture. Could Jesus' death, like John the Baptist's, be associated with his popularity among the crowds?[30] It is so difficult to determine what number would create a tipping point. The overall impression provided by the canonical gospels is of crowds composed of his followers from Galilee and Judea aware of (though perhaps misunderstanding) Jesus' teachings and miracles.[31] Jesus apparently exited and entered Jerusalem several more times without crowds praising him, suggesting that the event involved symbolism related to Israel's scriptures understood by his disciples, but perhaps restricted only to them or including a small circle outside that group.[32]

Jesus' manner of execution, then, fits the category of propaganda. Crucifixion as a crime deterrent was common within the Roman provinces. In the generation after Jesus, Titus' army would crucify Jews caught in the cross hairs of the Roman army's siege of Jerusalem. Josephus laments that crosses were placed in view of the city walls to 'induce the Jews to surrender in order to avoid the same fate. The soldiers themselves through rage and bitterness nailed up their victims in various attitudes as a grim joke until, owing to the vast numbers there was no room for crosses, and no crosses for the bodies' (*War* 5.450). 'Crucifixion broadcast Rome's zero-tolerance policy toward a perceived threat of sedition.'[33]

30. Fredriksen, *Jesus of Nazareth*, p. 247 declares, 'Jesus, the focus of this popular conviction, had in essence lost control of his audience'. She adds, p. 245, 'Jesus' authoritative proclamation of the Kingdom's immediately imminent arrival triggered for those pilgrims relatively new to his mission the conviction that, were the Kingdom on its way, Jesus himself would be its leader'.

31. 'Crowd' in the Gospels is a complex category involving various social strata in different gospel scenes, but we are unable to explore its variations here. Mark describes them as *hoi polloi*, the common folk who made up the vast majority of the Jewish population (Mk 11.8). Luke declares that they were disciples (19.37). Matthew writes that all of Jerusalem is astir about the identity of this man; the crowds identify him as 'Jesus, the prophet from Nazareth in Galilee' (21.11). John implies they were Judean pilgrims who knew Jesus mainly from the time he raised Lazarus (12.17-18).

32. Fredriksen, *Jesus of Nazareth*, p. 150.

33. Fredriksen, *Jesus of Nazareth*, p. 150.

Temple Cleansing and Jesus' Messianic Role

Thus while the Triumphal Entry likely put Jesus on the 'to be watched' list, it hardly justified immediate death in and of itself, from Pilate's perspective. I suggest it took the added weight of Jesus' temple action (and the subsequent decisions by the Sanhedrin) to tip the balance against Jesus.[34] In the temple, Jesus overturns tables and drives out sellers of sacrificial animals – why? This event raises numerous questions for historians, though few doubt its historicity. Traditional interpretations suggested that Jesus was upset at the commercialization of the temple, and was therefore *cleansing* it from its contamination of mammon. Rightly, however, that view has come under fire. Instead, Jesus' actions are seen in light of his eschatological promises of a renewed temple made by God[35] or the destruction of the current Temple due to its oppressive system[36] or as judgement by God.[37]

Criticism that God would soon destroy the temple (likely by the Romans) puts Jesus on a collision course with both the chief priests and Pilate, for different reasons. The chief priests need the authority of the Temple to uphold their own power. They rely on the economic benefits accrued to them by the smooth functioning of the temple, and their wealth forms a substantial base for their authority over the Jewish temple state. Pilate cannot afford any destabilizing of the Jewish status quo. He takes his cue from the Jewish leaders – if they are nervous, he is as well. Dunn concludes 'most likely it was because Jesus was seen as a threat...to the power brokers within Israel's social-religious-political system, [sic] that they decided to move decisively against him'.[38]

---

34. Sanders, *Historical Figure of Jesus*, p. 258, concludes that Jesus' words and actions were not merely predicting the temple's destruction, but were viewed by alarmed onlookers as threatening: not that Jesus and his few followers would raze it, but that God (less likely the Romans) would destroy it.

35. Sanders notes in *Jesus and Judaism*, p. 75, 'Thus we conclude that Jesus publicly predicted or threatened the destruction of the temple...that he probably also expected a new temple to be given by God from heaven, and that he made a demonstration which prophetically symbolized the coming event'.

36. J.D. Crossan, *Jesus: A Revolutionary Biography* (San Francisco: HarperSanFrancisco, 1994), pp. 127-33.

37. Wright, *Jesus and the Victory of God*, p. 417, states that 'when Jesus came to Jerusalem, he symbolically and prophetically enacted judgment upon it'. The strength of Wright's position, in my opinion, is its insight that Jesus critiqued the current Temple.

38. J.D.G. Dunn, *Jesus Remembered* (Grand Rapids: Wm B. Eerdmans, 2003), p. 786.

Jesus' actions in the temple must be understood both politically and religiously. Horsley chastises recent scholarship that operates with the modern dichotomy of separation between Church and State. He reminds us that in the Roman world, worship of the Emperor was not merely window dressing, but effectively held the Empire together, 'it integrated the Greek cities and, via the patronage system, their economies into the overall Roman imperial order centered in the emperor, the divine saviour of the world'.[39] Joel Green and John Carroll remind us that institutions like the Roman Empire or the Jewish Temple legitimate themselves by claiming divine prerogative. The socially constructed world proclaims that this is how it *should* be. From the authorities' perspective, not only did Jesus trespass against conventional wisdom, he also flouted the divine. Jesus' actions at the temple destabilized the status quo, even as his past behaviour on the Sabbath or eating with the 'unclean' called into question established social patterns. 'The moral order and distribution of power represented by the temple was at stake in Jesus' behaviour'.[40]

Many Jews at this time looked to the destruction and rebuilding of the Temple as a prime indication that God was restoring Israel.[41] For example, E.P. Sanders cites *1 Enoch* 90.28-30 as evidence among contemporary Jews for the Temple's destruction.[42] Moreover, we must also not lose sight of the fact that Messiah/Christ means 'anointed'. To hold that title directly challenged those who are also anointed, specifically the high priest who is anointed for his duties in managing the Temple. Thus when Caiaphas wonders if Jesus is the Messiah, he is contemplating a potential rival to the role of God's 'anointed one'.

In the end, any disruption of the temple system, any threat to its continuation, was a challenge to the status quo. The seemingly diverse acts of the Temple 'cleansing', the trial with its charge of blasphemy, and Pilate's judgment of King of the Jews resolve themselves into a coherent picture when we consider the expectations and role of the Messiah in much of Second-Temple Judaism. Jesus' actions (understood in light of his interpretation of Scripture) at the Triumphal Entry and in the temple suggest a claim to the title of Messiah (anointed one). As Wright notes, 'if Jesus has

39. Horsley and Tracy, *Christmas Unwrapped*, p. 116.

40. John T. Carroll and Joel B. Green, *The Death of Jesus in Early Christianity* (Peabody, MA: Hendrickson, 1995), p. 178.

41. George W.E. Nickelsburg, *Jewish Literature between the Bible and the Mishnah* (Philadelphia, Fortress Press, 1981), p. 18.

42. Sanders, *Jesus and Judaism*, pp. 77-90.

been doing and saying things against the temple, the natural implication is that he thinks he is the anointed one, the Messiah'.[43] Jesus' teachings about the kingdom of God were folded into a demonstration at the temple that the kingdom was at hand. Threats to destroy and rebuild the temple could not be taken lightly, especially if one insisted he was God's anointed sent to do so.[44]

Trial before the Sanhedrin

As the canonical gospels present it, Jesus would not have been crucified by Rome without the chief priests' charges. Yet the trial's historicity is debated vehemently among scholars. Some argue Jesus was too insignificant to warrant a meeting with the Sanhedrin, reaching this conclusion by isolating the event in the temple from Jesus' ministry and from the crowd's attention. The argument maintains that the chief priests would hardly spend so much of their time dealing with a man who makes no kingly or messianic claims and who tossed over a few tables in one corner of the colossal temple complex. Jesus is a threat neither to the Sanhedrin nor Rome; only a crowd's (false) opinion spiralling out of control could threaten him. Others believe the Sanhedrin meeting would have been unnecessary given (presumed) standing orders that any questionable trouble-maker would be summarily dispatched. Such scepticism is represented by John Dominic Crossan, for whom the whole trial scene is prophecy historicized, 'the Trial is, in my best judgment, based entirely on prophecy historicized rather than history remembered. It is not just the *content* of the trial(s) but the very *fact* of the trial(s) that I consider to be unhistorical'.[45]

The discussion about the Sanhedrin's involvement takes place in today's post-Holocaust setting, and many scholars (rightly) resist an anti-Semitic reading of the gospels. For example, Crossan correctly notes that while Christian propaganda that condemned the Jews and exonerated the Romans

43. Wright, *Jesus and the Victory of God*, p. 523. He notes that the question is not 'are you the second person of the Trinity'. Rather, the question reflects whether he is the fulfillment of 2 Samuel 7 or Psalm 2.

44. In this Jesus differed from the Essenes who also criticized the Temple, but did not mount a demonstration against it. Instead, they were waiting for the messiah(s) to restore Israel, the sons of light.

45. Crossan, *Who Killed Jesus?*, p. 117. He adds, p. 152, 'However explicable its origins, defensible its invectives, and understandable its motives among Christians fighting for survival, its repetition has now become the longest lie, and, for our own integrity, we Christians must at last name it as such'.

was harmless when the Christians were a tiny minority, it turned lethal when they took over Rome.[46] Certainly the goal of avoiding an anti-Semitic reading is laudable, but the historian must not ignore first-century realities simply because those 'facts' were later used in horrible ways by the Church against Jews.

Working backwards from the charge of 'King of the Jews' and forward from Jesus' temple action, a trial by the Sanhedrin makes a great deal of sense.[47] Caiaphas appreciated that Jesus and his motley gang could hardly take over the Temple, let alone Jerusalem; however, Jesus' charismatic power could rouse a multitude, and that spelled trouble with Rome. Assuming that Jesus was immersed in the theological debates of his day concerning messianic hopes and claims, a meeting with Jewish leaders (variously portrayed by the four Gospel writers) can be accepted as reflecting a historical event. In other words, the 'trial' coheres historically with Jesus' first-century environment and is consistent with Jesus' teachings and ministry.

Pilate was soon involved in the deliberation about Jesus. He was informed by the temple leadership as to the potential dangers of Jesus' message and/or its reception by the Jewish crowds gathered in Jerusalem to celebrate Passover. The pattern probably looked something like the scenario recorded by Josephus concerning Jesus ben Ananias (*War* 6.300-309). In 62 CE, this Jewish prophet, drawing on images in Jeremiah, began predicting daily the Temple's doom. His dire warnings upset the chief priests, who hauled him in for questioning. Though tortured, he remained silent. Next he was taken to Albinus, the Roman governor, who also questioned and tortured him. Again, he gave no defence, and Albinus tossed him out as a lunatic, not worthy of death. He was killed during the siege of Jerusalem by a rock thrown from a Roman catapult.

A comparison of ben Ananias and Jesus is instructive. Both spoke prophetically against the temple. Both were interrogated and beaten by the chief priests, who later turned the accused over to the Roman authorities. And both were questioned and abused by the governor. The basic process of justice is the same: arrested and questioned by the Jewish authorities, and then transferred to the Roman governor for further punishment. Because Jesus ben Ananias had no followers, and no ministry other

---

46. Crossan, *Who Killed Jesus?*, p. 152.

47. Using the criterion of historical coherence, Josephus' information supports the Gospels' record. Darrell L. Bock suggests that 'grand jury' might be a better term to use than 'trial'. Bock, *Jesus According to Scripture: Restoring the Portrait from the Gospels* (Grand Rapids, MI: Baker Academic, 2002), p. 371.

than shouting lamentations throughout Jerusalem and its temple, he was not executed. Because Jesus was not leading an insurrection, his followers were spared (though some were later killed by Rome).

Again, though post-dating Jesus' time, events surrounding another Jewish figure illumine nicely the collaboration between governor and chief priests in Jesus' own day. About a decade after Jesus' death, during the tenure of Cuspius Fadus (procurator-ship begun in 44 CE), a certain Theudas gathered a crowd and marched to the Jordon river, promising to part the waters. In all likelihood, Theudas was reenacting the crossing of the Jordan done by Joshua when he entered the land to claim it for Israel. Fadus reacted swiftly and violently, sending his army to subdue the (unarmed?) multitude. They captured Theudas and cut off his head.

Justice was swift and brutal, a characteristic of the Roman response in Judea. But Josephus' silence about why Fadus would be alarmed at a multitude watching for a miracle at the Jordon invites exploration. The likely source for such information is the chief priests whose responsibility it was to control the Jewish population. Quite possibly they alerted Fadus to the religio-political significance to Theudas' claims. The chief priests feared a new 'Joshua' taking over the 'promised land' and removing all pagans. Forewarned, Fadus quickly subdued the potential uprising. Theudas' death at the hands of the Roman army instead of on a cross is probably due to the battle conditions under which he was captured. The Roman soldiers could ride back into Jerusalem displaying the successful completion of their mission – the head of the ringleader. It likely had as significant an impact on the public imagination as would a crucifixion.

Pilate's Response

Pilate faced many challenges (some of his own making) with Jewish opposition to Rome's occupation. He learned first hand about many Jews' convictions about the sanctity of Jerusalem, the temple, and the money kept there. Events which occurred early in his tenure tainted his entire term. His distain for Jewish traditions is betrayed in his confrontational posturing and baiting of the Jewish crowds and leaders. The canonical gospels' presentation of Pilate's attempt to acquit Jesus before the Jewish leaders is not wholly driven by a concern to condemn the latter. It reflects as well the learned hesitancy governors of restless provinces showed when faced with potentially volatile situations.[48]

48. Dunn, *Jesus Remembered*, p. 776. He rightly concludes 'the primary responsibility for Jesus' execution should be firmly pinned to Pilate's record, and the first

We cannot look at Pilate in isolation from his collaborators in the temple, but we can briefly sketch who Pilate was and how he acted based on evidence from Philo, Josephus and Roman historians. From their stories emerge a man with a violent streak and a pugnacious personality willing to provoke his constituents for the sheer pleasure of watching their discomfort. He walked dangerously close to the line between taunting the people and driving them to riot.

Yet he was also a man who doubted himself, and backed down when confronted. He got ahead of himself when he provocatively brought Roman army standards into Jerusalem. Their images drew outrage from the Jews, who promised to die rather than have such offending symbols in the holy city.[49] He backed down from killing the protesters, but the sting of that failed showdown was partly assuaged when he again compromised the sacred Temple. He took *korbonas* (dedicated money) from it to build an aqueduct, and that inflamed the population. But he was ready for their mob reaction, and placed 'undercover' soldiers among them, who on his command began slaughtering the crowd.[50] Importantly, Pilate had access to this money only with the collaboration of the chief priests.

Ultimately Pilate's collaboration with the chief priests was his undoing. Pilate slaughtered a large group of Samaritans, apparently armed but claiming to be harmless.[51] The Roman legate in Syria called for Pilate to give an accounting in Rome. Fortunately for Pilate, the emperor died before he arrived. But the event raises several questions, not the least of which is why Pilate was condemned if the Samaritans did have weapons and were congregating around Mount Gerizim. The answer lies within Jewish history. The Samaritans killed were led by a prophet who claimed that he knew where the Temple utensils were buried. Once found, the Samaritan Temple would likely be rebuilt – an affront to the Temple in Jerusalem. Only a few generations earlier, Alexander Jannaeus destroyed the Samaritan Temple, and no chief priest worth his salt would allow it to be rebuilt under his watch. Likely Caiaphas warned Pilate against allowing this prophet to proceed, and to destroy his movement as a potential threat to Jerusalem. This reconstruction is supported by the fact that Caiaphas was

hints of an anti-Jewish tendency in the Gospels on this point should be clearly recognized and disowned', pp. 776-77.

49. Josephus, *Jewish War* 2.171-74; Josephus, *Antiquities of the Jews* 18.55-59. Probably also Philo, *Legatio ad Gaium* 301-302.

50. *War* 2.175; *Ant.* 18.60-62.

51. *Ant.* 18.88-89.

deposed at the same time as Pilate, suggesting that Caiaphas had a hand in the Samaritan incident.

This brief profile of Pilate suggests we are dealing with a man who is not especially clever, but, for his time, typically brutal. In this, he was not so different from other procurators in Judea, and he certainly would not be the worst. He was not a weak leader asking for guidance on how to run Judea. Nor was this a man sympathetic in any way to Judaism or Jewish problems. He was normally disinclined to give the Jews any favours; even more, he seemed to take pleasure in their misfortune. Darrell Bock remarks that when Pilate returns after questioning Jesus, 'one intuits that Pilate is having some fun with his Jewish neighbors'.[52] But even if he was loath to offer favours to the Jewish elite, Matthew's gospel suggests that they had a well-oiled relationship. They 'handed over' Jesus to Pilate, directly implying that his death was assured. Judas thinks so, because when he hears that Jesus has been given to Pilate, he knew Jesus' fate was sealed (Mt. 27.1-5) and he hangs himself.

Because the chief priests relied on the governor as the final keeper of the peace, it makes historical sense that they would hand over Jesus for punishment. Pilate's questioning of the chief priests and his taunting of the crowd is historically plausible if he was determined to maintain control of the situation. He could not risk the crowd rioting through premature condemnation of what could be a very popular figure.[53] By testing the waters, he was able to discern Jesus' popularity. He would likely have known about the temple incident, and could only imagine the outrage any desecration of the temple might cause. In fact, he could point to personal experience, when he brought shields into Jerusalem, and was humiliated with a show of non-resistance by the populace. He would not want a repeat performance.

The Pilate we know from history is not weak, nor given to offering favours to the priestly aristocracy. I suggest that in Jesus' case, Pilate enjoys the chief priests' dilemma: how to maintain their power and avoid killing a crowd favourite.[54] The Gospels' portrayal of his tormenting the priests by repeatedly declaring Jesus' innocence fits with what we know about his *modus operandi*. Pilate had no intention of turning Jesus loose

---

52. Bock, *Jesus According to Scripture*, p. 532.

53. It is also possible that Pilate is worried about Jesus' identity as a 'divine man'. Generally speaking, Romans believed that gods could appear in human form. He probably was aware that Jesus healed and performed other miracles. The Gospels indicate he was surprised at Jesus' lack of power when he questioned him.

54. Carter, *Roman Empire and the New Testament*, pp. 30-31.

after his informers/collaborators determined he was a threat to peace. But he enjoyed their squirming as he teased them with his power. He offered them the horrible choice of which Jew they wanted to see die. He made them complicit in Rome's crucifixion of a Jew. While they tried to toss the responsibility of Jesus' death onto Pilate (and he certainly bears the blame as the one who ordered the death), Pilate lobs the ball back into their court. He demands that they show their allegiance to Rome. The match between these unwilling partners ended in a draw, each achieving their immediate goal, but neither obtaining the upper hand.

Whether Pilate would have acted against Jesus had the chief priests not raised the complaint is more difficult to answer.[55] Pilate cared not at all for Jewish religious questions, but was consumed with concern about Jewish rebels. In fact, the two 'thieves' crucified with Jesus were not really thieves in our sense of the word. The Greek term carries the meaning of bandit or brigand – a political insurrectionist. Would Jesus' Triumphal Entry or temple activity have created enough concern for Pilate to pursue Jesus apart from any charges leveled by the Jewish leaders? The answer depends in part on the size and composition of the Jewish crowd who welcomed him. If Pilate viewed the crowd or the followers of Jesus[56] as mounting an uprising against Roman occupation, he would likely be expected to act swiftly and harshly against both Jesus and his followers. That he did not suggests several interesting ideas. First, likely Pilate viewed the temple guards and high priests as the front line of defence against riots during the high holy days. He would depend on them to spot the first signs of uprising, and he was not expecting such from Jesus. Second, the relative freedom of movement Jesus enjoyed during his three-year ministry denotes that he did not organize a band of Roman resisters. The ever-changing crowds who heard him speak or watched him heal did not coalesce into a force intent on winning Israel's freedom from Rome. Jesus remained, in Pilate's mind, another Jewish teacher speaking to other Jews about their God – until news of his anointed status is thrown in the mix.

So why did the chief priests not demand that Pilate also destroy Jesus' disciples? Is it because they were so few in number (Acts 1.15 claims 120 followers before Pentecost) as to represent no threat at all? Yet Roman

---

55. Crossan believes that Pilate would go after Jesus as a trouble maker upsetting the social status quo. He removes almost all religious overtones (content) from Jesus' ministry.

56. Fredriksen's argument (*Jesus of Nazareth*), hangs on the distinction between the crowds unaware of Jesus' real message, and his disciples who know he is not the Messiah (and thus are not a threat to Rome).

policy did not take into account the size of the group challenging their authority – any opposition to Roman supremacy was punished with excessive force. Perhaps the chief priests counselled Pilate that the crowds would quickly forget Jesus because he was a fraud, and thus his fame would fade with his ignoble death.[57]

I suggest that both Pilate and the chief priests saw Jesus as a threat to their precariously established status quo, in other words, as a political and social concern. The reality of collaboration between the 'religious' elite running the temple, and the Roman elite ruling the province is often under appreciated. Categories of wealth and commitment to the current state of affairs often trump religious and ethnic differences, and pursuit of power makes strange bedfellows. The charge 'King of the Jews' by which Jesus was crucified reveals a complex relationship between the Roman and Jewish ruling classes which sought to maintain the state's stability (and their power) by removing a potential threat to their hegemony. Josephus paints a picture of social tension at the time of Pilate, 'the multitude contended with the nobility, and both sent ambassadors [to Rome]; for the men of power were desirous that their form of government might be changed into that of a Roman province; as were the multitude desirous to be under kings, as their fathers had been' (*Ant.* 18.3.5). Into this hostile setting rides Jesus, proclaimed and mocked as a king.

Pilate: A King Maker?

The charge 'King of the Jews', is formally placed on Jesus' cross.[58] Identifying a criminal's offence at the place of execution was not unknown in the Roman period. Twice Suetonius mentions criminals whose crimes are announced on placards. For example, a slave accused of stealing a strip of silver from a couch has his hands cut off and hung about his neck, and a placard listing the reason for his punishment precedes his parade among the banquet guests.[59] John states that the notice was written in three

---

57. Yet frustratingly for the temple elite, Jesus' followers hailed him as Messiah.

58. The Gospel of Peter, which describes the Jewish elite as directly responsible for Jesus' death, identifies Jesus on the cross as 'King of Israel'. Mk 15.26 declares Jesus is 'the King of the Jews'. Mt. 27.37 reads 'This is Jesus, the King of the Jews'. Luke writes 'This is the King of the Jews' (23.38). John gives the longest title, 'Jesus of Nazareth, King of the Jews', (Jn 19.19-22). All the gospels attribute the title to the Romans – John most directly to Pilate, while the Synoptics vaguely suggest the soldiers (presumably under orders from Pilate).

59. Suetonius, *Caligula* 32.2. See also *Domitian* 10.1 and Cassius Dio, *History*

languages: Hebrew, Greek, and Latin. We have examples of formal proc-
lamations written in Greek and Latin. Moreover, Josephus tells us that the
signs warning gentiles from proceeding further into the temple complex
were written in both Greek and Latin.[60]

With the title 'King of the Jews' Pilate declared that Jesus fitted into a
well-known category of rebels who sought the downfall of the Roman
Empire or at least the freedom of Israel. But additional meanings of the
phrase acted as ripple effects from a stone thrown onto a pond.[61] Pilate
shamed the chief priests by publicly parading an 'anointed' Jew to the
cross – once again Rome shows its superiority over Jews. Pilate perhaps
intended to humiliate those Jews who hoped for a king on the grand scale
enjoyed by Herod the Great. Pilate mocked the dreams and desires of the
populace, sneering at their futile hopes that their God might rescue them
from Rome's domination. With the death of yet another Jewish 'king',
Rome's power stands supreme, the Emperor's honor secure, and Pilate's
dominance over the Jews further imposed.

54.3.7, who describes a condemned slave led through the Forum with an inscription
announcing the reason for his death by crucifixion.

60. *War* 6.4.2, 125.

61. Nils A. Dahl, explains 'that Jesus was crucified as King of the Jews is not a
dogmatic motif that has become historicized in the passion narratives; precisely to the
contrary, it is a historical fact that became centrally important for the formulation of
the first Christian dogma: Jesus is the Messiah'. He continues that this confession
represents a 'thorough, radical Christianizing of the Jewish title of Messiah'. Nils A.
Dahl, *Jesus the Christ: The Historical Origins of Christological Doctrine* (Minneapolis: Fortress Press, 1991), p. 40.

Jesus as *Mamzer* ('Illegitimate Son')

Scot McKnight

Introduction

What, we are asking in this book, can be learned about Christology – or the nascent beliefs about Jesus – by examining the accusations against him by his opponents?[1] Do these accusations, made public and even performative in coming into verbal form as a label, reveal hidden claims on the part of Jesus, his family,[2] his relatives, his friends, or his followers? What value is there in an accusatory label? As Bruce Malina and Jerome Neyrey have stated:

> To label a person or group negatively is a social act of retaliation for some alleged deviance... In the hands of influential persons or powerful groups, they [labels] can inflict genuine injury, since they serve to define a person as out of social place, hence as permanently deviant... in a society built on grades of status, degrading terms that stick almost necessarily lead to collective avoidance, ostracism and isolation.[3]

The general implication is obvious: calling Jesus *mamzer* was a way of denouncing him, and the way of denouncing him was to call into question

---

1. This chapter is rooted substantially in my article 'Calling Jesus *Mamzer*', *JSHJ* 1 (2003), pp. 73-103. Portions of the chapter are lifted from that article, though now explored in a different direction. This piece is also indebted to a response paper I gave to John Miller at the SBL Historical Jesus section in the 2005 meeting at Philadelphia.

2. I do not accept the general thesis of James Tabor but I do think more attention needs to be given to the family of Jesus. Though the details cannot be defended here, Richard Bauckham's research into the family of Jesus commends itself more. On James Tabor, see *The Jesus Dynasty: The Hidden History of Jesus, His Royal Family, and the Birth of Christianity* (New York: Simon & Schuster, 2006); R. Bauckham, *Jude and the Relatives of Jesus in the Early Church* (Edinburgh: T & T Clark, 1990).

3. B.J. Malina and J.H. Neyrey, *Calling Jesus Names: The Social Value of Labels in Matthew* (Sonoma, CA: Polebridge, 1988), p. 37.

his origins – he was not a legitimate Israelite male and therefore, one would think, his teachings and his mission and his vision are all called into question. One can suggest that calling Jesus *mamzer* was perhaps a response to those who were claiming already during the lifetime of Jesus a supernatural origin.

A recent, gently rolling wave of scholarship has argued that Jesus was assigned the label *mamzer* ('bastard', 'illegitimate son') by his contemporaries and that far-reaching conclusions about Jesus' mission can be derived from the status that would result from such an accusation. In this piece, we are concerned with not only the social status of Jesus but even more with the insights such a label might shed on what Jesus and others may have believed about Jesus' origins. The recent use of *mamzer* for understanding Jesus' social status must be assigned to a list of breakthroughs, and it is to the credit of Bruce Chilton that the category is to be given a front-row seat in recent discussion.[4] I am unaware that any scholar, prior to Chilton, has given the category the attention it might deserve.

The Accusation: Mamzer

One can infer that early Christians did not invent such a social status for Jesus and we can see their straining already in Matthew's own genealogy. Here we find a series of names, punctuated by women with a reputation (Mt. 1.1-17: Tamar in v. 3, Rahab and Ruth in v. 5, the wife of Uriah in v. 6) who are then used to set the stage for Mary. Evidently, we are to understand Mary as such a woman, though she is guiltless since the conception in her case was virginal (1.16, commented on in 1.18-25). Some scholars, like Joel Marcus and Stephen Wilson,[5] remain convinced that the language of Mark 6.3 (ὁ υἱὸς τῆς Μαρίας, 'the son of Mary')[6] reflects

---

4. B. Chilton, *Rabbi Jesus: An Intimate Biography* (New York: Doubleday, 2000 [Peekamoose]); 'Jésus, le *mamzer* (Mt 1.18)', *NTS* 46 (2001), pp. 222-27.

5. Joel Marcus, *Mark 1–8* (AB, 27; New York: Doubleday, 2000), p. 375; Stephen G. Wilson, *Related Strangers: Jews and Christians 70-170 C.E.* (Minneapolis: Fortress Press, 1995), 188. Richard Bauckham, 'The Brothers and Sisters of Jesus: An Epiphanian Response to John P. Meier', *CBQ* 56 (1994), pp. 686-700, contends that 'son of Mary' serves to indicate that the 'siblings' of Jesus had a different mother than did Jesus. See also now James F. McGrath, 'Was Jesus Illegitimate? The Evidence of his Social Interactions', *JSHJ* 5 (2007), pp. 81-100.

6. For the text-critical issues, cf. R.E. Brown, *The Birth of the Messiah: A Commentary on the Infancy Narratives in the Gospels of Matthew and Luke* (ABRL; New York: Doubleday, 2nd edn, 1993), pp. 537-39.

accusations and labels at the time of Jesus, which Matthew felt uncomfortable with and so changed to 'the son of the carpenter' (13.55): the normal *Yeshua ben Yosep* is abandoned in favor of the scurrilous *Yeshua ben Miriam*.[7] Since scholars today are re-thinking John's Gospel as a legitimate source for information about the historical Jesus,[8] we are possibly

7. E. Stauffer, 'Jeschu ben Mirjam (Mk 6:3)', in *Neotestamentica et Semitica: Studies in Honour of Matthew Black* (eds E.E. Ellis and M. Wilcox; Edinburgh: T & T Clark, 1969), pp. 119-28. 'Alle mysteria Christi sind paradoxe Tatbestände, die eine dialektische Deutung hervorrufen, positiv oder negativ, doxologisch oder polemisch. Das gilt von der Geburt Jesu genau so wie vom Faktum des Leeren Grabes, von seiner Wundertätigkeit genau so wie von seinem Selbstzeugnis. Darum entfaltet sich die christliche Jesusbotschaft a principio in der Kontroverse' (p. 128). For others who see a slur here, cf. M.D. Hooker, *The Gospel According to Saint Mark* (London: A & C Black, 1991), p. 153; J. Marcus, *Mark 1–8* (AB, 27; New York: Doubleday, 1999), pp. 374-75. See also H.K. McArthur, 'Son of Mary', *NovTest* 15 (1973), pp. 38-58; R.E. Brown *et al.*, *Mary in the New Testament* (Philadelphia: Fortress Press, 1978), pp. 59-67; R.E. Brown, *Birth*, pp. 537-41; J.P. Meier, *A Marginal Jew*, I, pp. 225-27; T. Ilan, '"Man Born of Woman ..." (Job 14:1): The Phenomenon of Men Bearing Metronymes at the Time of Jesus', *NovTest* 34 (1992), pp. 23-45. In spite of this trend to find in 'son of Mary' little more than an ordinary remark, (1) the oddity of the expression – since sons were named by their father unless the mother's lineage was superior, (2) in a context of conflict, (3) where later Evangelists modify the language, and (4) for a woman who at least later is to be accused of illicit sexual union, begs for explanation and one solid such explanation is that it hints at illegitimacy. Furthermore, Meier offers the suggestion that the statement is 'flip' without a shred of evidence. Also, that the 'brothers and sisters' are mentioned in Mark 6.1-6 does not necessarily include them in the same accusation. Finally, it should not be argued that 'son of Mary' was, as a form, indicative of illegitimacy; there could be other motives for labelling a son by his mother. I am of the suspicion that too much of this scholarly trend seeks to find the Jewish accusation later than the Christian affirmation, rather than the reverse. From a completely different angle, and with far less care at the historical level, cf. J. Schaberg, *The Illegitimacy of Jesus: A Feminist Theological Interpretation of the Infancy Narratives* (San Francisco: Harper & Row, 1987), pp. 160-64. For her response to some caustic reactions to her study, see J. Schaberg, 'A Feminist Experience of Historical-Jesus Scholarship', in *Whose Historical Jesus?* (Studies in Christianity and Judaism, 7; ed. W.E. Arnal, M. Desjardins; Waterloo: Wilfrid Laurier University Press [Canadian Corporation for Studies in Religion], 1997), pp. 146-60.

8. See J.A.T. Robinson, *The Priority of* John (ed. J.F. Coakley; Oak Park, IL: Meyer-Stone, 1985); M. Hengel, *The Johannine Question* (Philadelphia: Trinity Press International, 1989); D. Moody Smith, 'Historical Issues and the Problem of John and the Synoptics', in *From Jesus to John* (ed. M.C. de Boer; Sheffield: JSOT Press, 1993), pp. 252-67; J. Ashton, *Understanding the Fourth Gospel* (Oxford: Clarendon Press, 1991) and *Studying John: Approaches to the Fourth Gospel* (Oxford: Clarendon Press,

justified to find historical confirmation of our issue in John 8.41, where the Jews/Judeans (John's problematic term for Jesus' opponents) protested to Jesus: ἡμεῖς ἐκ πορνείας οὐ γεγεννήμεθα, ἕνα πατέρα ἔχομεν τὸν Θεὸν ('we are not illegitimate children; we have one father, God himself'). That is, their claim probably labels Jesus one more time with his suspected illegitimacy.[9] The Hebrew equivalent here would probably be 'offspring of fornication' (*yaldey zenunim*). This suspicion is covered rather gently by John in 6.42 with the following: 'Is not this Jesus, the son of Joseph...?' No need, so reasons John, to poke at a deep wound. That the audience accuses Jesus of being a 'Samaritan' and 'demon-possessed' in John 8.42 probably speaks to the same suspected status of Jesus, and it may just as well lurk behind John 9.16 ('a sinner').

That Mary was pregnant before cohabiting with Joseph is indisputable; no Christian would have invented the problem of Jesus' claimed irregular, divine origins and accusations in order to dismiss the accusations. How the pregnancy was discovered (prior to cohabitation or a birth too early not to be noticed), or *why* or *how* Mary was impregnated was explained differently. By the followers of Jesus, Jesus' irregular origin was explained from a virginal conception (hence, Mt. 1.18-25; Lk. 1.26-38;[10] *Prot. Jas.* 7.1–16.2; *Ps.-Mt.* 6-12).[11] For others in the Diaspora, from the mid-second century CE onwards, Mary had been caught *en flagrant* – Mary and someone other than Joseph had intercourse, and she was discovered when signs of pregnancy were visible (cf. Origen, *Against Celsus* 1.28 [Mary is cast out by Joseph for adultery with a certain Panthera], 32-33, 69; 2.5, 8-9, 31; Tertullian, *de Spectaculis* 30.6; *Gosp.Thom.* 105; *Acts of Pilate* 2.3; *m. Yeb.* 4.13; *t. Hul.* 2.24; *b. Sanh.* 67a; *y. A.Z.* 40d; *y. Shabb.* 14d).[12] On the issue of Galilean customs differing from Judean customs, the evidence

1994); D. Tovey, *Narrative Art and Act in the Fourth Gospel* (Sheffield: Sheffield Academic Press, 1997); S. Byrskog, *Story as History – History as Story* (Tübingen: J.C.B. Mohr, 2000); R.T. Fortna and T. Thatcher (eds), *Jesus in Johannine* Tradition (Louisville, KY: Westminster/John Knox, 2001). A marshalling of the scholarship and some discussion of some evidence can be seen in C.L. Blomberg, *The Historical Reliability of John's Gospel* (Downers Grove, IL: InterVarsity Press, 2002).

9. So Schaberg, *Illegitimacy*, pp. 157-58 (with n. 39); *pace* J.P. Meier, *A Marginal Jew*, I, pp. 227-29; R.E. Brown, *Birth*, pp. 541-42.

10. For a fair-minded, though slightly overdone, discussion of the value of the infancy narratives, cf. J.P. Meier, *A Marginal Jew*, I, pp. 208-14.

11. For study, cf. R.E. Brown, *Birth*, pp. 517-33, 697-712; Schaberg, *Illegitimacy*, pp. 178-92; J.P. Meier, *A Marginal Jew*, I, pp. 220-22.

12. Cf. R.E. Brown, *Birth*, pp. 534-42; Schaberg, *Illegitimacy*, pp. 169-74.

is unclear for the first century and should not be factored into the discussion.[13] Jane Schaberg is correct in what follows and an important corollary follows my quotation of her: 'In the absence of a trial or hearing, and in the absence of any punishment or repudiation, suspicion of illegitimacy – whether sincere or prompted by the desire to discredit Jesus – could thrive only on the admission of someone involved.'[14]

The corollary is clear: Joseph, somehow, was disentangled from the mess and was seen as innocent (*dikaios*; Mt. 1.19). He was not the father of the baby; but Mary was the mother. The father had to be someone else. Someone, as they say in our Southern States, 'fessed up'. Presumably, Mary made the claim that Joseph was not the father[15] or, what is clear from the Gospel records (Mt. 1.18-25), Joseph was surprised and/or stated that he was not the father. The word, however, got out.

The social stigma attached to Mary, that is, the label that gave to her a 'master status' of some sort, would have been telling (cf. Wisd. 4.3-6). The Christian tradition claims Mary was saved by a benevolent act of Joseph.[16] He avoided the public-shaming event described or alluded to in *m. Sot.* and broke Jewish custom by marrying her, cohabiting with her, and raising Jesus (and the other children). Whatever explanation one prefers today is not the issue; clearly, Jesus' origins were *irregular* and that irregular origin gave rise to an accusation. Jesus may have been labelled by his contemporaries as a *mamzer*. And such a label would have carried with it socio-religious implications with a powerful significance for Jesus. As Malina and Neyrey have argued, though they failed to note that *mamzer* may have been one of the labels pinned to Jesus:

> ...negative labelling bears the force of stigma. When carried out publicly or at times secretly, such labelling can carry with it an institutional sanctioning of overwhelming proportions: positively by granting symbolic reward potential, negatively by granting symbolic devastation potential,

13. That Jews in Galilee were more strict on premarital customs than Jews in Judea can be seen in *t. Ket.* 1.4; *Ket.* 9b, 12a; but cf. the earlier text at *m. Ket.* 1.5 where the distinction is not raised. Scholarship is not decided on the feasibility of this distinction for first-century Judaism and neither have many paid sufficient attention to the context of these statements; cf. B. Chilton, 'Jésus, le *mamzer*'.

14. Schaberg, *Illegitimacy*, p. 153.

15. *m. Ket.* 2.5-6, for instance, shows that the woman's testimony is deemed worthy with respect to her sexual experience.

16. The deliberations behind Mt. 1.18-25 concern Deut. 22.13-21, 23-27, 28-29, and pertain to Mary's motives and options, as well as to Joseph's options.

> both of deep and enduring quality... Labelling is intended to create a master status...[17]

Before exploring a Christology from the side, we need to wade through the waters of the historical evidence to see what we can discover on the significance of labelling Jesus as a *mamzer*. Only as a result of patient examination of this evidence can we discover the assumptions behind the label.

The Implications: Social Sketch

Far-reaching implications have been drawn by several scholars,[18] especially Bruce Chilton, on the basis of this 'master status' of Jesus as a *mamzer* and, in addition, that status had 'profound influences on Jesus' personal development'.[19] The following factors of Chilton's theory may be noted.[20] Joseph, a journeyman who visited Mary's parents for repair work, and Mary began to sleep together before their marriage [pp. 6-7],[21]

17. Malina and Neyrey, *Calling Jesus Names*, pp. 38, 39.

18. It is unfortunate that John Miller's study, *Jesus at Thirty: A Psychological and Historical Portrait* (Minneapolis: Fortress Press, 1997), fails to take note of Jesus' *status* as a *mamzer* in Jewish society (*pace* pp. 41-42). In spite of the potential significance of the question and its answers, others have also not asked the question about Jesus' status in Jewish society: e.g., J.P. Meier, *A Marginal Jew: Rethinking the Historical Jesus* (3 vols.; ABRL; New York: Doubleday, 1991), I, pp. 332-45, where it would make a difference.

19. Chilton, *Rabbi Jesus*, here p. 6. For those unfamiliar with Chilton's new book, the following points should be mentioned: (1) his Jesus is a combination of his *mamzer* status, runaway for several years, Throne/Chariot mysticism, consciousness of endowment by the Spirit, and *Tradent* of his various dimensions of *kabbalah*; (2) his concerns are purification [Jesus came to the conviction, partly through his encounter with the Samaritan woman now seen in John 4, that all Israel was in fact pure and so broke from John and replaced baptisms with meals as the venue of purity], exorcism, miracles, and even nature control; (3) his identity shifts through phases of being a *mamzer*, a *talmid* of John, a rabbi, a messianic exorcist, a *chasid*, a prophet, and an angel; (4) the gospel records are unusually confused chronologically and Chilton's study is an attempt to re-align numerous sayings/events with the order seen in (3) above; (5) most importantly, the final phase of Jesus' mission was to actualize the Zecharian vision of pure Temple worship and sacrifice, brought to the fore when Jesus attempted an occupation of the Temple but, after failure to accomplish his mission, re-vitalized when Jesus began to see his meals as a 'replacement' (p. 254) of the Temple sacrifices.

20. Pagination is in brackets.

21. Two comments are in order here: (1) it is never quite clear to me if Chilton thinks the father was Joseph or someone else – pp. 6-7 and 200 suggest Joseph, but p. 20 suggests someone else; and (2) the child resulting from premarital intercourse

and so the circumcision was performed, in part, to bring Jesus into the *berith* ('covenant') [pp. 9-12]. This relation made Jesus a *mamzer*,[22] and thus Jesus 'negotiated the treacherous terrain between belonging to the people of God and ostracism in his own community' as (my expression) a special kind of pariah of society.[23] Concluding that Jesus was socially classified as a *mamzer*, and assuming that *mamzerim* could survive (*b. Yeb.* 78b [R. Zera]) and were known in Jewish society (cf. *b. Ket.* 14b [R. Simeon ben Menasia]), Chilton draws out the following fifteen historical

by a couple intending to marry (i.e., Joseph and Mary) is not, to my knowledge, labelled a *mamzer* in the earliest evidence I have seen (cf. Deut. 22.28-30). I can fully agree that such a child may have been seen as inappropriate and the like, but the Jewish evidence does not suggest that such a couple's child cannot enjoy full Jewish society. It is unclear to me if Chilton thinks Joseph was unfaithful to his (presumed) first wife (not Mary) – in which case, since Mary is unmarried, the child would not be a *mamzer* but a child of polygamy, or if their relations were just prematurely sexual, in which case again the child would not be a *mamzer*. Because Chilton's book is not a technical monograph, but a popular (and beautifully styled) biography, some of these details appear to me to be suggestive rather than definitive and determinate. On the other hand, because of Chilton's status in historical Jesus research, none of his statements can be taken casually. On p. 13 Chilton says, 'An unmarried woman impregnated by a man outside her community was in an invidious position, suspected of illicit intercourse'. The public knowledge that Joseph was doing repairs at her father's home would have been knowledge enough. On the same page, Chilton rightly observes that sexual relation before marriage 'was broadly tolerated' and, furthermore – what he does not note, is that such relations led to a marriage that could not be broken (Deut. 22.28-29). Chilton appeals to *m. Ket.* 1.8-9 for the view that unknown fathers are deemed *mamzerim* or *Netin* (descendants of the Gibeonites; cf. *m. Qid.* 4.1, 3). However, this conflicts at times with Deut. 22.28-29. One may presume that, *if* a male chooses to marry the impregnated woman, it is likely he is the father, in which case the father's status is determinative of the child (e.g., if Joseph is an Israelite, Jesus is not a *mamzer*). Thus, the 'evidence' brought forward by Mary would have been Joseph's decision to marry her and name the child.

It might be argued that Chilton's book is popular and, therefore, subject to less of a historical critique. My reply is simple: nothing Chilton writes is without scholarly merit. Furthermore, we should not be fooled by Chilton's easier style in this book: this is a rigorously defended book in that it offers evidence – even if never complete evidence – at every important juncture. To be sure, the format prevented Chilton from presenting the requisite footnotes, bibliographic discussion, and evidential displays. Nonetheless, because Chilton has published so many items leading to his *Rabbi Jesus*, the book becomes a monument to his scholarly enterprise on Jesus.

22. So Chilton, 'Jésus, le *mamzer*', p. 224.
23. Chilton, *Rabbi Jesus*, p. 13.

conclusions, conclusions over which the dark cloud of using later rabbinic information certainly looms large.[24]

(1)   Jesus would have lived in a caste apart [p. 12];
(2)   Jesus was unable to marry within established bloodlines [p. 12];
(3)   Jesus was often excluded from the mainstream of religious life [p. 12] by the elders and fellow villagers [15, 21];
(4)   Jesus' voice was silenced[25] in public congregations [p. 13];
(5)   Jesus was an 'untouchable... for ten generations' [p. 14];
(6)   The community felt imperiled both viscerally and communally [p. 15];
(7)   Jesus' status was doubly-deficient when Joseph died [p. 20];
(8)   Jesus was accepted as a *talmid* of John in spite of his status [pp. 34, 40];
(9)   Jesus' brothers, especially James, resented his status [p. 42];
(10)   Mary would have had difficulty finding a she-*mamzer* for Jesus to marry [pp. 72-73]; Miriam was possibly such a person (Lk. 8.2) [pp. 144-145];[26]
(11)   Jesus' retreat of twenty-one miles to Capernaum was outside the limits of his reputation as a *mamzer* [p. 95];
(12)   Jesus' rejection at Nazareth was provoked in part because of his *mamzer* status [pp. 97-102];
(13)   Jesus' teachings in Jerusalem are challenged because of his *mamzer* status [p. 121, here anchoring comments in Jn 8.19];
(14)   Jesus, in spite of his *mamzer* status, becomes an Elijah-like prophet and symbol of Galilean resistance to and liberation from Rome [pp. 168, 185];
(15)   Jesus' followers rejected the stories that Jesus was a *mamzer* [p. 200];

In addition to these claims, Chilton psychologizes in an imaginative vein with the following statements:

(A)   'It is hard to exaggerate the isolation and unease the boy would have felt growing up as a *mamzer* in Nazareth' [p. 14];

24. His definition: 'an Israelite of suspect paternity' (p. 12).

25. Here Chilton combines *mamzer* and *shetuqi*, 'silenced ones' (from *m. Qidd.* 4.1). A *shetuqi* is one who knows his mother but not his father. That Joseph married Mary suggests to me that Jesus knows his 'father' and that means he would not technically be classified as a *shetuqi*. But, see below at definition 9 p. 153.

26. The later rabbinic formula is from *b. Yeb.* 37a: 'Persons of confirmed illegitimacy may [intermarry] with others of confirmed illegitimacy, but those of confirmed illegitimacy may not intermarry with those of doubtful illegitimacy; nor those of doubtful, with those of confirmed illegitimacy; nor those of doubtful, with others of doubtful illegitimacy'. Chilton imagines here Mary seeking out a female of confirmed illegitimacy, a she-*mamzer*.

(B)   'But Jesus was forced by the circumstances of his birth to look outside the provincial establishment for an understanding of who he was and what it meant to be an Israelite' [p. 16];

(C)   'Insults such as exclusion from the synagogue were a regular part of Jesus' childhood' and behind Luke 7.31-33 [parable of the piping and wailing], Chilton confesses, 'I see a small child, standing apart from other children, wishing to play but not being included, defensively ironic about the gang's incapacity to agree on a game' [p. 16];

(D)   Chilton contends Jesus' intense personal vision, gregariousness, and inclusive vision were shaped on the anvil of his *mamzer* status that led to loneliness and wanderings on foot and in thought [pp. 16-17];

(E)   Jesus' understanding of God as his *Abba* emerges from his status [p. 17], and thus, 'If Joseph's fatherhood was in doubt, God's father-hood was not' [p. 17];

(F)   When Joseph died, and was buried on the same day, Chilton sur-mises: 'On the saddest day of Jesus' young life, the synagogue would still have excluded him from their midst' [p. 21];

(G)   Because of the 'synagogue's disdain for him' Jesus had a 'deep skep-ticism about religious authority' [p. 21] and the deep divide between Christianity and Judaism derives in part from Jesus' *mamzer* status and exclusion from his father's funeral [p. 21];

(H)   'The death of his father brought an emotional truth home to Jesus: the Kingdom of God was his only support' [p. 22];

(I)   As an adolescent, Jesus' family visited the Temple and led to a trans-formation for Jesus: 'The *mamzer* from Galilee had come to the place where God's presence was more palpable than anywhere else on earth. And he was part of it, in the house of his *Abba* (Luke 2.49). Gone was the exclusion he felt from Nazareth's synagogue, as he stood at the heart of the sacred, vouched for as an Israelite by his family' [p. 32][Chilton imagines that Jesus ran away from his family for a few years as a result of this experience at the Temple; he finds himself as a *talmid* of John the Baptist, only much later returning home][see also pp. 34, 37, 42];

(J)   'The hurt inflicted during his childhood, the sense that he was an out-cast, in the wrong through no fault of his own, was healed through his repeated immersions. The Jordan's waters washed away his feeling of estrangement. He repented of his anger he had felt, of his resent-ment against his own people in Nazareth' [p. 49]; it was from John that Jesus learned of Chariot mysticism [pp. 50-58];

(K)   'His tangible experience of God overwhelmed the feeling of rejec-tion he had known as a *mamzer* in Nazareth, and he conveyed his newfound sense of inclusion to others' [p. 60]; 'If God was there for an alleged *mamzer*, God was also there for a Samaritan. His pain and anxiety is part of the maturing of many religious personalities: the shedding of conventional identity in order to define a new self, framed by contact with the divine' [p. 70; cf. also p. 89];

(L)   Jesus returns to Nazareth to escape death at the hands of Antipas, but is not feted as his prodigal son parable would imply because of his *mamzer* status [p. 63];

(M)   'What did his repute as a *mamzer* matter to this strong, mature young man, a survivor of hunger, cold, thugs, and Herod Antipas' attack on John? … Jesus found his voice as a teacher and story-teller…' [p. 73].

It is appropriate to distinguish Chilton's fifteen historical claims from the implications he draws out in a more psychological vein. I do not doubt that psychology can help us to understand Jesus though studies demonstrate significant correlations between one's self-image and one's image of Jesus.[27] Neither do I doubt that being classified publicly as a *mamzer* would have had psycho-social consequences for Jesus' personal, social, and religious development. In principle, then, I am opposed to neither of the two categories of Chilton's imaginative reconstruction of Jesus. And, neither am I opposed to the use of imagination in history.[28] One of the solid features of E.P. Sanders' studies of Jesus is his ability to re-imagine what the world of Jesus was like, and one thinks of other fields where the same applies.[29] Peter Brown's studies, for instance, reveal the enlightening power of a historically-based imagination.[30] But it is the place of the

27. On which, cf. the insightful study of L.J. Francis and J. Astley, 'The Quest for the Psychological Jesus: Influences of Personality on Images of Jesus', *Journal of Psychology and Christianity* 16 (1997), pp. 247-59.

28. For my own views on historiography, see *Jesus and His Death: Historiography, the Historical Jesus, and Atonement Theory* (Waco, TX: Baylor University Press, 2005), 3-46.

29. *Jesus and Judaism*; see also his *The Historical Figure of Jesus* (London: Penguin, 1993). Other Jesus scholars, whose books cannot be cited here, with such an imagination include A. Schweitzer, R. Bultmann, H.J. Cadbury, W. Manson, J. Jeremias, C.H. Dodd, R.A. Horsley, M. Borg, J.D. Crossan, G. Vermes, G.B. Caird, and N.T. Wright. Unfortunately, J.P. Meier's three volumes each lack this imaginative power.

30. P. Brown, *The Making of Late Antiquity* (Cambridge, MA: Harvard University Press, 1978); *Augustine of Hippo: A Biography* (Berkeley, CA: University of California

historian to use an imagination backed by secure data, as do Sanders and Brown, and it is to these data that we should turn to find the meaning of being called *mamzer* and its implications for Jesus' life.[31]

Another word pertaining to method: the rabbinic definition of *mamzer*, even a definition in flux, should probably be distinguished from social innuendo and social labels. It follows from this that different Jewish persons may have had tighter or looser definitions of a *mamzer*. For one person Jesus might have been a *mamzer*, to another he might not have been. But we should not assume either that the rabbinic definitions were clearly known and applied, and neither should we assume that contrary views might have obtained.

Definition: Mamzer *and Jesus*

We should begin with the common assumption that a Jew is one who can marry other Israelites, and who can function within Israelite society and worship because his or her mother was Jewish. Contrary to such a Jew, a *mamzer* would be a child born of a prohibited marriage (cf. *m. Qidd.* 3.12) or sexual union that is punishable by *karet* (extirpation) or death.[32] In general, the label *mamzer* not only called into question but designated a person as 'not a legitimate Jew' and therefore restricted from the benefits granted to legitimate Jews. For Jesus' contemporaries to have called Jesus *mamzer* was a potent way to discredit whatever it was that he was claiming or doing or teaching.

In the *Encyclopaedia Judaica*, Schereschewsky contends, in glaring contrast to the inferences drawn by Chilton, that a *mamzer* has only one restriction in Jewish society: marriage.[33] That *m. Hor.* 3.8 classifies a scholarly *mamzer* above an ignorant high priest confirms the view that *mamzerim* functioned freely within Jewish society. In fact, this text may level the discussion of Chilton and should perhaps be given more importance than it has been given. Neusner translates as follows:

(A)   A priest takes precedence over a Levite, a Levite over an Israelite,

---

Press, 2nd edn, 2000); *The Rise of Western Christendom: Triumph and Diversity, A.D. 200-1000* (Cambridge, MA: Blackwell, 1996).

31. For an early critique of Chilton's use of *mamzer*, see the review of J. Klawans, 'Filling in the Gaps', *Bible Review* (February 2002), pp. 42-44, who calls the author to task for his definitions of *mamzer* and *rabbi*.

32. So defined by Ben Zion (Benno) Schereschewsky, 'Mamzer', *EncJud* XI, p. 840; see also the insightful remarks of B. Chilton, 'Jésus, le *mamzer*', pp. 225-26.

33. Schereschewsky, 'Mamzer', p. 840.

an Israelite over a mamzer, a mamzer over a Netin, a Netin over a
proselyte, a proselyte over a freed slave.

(B)   Under what circumstances?

(C)   When all of them are equivalent.

(D)   But if the *mamzer* was a disciple of a sage and a high priest was an
*am haare*s, the *mamzer* who is a disciple of a sage takes precedence
over a high priest who is an *am haares*.

We have then two widely divergent views on the meaning of *mamzer*
and, therefore, two massively different kinds of implications drawn for
the functioning of a *mamzer* within Jewish society. For Chilton, a *mamzer*
is an outcast; for Schereschewsky, a *mamzer* has one small limitation: he
or she can not marry a full Jew. For Jesus this would mean that, according
to Chilton, Jesus had to play dodge ball his entire life in order to accomplish his will; for Schereschewsky, Jesus simply was prohibited from
marrying a woman who had full standing in Jewish society. Nothing
more. Both views offer credible social circumstances for explaining, in
part or in whole, Jesus' celibacy, but the first view explains at a radical
level Jesus' mission and message. In light of this extreme set of alterna-
tives, we need to examine the surviving evidence about the *mamzer* in
Jewish society and how a person's status was determined.[34]

As far back as Ezra's priestly declarations for endogamy and divorce in
order to purity the community of Israel (Ezra 9–10), where the non-Jewish
women and their children (perhaps seen as *mamzerim*) were divorced and
sent away, there is evidence for determining one's status by the Jewishness (or non-Jewishness) of one's mother.[35] Centuries later, Josephus, in
his *Antiquities* (14.399-405), labels Herod the Great a 'commoner and an
Idumaean, that is, a half-Jew' (ἰδιώτῃ τε ὄντι καὶ Ἰδουμεαίῳ, τουτέστιν
ἡμιιουδαίῳ; *idiote te onti kai Idoumeaio, toutestin hemi-ioudaio*). The
label may derive from the matrilineal principle of determining one's
Jewish status by the status of one's mother: Josephus' father, Antipater,
was a descendant of those forcibly converted under Hyrcanus, but his

34. For a good discussion of the term in Medieval studies, cf. S.M. Passamaneck,
'Some Medieval Problems in *Mamzeruth*', *HUCA* 37 (1966), pp. 121-45.

35. See on this the careful discussion of S.J.D. Cohen, 'The Origins of the Matrilineal Principle in Rabbinic Law', *Association of Jewish Studies Review* 10 (1985), pp.
19-53; *The Beginnings of Jewishness: Boundaries, Varieties, Uncertainties* (Berkeley,
CA: University of California Press, 1999), pp. 263-307. Cohen's conclusion that the
matrilineal principle is not known until the time of the Mishnah minimizes, I think,
the evidence of Ezra, even if I concur that other evidence until the Mishnah is unclear.
See also D. Bossman, 'Ezra's Marriage Reform: Israel Redefined', *BTB* 9 (1979),
pp. 32-38.

mother, Cypros, was a Nabatean and, therefore, handed her status to Herod. And, the standard explanation of the confusion over Timothy's status (Acts 16.1-3) is that, though Jewish through his mother's status, his lack of circumcision rendered his status ambiguous; consequently, Paul circumcises him. The implications are clear: (1) by circumcision, Timothy obtains an unambiguous Jewish status; (2) had his status been determined by his father, a Greek, or by an illegitimate marriage, then such an act by Paul would be a deconstruction of Paul's own agenda since it would have made Timothy first a proselyte to Judaism; and (3) his mother's status determined Timothy's status, but his lack of circumcision made him suspect.[36] The circumcision of Timothy suggests that the matrilineal principle is at work in this passage.[37] In spite of a lack of overwhelming evidence, we may conclude as a general principle that a person's Jewish status at the time of Jesus was determined by his or her mother. This means that, since Mary, the mother of Jesus, was a Jew, Jesus was legally a Jew unless his father was a man who rendered Mary's children otherwise.

But was Jesus a *mamzer*? That is, though Jewish through his mother, was he a Jew of low estate because of some irregular union? The answer hangs on how we define *mamzer* and the evidence is not clear even at its inception.[38]

We begin with Deuteronomy 23.3 (ET 23.2): 'No one misgotten (i.e., *mamzer*) shall be admitted into the congregation of the LORD; none of his descendants, even in the tenth generation, shall be admitted into the congregation of the LORD (JPS)'. Not uncommon for biblical legislation, the term comes out of the blue. In the code of Deuteronomy 23, the *mamzer* is classed with those who are emasculated by crushed testicles (23.2) and with the Ammonites and Moabites (23.4-7). If these three sorts are 'abhorred', Israelites are not to abhor the Edomites or Egyptians, for ancestral and historical reasons (23.8-9). The children of Edomites and Egyptians may be admitted in the third generation while the 'tenth generation' exclusion of the *mamzer* clearly means 'forever'.[39] Such are not to be

---

36. For discussion of this passage, cf. C.K. Barrett, *The Acts of the Apostles* (ICC; 2 vols.; Edinburgh: T & T Clark, 1994, 1998), II, pp. 758-63.

37. But cf. Cohen, *Beginnings of Jewishness*, pp. 363-77; for a response cf. I. Levinskaya, *The Book of Acts in its Diaspora Setting* (The Book of Acts in its First Century Setting, 5; Grand Rapids: Eerdmans, 1996), pp. 12-17.

38. Cf. Louis Epstein, *Marriage Laws in the Bible and the Talmud* (Cambridge, MA: Harvard University Press, 1942), pp. 279-96.

39. Later rabbinic texts, feeling the sting of permanent exclusion and knowing the realities of social and religious life, debated 'for all time' (*b. Yeb.* 78b): 'R. Zera

admitted to the covenant people and they become, as a living embodiment, a witness to the kinds of sins that cannot be rectified.

But does non-admission to the congregation of YHWH refer to limitations in 'marriage' or in 'public participation in worship at the Temple' or might it mean 'exclusion from community participation' in a general sense?[40] There is no answer in the text of Deuteronomy. We have a legal ruling and a sociological label (*mamzer*) but no definition and no explication. Time will unravel its meanings and its implications.

Definition 1: Mixed Marriage Child

Zechariah 9.6 intimates that *mamzer* refers to the children of 'mixed marriages', for here the prediction is that the downfall of Philistia will result in a 'mongrel people' (*mamzer*)[41] settling in Ashdod because of the Lord's hand of judgment on the place.[42] Oddly, these people will apparently observe Jewish food laws and worship the one, true God (9.7). The text seems to suggest that a *mamzer* was of mixed parentage, a child born of an interdicted union. Such a definition of *mamzer*, however, is not consistently applied in later Jewish traditions (cf. *b. Yeb.* 16a for R. Johanan; but see *Avot R.N.* 16).[43] Rabbah b. Bar Hana, in the name of R. Johanan, thought that if a slave or an idolater impregnated an Israelite girl, that child would be a *mamzer*, but R. Simeon b. Judah, consistent with most of the rabbinic traditions, narrowed the definition to what will be seen in (4) below (*b. Yeb.* 44b-45a). Rabbah b. Bar Hana's definition borders on the apparent understanding of *mamzer* in Zechariah 9.6. And the same may be said of the view of R. Hiyya b. Abba, who along with R. Johanan,

replied: It was explained to me by Rab Judah that those who are known [to be *mamzerim*] survive [and marriage is forbidden]; those are not known do not survive; and those who are partly known and partly unknown survive [as *mamzerim*] for three generations but no longer'.

40. *B. Yebamoth* 78a tells the story of a certain Menjamin who said, 'I am an Egyptian ... and I shall arrange for my son to marry an Egyptian wife of the second generation in order that my grandson shall be eligible *to enter the congregation*'. Menjamin has in view full rights to Jewish society, including marriage of an Israelite girl.

41. An etymology from an older generation of scholars for the term *mamzer* was *m'm zr* ('from a foreign people').

42. *Tg. Zech.* 9.6: 'And *the house of Israel* shall dwell in Ashdod *where they were as foreigners*, and I will *put an end to* the Philistines' acendancy'. The targumist makes Israelites foreigners rather than seeing here a 'mixed marriage'.

43. Some older Jewish scholars held to such a definition; cf. Epstein, *Marriage Laws*, p. 184.

considered the children of women who had married proselyte men – who, however, had not been immersed – *mamzerim* because they openly violated the law in this and other matters (*b. Yeb.* 46a). Therefore, if it is argued, as some later Jewish accusations in both Jewish and Christian sources reveal, that Mary's 'partner' was a foreigner (e.g., Pantera),[44] then it is likely Jesus would be classified as a *mamzer* because his father would have been a Gentile and Jesus would be the product of a mixed marriage. In such cases, the suspected and now defined legal status of Jesus brought into question his claims, his teachings, and his missions – not to mention all those who followed him.

Definition 2: Seducer (?)

The rest of the Jewish tradition on this term implies exegesis of Deuteronomy 23.3 and Leviticus 18.6-8. The Dead Sea Scrolls, for example, do not help with definition; instead, the texts use this term as a label for persons who are somehow outside the people of God and who pollute the purity of Israel. That is, the texts uphold the ruling of Deuteronomy 23.3. Thus, *4Q174* 3.4, an eschatological text that envisions the Temple worship of the final days, commenting on Exodus 15.17-18, says, 'This passage describes the temple that no [man with a] permanent [fleshly defect] shall enter, nor Ammonite, Moabite, bastard [i.e., *mamzer*], foreigner, or alien, forevermore'.[45] The same upholding of Deuteronomy 23.3 is found throughout the scrolls, but no definition is found (cf. *4Q394* 13.39; *4Q444* frg. 1 1.8). The use of the 'spirits of bastards' in incantations suggests the danger posed by a *mamzer* as a seducer, but this is only a possible understanding of the term and it may be merely metaphorical (*4Q510* frg. 1.5; frg. 2 2.3; frg. 35.7). There is no evidence that Jesus fits this possible definition of a *mamzer*, if it is a definition.

These two definitions of the term *mamzer*, if the second one is even that, carry the load for at least a millennium, for we find no clarification of our term until the rabbis. Thus, from Deuteronomy 23.3 until the *Mishnah* we find no conscious definition of the term. This cannot go unnoticed, and

44. See the unimaginative repetition of this belief in J.J. Rousseau, R. Arav, *Jesus and His World: An Archaeological and Cultural Dictionary* (Minneapolis: Fortress Press, 1995), pp. 223-25. An imaginative re-vitilization of this view can be seen in M. Sawicki, *Crossing Galilee: Architectures of Contact in the Occupied Land of Jesus* (Harrisburg, PA: Trinity Press International, 2000), pp. 192-97.

45. The translation is that of M. Wise, M. Abegg, Jr, and E. Cook, *The Dead Sea Scrolls: A New Translation* (San Francisco: HarperSanFrancisco, 1996).

should force the historian to operate with considerable caution in drawing conclusions. That Jews knew who was 'in' and 'out' should not be contested; that a firm and clear category existed for a *mamzer*, however, must at least be treated with caution. Even more, I am no expert in rabbinic laws and their development so it is with a certain hope of general accuracy that I put forward the following suggested definitions of what *mamzer* might have meant at the time of Jesus.

Definition 3: Akiva – Children of Those Not Permitted to Enter the Congregation

If Deuteronomy 23.3 and the DSS do not clearly define the term, later rabbinic and targumic renderings do clarify the meaning of the term and to these various definitions we now turn, in the hope that they may offer insight into what might have been meant had Jesus been stigmatized as a *mamzer*. The standard definition is found in *m. Yeb.* 4.13, and I quote here from J. Neusner's translation:

(A) What is the definition of a mamzer?

(B) '[The offspring of] any [marriage of] near of kin which is forbidden under the rubric, He shall not come into the congregation of the Lord' (Deut. 23.3), the words of R. Aqiba.

(C) Simeon of Teman says, '[The offspring of] any [marriage] for which the participants are liable to extirpation by Heaven'.

(D) And the law follows his opinion.

(E) R. Joshua says, '[The offspring of] any [marriage] for which the participants are liable to be put to death by a court'.

(F) Said R. Simeon b. Azzai, 'I discovered a family register in Jerusalem, in which was written: "Mr. So-and-so is a mamzer, [having been born of an illicit union] of a married woman [and someone other than her husband]"'—

(G) so supporting the opinion of R. Joshua.

(H) (1) His wife who died—

(I) he is permitted to marry her sister.

(J) (2) [If] he divorced her and afterward she died,

(K) he is permitted to marry her sister

(L) (3) [If] she was married to someone else and died,

(M) he is permitted to marry her sister.

(N) (4) His deceased childless brother's widow who died—

(O) he is permitted to marry her sister.

(P) (5) [If] he performed the rite of halisah with her and she died,

(Q) he is permitted to marry her sister.

Three nuanced definitions are here given: (1) R. Akiva judges that a *mamzer* is a child of a marriage of partners of a near kinship that is prohibited by connection to the expression, from Deuteronomy 23.3, 'he shall not come into the congregation of the Lord' (*lo-yavo mamzer biqᵉhal YHWH*). Akiva is not entirely clear and, perhaps, he considers the *mamzer* he or she who is deemed the result of 'incest' (cf. *t. Yeb.* 1.9);[46] (2) R. Simeon ben Teman judges that a *mamzer* is a child of an interdicted union liable to the laws of extirpation (e.g., Lev. 18.6-18, 29; *m. Ker.* 1.1); and (3) R. Joshua judges a *mamzer* is a child of a marriage whose partners are liable to punishment by a court (*m. Sanh.* 7.4), and he is supported by Simeon ben Azzai. The appended details (H.-Q.) pertain to rulings on marrying one's wife's sister.

For Akiva, Jesus would be called *mamzer* if Mary, by contextual association, were divorced and her son from that former marriage engaged in relations with her (Deut. 23.1), or if she had relations with a man whose testicles were crushed (23.2) – which would have its own drawbacks, or if she engaged in relations with an Ammonite or a Moabite (23.4-7; cf. Neh. 13.1). The later *b. Yeb.* 44a clarifies the definition of Akiva with this: 'Who is a bastard? [The offspring of a union with] any consanguineous relative with whom cohabitation is forbidden'. The evidence for Mary fitting Akiva's (apparent) definition is lacking.

Definition 4: Simeon – Children of Parents Guilty of Extirpation
Fundamentally for Simeon ben Teman, as the *Bavli* will show in its explications and in the views of both Beth Hillel and Beth Shammai (e.g., *b. Yeb.* 14a-14b), a *mamzer* is the child of a marriage of forbidden degrees found in Leviticus 18.6-18. The act of such intercourse leads to extirpation. Simeon's ruling becomes the *halachah*. The connection of *mamzer* in Deuteronomy 23.3 with Leviticus 18.6-18 may result from the explicit prohibition of a man to marry his father's former wife in Deuteronomy 23.1. Regardless of possible origins for the connections, from Leviticus 18.6-18 we learn that one is not permitted intercourse with one's mother or (what we now call a) 'step-mother', one's sister – whether the child of one's father or mother, a grandchild, a 'step-sister', one's paternal or maternal aunt, one's paternal uncle, one's daughter-in-law, one's sister-in-law, or with a female *and* her daughter or granddaughter or her sister (while the original female is alive). Later rabbinic documents amplify this meaning to include the *levir* (male who is to fulfill the levirate marriage law) who does not marry his brother's widow with the proper motive – in

46. On the later discussions of R. Akiva's understanding, cf. Epstein, *Marriage Laws*, pp. 281-82, who contends that Akiva's perception of the term pertaining to incest is not consistently maintained.

other words, if he married her for her beauty or to gratify his desires (*b. Yeb.* 109a). Any child from such a union is a *mamzer*, according to Abba Saul. And, if a write of divorce (*get*) were not properly explicated the divorce is not considered legitimate, and any children from such a union would be *mamzerim* (*b. Git.* 86a; *b. B.M.* 55b).

If this definition is followed, Jesus could have been legally labelled a *mamzer* if the accusation was that (1) Joseph was not the father; (2) an identifiable other who fitted these rulings was the father. The label, in all these cases, then is directed at Mary for an illicit union and at Jesus, solely for being the child of such a union. To be called *mamzer* according to Simeon, then, Mary – assuming she is young and betrothed – would have had to have had intercourse with and conceived by her brother, or her 'step-brother', or her brother's or sister's son, or her uncle, or her brother-in-law (while her sister is alive), or a married man other than her betrothed. There is no evidence for such a definition of *mamzer* in the case of Mary, Joseph, and Jesus. In a discussion of a Christology from the side, such a label might tell us more about Mary's observance (or non-observance) of Torah than it would Jesus.

Definition 5: Joshua – Children of Parents Guilty of Punishment at the Court

Rabbi Joshua, however, stipulates that a *mamzer* is the child of parents who are liable to punishment at the hand of a court – a court conveniently defined for capital crimes in *m. Sanh.* 7.4. Operating under this definition, Mary would be found guilty for impregnation as a result of sexual relations with her father, or her 'step-father', or another man who is betrothed. On the other hand, another set of categories can be brought in for classifying Jesus as a *mamzer*: if Mary committed some heinous sin, like Sabbath profanation, cursing her parents, bestiality, or leading others into idolatry, she would be guilty of a capital crime and her son would then be a *mamzer* – according to R. Joshua. In the former case, the offending parties would have to be known, and would probably have shown up in some record – and in the case of *Bavli*, we are told that Mary's suitor was a certain ben Pantera (*b. Sanh.* 67a; *b. Shabb.* 104b).

In short, for Jesus to have been called *mamzer* under Joshua's categories, Mary would have had to have sexual relations with one of these forbidden persons or have committed some violent sin. The latter is only a last resort. The evidence we do have from later accusations against Jesus and Mary, however, leads us to think the charge against Jesus by his contemporaries was generated by his mother's sexual relations with a forbidden man. It needs to be observed here, in light of the ambiguity in Chilton's definition of Joseph and Mary's relations, that in no case so far is the child born of pre-marital intercourse by a betrothed couple called a *mamzer*.[47] If Jesus was called a *mamzer*, it would have been based on a conviction that Joseph was not the father – a firm dimension of the infancy traditions of Matthew and Luke.

We should note that one statement in *m. Sanh.* 7.4 connects this law with the situation described in the Gospels for Mary: 'he who has sexual relations with a betrothed maiden' (7.4 G). Though written for a male, this casuistic stipulation, by inference, applies as well to Mary. She, as a betrothed maiden, so the accusation goes, had sexual relations with someone other than her betrothed and that means extirpation. I say 'probable' because the rabbinic evidence does not call the child of any of these relations a *mamzer* by a rabbi of the earliest periods.

There are two problems with this inference: first, there is no direct evidence that this inference was made by rabbis of the earliest periods, though there is indirect evidence in *m. Sanh.* 7.4 and *b. Yeb.* 69b, and – what is more important – none of these situations exactly describes what the Gospels record of Mary and Joseph. In their case, they are already betrothed; if they are accused of responsibility for conceiving a child prior to marriage (as Chilton seems to allege), it is only remotely possible that their child would be called a *mamzer*. More likely, they would have been required to marry; their children would be Jews (since Mary is a Jew); and the status of the children would probably be normal.[48] Finger-pointing would have occurred, no doubt, but that is social commentary and not necessarily legal status. The best conclusion we can draw from this 'guesswork' in light of R. Joshua's definition and the casuistic laws of Deuteronomy 22 is that, if Jesus was classified as a *mamzer*, it would have been because some were convinced that Mary conceived illicitly. It is only remotely possible that a child of both Mary's and Joseph's conception would be called a *mamzer*. The category of Matthew 1.19, that Joseph was a *tsadiq*, is most likely confirmed if it is the case that Jesus was classified by some as a *mamzer*.

---

47. We do not have sufficient evidence to claim (1) that the Galilean strictures on pre-consummation relations were broken and (2) that such a breaking of the rules led to a *mamzer* status for the child.

48. See J. Schaberg, *Illegitimacy*, p. 152.

Definition 6: Children Conceived During Betrothal (If Suspicion Is Present)

From a much later period to be sure, but the evidence from *b. Yeb.* 69b may provide the most direct evidence we have of the accusation levelled against Mary and therefore descriptive of the status of Jesus: 'It was stated: Where a man cohabited with his betrothed in the house of his [future] father-in-law, Rab said: The child is a bastard [*mamzer*]; and Samuel said: The child is a *shethuki* ["silenced one"]' (Soncino). The concern of the *Bavli* here is with a priest's daughter eating the *terumah* ('heave offering'; Num. 18.8-10) and not with the ordinary Israelite woman's situation (cf. *b. Yeb.* 69b-70a). And, furthermore, Raba – and his view seems to prevail and it is more lenient – thought Rab's view only permissible if the girl could have at the same time had sexual relations with a male otherwise prohibited (hence, *shetuqi*). If she was not, then the child is assigned to the father and obtains the appropriate status. It is probably this context that best explains that Mary's motives and actions are not impugned in the Christian records.[49] Leniency was the rule of the day on such matters.

If it is the case that some thought ill of Jesus because they thought Mary and Joseph conceived prior to the official marriage bed, then there was (eventually) dispute over the status of such an accused offspring: one says *mamzer*, another one says *shetuqi* (because the father was unknown because no one confessed?). It should be observed that the two classifications here are given to a situation described in Deuteronomy 22.28-29, though there no label is affixed to either partner in the premarital conception. Like most of this evidence, dating is a problem and there is not a firm view that premarital conception rendered the child a *mamzer*. That the mishnah and the commentary are concerned with eating the *terumah* by the daughter of a priest renders the textual evidence of limited relevance to our concerns.

We have now five, and possibly, six definitions of a *mamzer*: (1) the child of a mixed marriage as seen in Zechariah 9.6; possibly (2), as is seen in the scrolls found in cave four, a seducer of the nation; (3) the child of parents who were not to be admitted to the congregation as is seen in Akiva's judgment; (4) the child of parents who were liable to extirpation as is seen in Simeon ben Teman's exegesis; (5) the child of parents who are liable to punishment by the court as is seen in R. Joshua; (6) the child of premarital conception. There are at least three other definitions found in the Jewish evidence that could shed light on Jesus as a *mamzer*.

---

49. See J. Schaberg, *Illegitimacy*, p. 146.

Definition 7: Children Born of Cult Prostitution
In his commentary on Deuteronomy, because the meaning of the term
mamzer is unclear through its etymology and contemporary usage, Peter
Craigie suggests that *mamzer* derives from *nzr*, with the latter pertaining
to consecration and dedication. He speculates that the consecration would
have been by pagan cult prostitutes and their children, *mamzerim*, would
have been previously dedicated to pagan gods and, therefore, unfit for
entrance into the congregation of the Lord. There is as little to discount
this view as there is to count it; in the absence of such evidence, we leave
it as a possibility that *mamzer* derived from pagan cult prostitution. If that
was its origin, that meaning was almost certainly lost by the first century
of the Common Era. It has nothing to do with Jesus.

Definition 8: Children Born of Theological Apostates
One finds in *t. Shehitat Hullin* 2.20-21 that the children of *minim* (probably 'apostates') are also classified as *mamzerim*:

> The sacrifice of a *min* is idolatry. Their bread is the bread of a Samaritan,
> and their wine is deemed the wine of idolatry, and their produce is deemed
> wholly untithed, and their books are deemed magical books, and their
> children are *mamzerim*.

In effect, one finds here the belief that apostasy renders a person's children unclean, unfit for Israelite society and worship, and therefore labelled
mamzerim. But, we are probably dealing with a non-issue: their children
probably also apostasized with them and therefore no longer had any
interest in Jewish society and worship. In the former, we are probably
dealing with non-realities, other than the sincere belief that intermarriage
between the Schools ought not to occur. It reflects a sectarian mentality
about what constitutes true Judaism. This view, also, has nothing to do
with Jesus.

Definition 9: A Shetuqi – *One Who Knows his Mother but not his*
Father; An Asufi – *a Foundling Who Knows Neither Mother or Father.*
Philo informs us that children of 'prostitutes' (and he is probably not
referring here to cult prostitution) are *mamzerim* because their fathers are
unknown due to the number of partners for the mother (*Spec. Leg.* 1.326).
The category used here could be the 'mixed marriage' of (1) above, or his
understanding might fit untidily into one of the rabbinic definitions, but it
seems that Philo's definition is more like that of the *shetuqi* than any of
the other definitions above. Josephus seems also to know this definition

(*Ant*. 4.244). In *m. Qidd*. 4.1-2 a *shetuqi* is defined as a 'silenced one' or a 'hush-child' because he knows his mother but not his father. Abba Saul, in a pun, called such a one a *beduqi*, 'one who was to be examined' (for status). Since Jesus is technically nowhere called a *mamzer*, it makes sense also to look to such a term as *shetuqi* – as does Chilton[50] – to define his status. In this case, the *shetuqi* is classified as a 'doubtful *mamzer*'. In this case, the mother is to be asked, and several different rulings apply (and debates ensure) depending on her answer (*b. Qidd*. 74a). Again, the discussion begins with Abba Saul, but it is Rabbi Gamaliel's ruling that appears to be the *halachah*, even though Raba rules in favor of Abba Saul (who is not as lenient on the mother's words). However, the rulings tend to favor the word of the mother and in most situations the child would be considered acceptable. In this case, if Mary claims Joseph is the father, the child would probably be accepted; if she says he is the child of someone else, the child is a *mamzer* as a result of examination; if she says the child is from God, the child would also be considered a *mamzer*. We are back, no doubt, to the same category for understanding Jesus' social status. In the case of the *asufi*, the 'foundling', the same principle obtains: the child is of suspected parentage, though in many cases considered pure (*b. Qidd*. 73a-73b). Since we know Jesus' mother, the category is useless to this discussion (*m. Qidd*. 4.1A, D).

Conclusion: Jesus the Mamzer

First, because of a lack of evidence, we do not know precisely what *mamzer* meant at the time of Jesus and, therefore, all logical inferences from accusation to a Christology from the side must be cautious. The evidence of Deuteronomy is unclear and the definition of Zechariah appears not to be the norm; if Zechariah 9.6 is given the guiding hand, a *mamzer* is one born of a mixed union (e.g., Jewish society would have had to classify Jesus as the son of a gentile male). The evidence from the Dead Sea Scrolls simply affirms the demand of Deuteronomy 23.3, but that evidence does not define the term. By inference, we can give the nod to the generic definition of the rabbis, that is, that *mamzer* refers to *a child born of an illegitimate union that led to an interdiction of marrying someone who was fully accepted as a Jew in Jewish society*. That is, roughly, someone who fits definitions 3–6. We must leave open the possibility, however, that at the time of Jesus – if we take Hillel as offering the ruling *halachah*

---

50. See Chilton, 'Jésus, le *mamzer*', pp. 225-26.

(cf. *b. Qidd.* 69a, 75a) – the term *mamzer* may have referred exclusively to a child of mixed parentage. It is reasonable to think some in Jewish society would have classified Jesus as *mamzer* according to this understanding.

It is also reasonable to see behind Matthew 1.18-25 a genuine memory of Joseph's adoption of Jesus as his son. If this is so, and if later rabbinic rulings were in general force that a child's status would have been clarified by such adoption (cf. *b. Qidd.* 73b) – and the second 'if' is more difficult to establish than the first 'if' – then it is theoretically possible that Jesus would have grown up with absolutely no stain against his classification – in which case Chilton has misconstrued the gospel evidence and the 'story' of Jesus. This view must remain possible. However, I find this theory less likely than that Jesus would have been classified as a *mamzer*, even if our perception of the precise definition of his status is unclear. In my judgement, the evidence of Matthew 1, Luke 1–2, Mark 6.1-6, and John 8 suggests that accusations were made against Jesus; if accusations were made, any such adoption would not have completely cleared up the issue of classification.

Second, we are nonetheless justified, because of the uniformity of the later evidence and the sheer likelihood from logic and the social sciences that a person with a questionable parentage would have been classified of lower status by society (whether it was technically legal or not), in suggesting that the term *mamzer* in the first century would probably have meant *'someone who was born of at least one parent of questionable status'*. If we infer that both Mary and Joseph were Israelites, then we are driven to infer that any accusation against Jesus that he was a *mamzer* would at the same time very probably be *an accusation that Joseph was not the father and that someone else was that father*. Anyone who surmised that Joseph was the father of Jesus would probably not have accused Jesus of being a *mamzer*. The evidence for that view, though not non-existent, is from a much later date. In other words, to be called a *mamzer* the community knew (1) Jesus' father as someone other than Joseph, (2) knew Jesus' father as someone who was not fully Israelite, or (3) did not know Jesus' father but had a suspicion about who he might have been. Rumour and innuendo are part and parcel of any society, not the least an ancient Galilean hamlet hemmed in by Roman occupation, but it should be noted that the rabbis, at least, were conscious of the problem of rumour and warned people to do careful inquiry before classifications were made (*b. Git.* 89a).

Third, it must be recalled that a *mamzer* could change his or her status. It is not clear what specific mechanisms were triggered to make the transition, but it is clear that 'until the tenth generation' was not as irrevocable as one might think. Thus, *Tg. Deut.* 23.3 introduces the notion of purity into the status of a *mamzer* by denying what was evidently (for the targumist) a problem in society: 'Neither is a bastard *considered purified for admission* into the congregation of the Lord, even in the tenth generation will he not be *considered purified* for *admission* into the congregation of the Lord'. But, *m. Qidd.* 3.13 reads, 'R. Tarfon says, "*Mamzerim* can be purified [from the taint of bastardy]. How so? A *mamzer* who marries a slave girl – the offspring is a slave girl. [If] he then freed him, the son turns out to be a free man". R. Eliezer says, "Lo, this is a slave who also is in the status of a *mamzer*" '. Thus, the son of a *mamzer* can become an Israelite if manumitted. B. *Qidd.* 71a reveals that money can purify a *mamzer* (cf. also *b. Qidd.* 69a). But, as is usually the case, the rabbis debated the issue and did not agree: 'Our Rabbis taught: *Mamzerim* and *Nethinim* will become pure in the future: this is R. Jose's view. R. Meir said: They will not become pure' (*b. Qidd.* 72b). The point to be made is that the 'tenth generation' may well not have been taken by Jesus' contemporaries as an irrevocable status. Steps may have been permitted to eliminate the taint of the status, though, as Jonathan Klawans has pointed out to me, this entire concern of changing status may be eschatological (*m. Ed.* 8.7). One might suggest that Joseph's marriage to Mary, or perhaps even the circumcision ceremony itself – upon which Chilton leans so heavily, could have functioned as such a transitional act. Evidence is not available for our period to permit confident judgement.

Fourth, when it comes to specific *social manifestations* of the *mamzer's* status deprivations, however, we are at a historian's loss of confidence. The evidence is not firm. If we can say, in general, that a *mamzer* would most likely have been socially- and religiously-restricted, we are unsure what that might mean. Could Jesus enter a synagogue – if there was a designated building? Could Jesus enter the Temple? All the way to the boundaries of the holy place? Could Jesus have married an Israelite girl? Could Jesus have participated in the annual feasts? In particular, at *Pesach* could he have offered his own lamb for sacrifice?

For the rabbis, who constructed an ideal society that probably diverged in many ways from the ideal, a *mamzer* was in general a lower-class member of society. However, even among those who thought a *mamzer* was not to marry an Israelite girl there is clear social adjustment. Rabbis permitted the *mamzer* to serve in civil trials, though not in capital cases (*b. Sanh.* 36b; *b. Nid.* 49b). If the *mamzer* could sit in trial in a civil case, it is highly likely that the *mamzer* was integrated into society in many other ways.[51] In fact, Passamaneck has concluded (for the Talmudic evidence): 'Clearly the Talmud did not exclude the *mamzer* from participating in many areas of Jewish life, and it is safe to assume that theoretically at least, the *mamzer* led a normal life except for his limited marriage opportunities'.[52]

It is time now to turn to each of Chilton's conclusions to draw together what can be known and what was most likely the case for Jesus. (Numbers and letters refer to the enumerated and lettered points above.)

Disagreements

First, I refer to points made by Chilton (pp. 140) where I think the evidence is insufficient to shoulder his historical conclusions. There is not sufficient clarity pertaining to conclusions 1 or 3 for them to be useful for understanding Jesus. The term 'caste' is problematic, as is the evidence that we do have that Jesus was not fundamentally separated from Jewish society. There is no evidence that Jesus was 'silenced' in public congregations (conclusion 4); in fact, Chilton makes much of Jesus' public speech in Nazareth. Perhaps Chilton would argue that Jesus' baptism purified Jesus from his *mamzer* heritage, but that supposition would almost certainly not have been held by the elders in the synagogue at Nazareth. I doubt very much that the community surrounding Jesus felt imperiled because of his *mamzer* status (conclusion 6).

I am not sure why Chilton thinks Jesus' status was lowered when his father died (conclusion 7). Jesus' status was determined as a *mamzer* because of his mother's illicit union. If Joseph adopted Jesus, then Jesus' status was elevated by that adoption and (only perhaps) by the rite of circumcision. Joseph's death, to my knowledge, would not have impacted Jesus' status for that status would have been sustained by the adoption. In light of the later evidence that an intelligent *mamzer* was of a higher status than an ignorant high (!) priest (*m. Hor.* 3.8), I am doubtful of Chilton's conclusion that there was anything particularly offensive about Jesus becoming a *talmid* of John (conclusion 8).

And, if Chilton wishes to remain consistent with this point, he should re-consider conclusions 11 and 13, as well as (I): if it was offensive to become a *talmid* of John, it would have been difficult to find a platform in Capernaum. And, if it was easy to get out of range by running off to Capernaum, certainly he was also safe in Jerusalem (conclusion 13). But,

51. For the record, the standard rabbinic classification is as follows: priests, Israelites, *mamzerim*, *nethin*, proselytes, and freed slaves (*b. Hor.* 13a).

52. Passamaneck, 'Some Medieval Problems', p. 124.

since I doubt conclusion 8 is secure (a *mamzer* status would not have prevented Jesus from being John's *talmid*), I would agree with conclusion 11 for other reasons: I find it unlikely that a *mamzer* would have been restricted at this level. And, therefore, I find it unlikely that Jesus would have found the Temple any more evocative of God's presence than any other Jews' sense when entering the Temple (I).

That Jesus could become a prophet-like leader is permissible to a *mamzer*, and I have seen no evidence that a *mamzer* could not operate in such a manner (conclusion 14). Deuteronomy 23.3 might restrict a *mamzer* from Temple and marriage, but it does not prohibit him from operating in society in a normal way. I am non-plussed by Chilton's contention that Jesus found in the Temple the palpable presence of his *Abba* (I), though he founds many of his observations about Jesus' *mamzer* status ultimately on Deuteronomy 23.3.

It is my judgement that it is quite easy to exaggerate Jesus' isolation (A) in that the evidence is not clear enough to know the full implications of being classified as a *mamzer*. Furthermore, the second we truck into the issue of self-identity and postulate that a *mamzer* status would have dramatically altered where Jesus found identity (B, D, E, K), we are entering into unacceptable guesswork: identities are shaped in any number of ways. Children who grow up in troubled homes sometimes have wonderful identities; children who grow up in healthy homes are sometimes troubled themselves. And, it should be observed here that John Miller postulates that Jesus' turning to *Abba* was indicative of a healthy, loving relationship with Joseph while others have argued that *Abba* emerged from a torn and battered relationship, and others from the death of his father. We should just knock this kind of speculation off; we do not know the hidden factors contributing to Jesus' use of *Abba*, though there is something to say for each view. At least Miller's work reveals patient and careful work with psychological research. That one's image of one's parents shapes one's image of God is founded upon firm studies;[53] that one can infer from one's view of God back to one's father is not. A recent study by D. Jacobs-Malina argues, in fact, that Jesus' vision of the Kingdom was more shaped by the ideal woman with an absent husband. Enough said; our data are insufficient to make too strong claims from Jesus' use of *Abba*.[54]

53. Important research includes A. Vergote *et al.*, 'Concept of God and Parental Images', *JSSR* 8 (1969), pp. 79-87; A. Vergote and A. Tamayo, *The Parental Figure and the Representation of God* (Religion and Society, 21; New York: Mouton, 1981).

54. D. Jacobs-Malina, *Beyond Patriarchy: The Images of Family in Jesus* (Mahwah,

Was Jesus excluded from the synagogue (C)? The evidence for this is three-fold: (1) that Deuteronomy 23.3 could be taken this way; (2) that the rabbinic sources do reveal that *mamzerim* could do just about everything in Jewish society; and (3) that the Gospel records show a Jesus who freely moved in and out of synagogues.

Chilton's contention that Jesus was excluded from his father's funeral because he was a *mamzer* borders on the sensationalist for me (F). The rabbinic traditions reveal a consistent and fundamental mercy when it comes to such matters; the rabbis dropped even the most basic commands for the funeral of one's father. That the parable of the prodigal son mimics Jesus' own life, and yet that Jesus himself was not feted because he was a *mamzer* (L), are neither probative at the historical and evidential level. Ultimately, it comes down to what Deuteronomy 23.3 implies by non-admission, and I doubt very much that there is sufficient evidence to suggest that Jesus would not have been given a welcome because he was a *mamzer*.

Agreements

I take it to be the case that conclusion 2 is justified on the basis of Deuteronomy 23.3 and the problems arising in Jewish society over marriage. That Jesus was an 'untouchable' for ten generations is both rhetorically overdone but also probably accurate, though there is clear evidence that a *mamzer* could change his status, though we are not sure when that might occur (see my third conclusion above). To be untouchable for ten generations affirms Deuteronomy 23.3, if the stipulation was in force. It is highly likely that Jesus' brothers resented his *mamzer* status (conclusion 9) and it is likely that Mary, had she wanted to, would have had difficulty finding a she-*mamzer* for Jesus (conclusion 10). That Jesus' rejection at Nazareth was in part related to his status seems to be quite reasonable (conclusion 12). It is certain that Jesus' followers rejected the accusations that Jesus was a *mamzer* (conclusion 15). And I would think that *Abba* language and Kingdom hope are partly to be explained in light of Jesus' *mamzer* status, though I retain the hesitations expressed above (E, H).

That Jesus' status was an issue in Jerusalem and that Jesus was antagonistic toward Israel's leaders are, in my view, perhaps Chilton's most enduring insights into Jesus in light of his *mamzer* status (Definition 13; cf. also G). It is this status that might explain Jesus' joining of John's somewhat anti-Temple attitudes as well as his outburst in the Temple. This raises, in its tow, the attitude Jesus had toward the Temple and its authorities in several instances. Each of these might be plausibly connected to Deuteronomy 23.3, if it be understood as Jesus' restriction of movement in the Temple. Thus, the so-called 'cleansing' might be a tirade related to the area where Jesus was in fact permitted. His action was a defence of his own: as a *mamzer* was he limited to the Court of Gentiles?

When Chilton surmises that the deep divide between Christianity and Judaism is in part related to Jesus' *mamzer* status, it has within it a kernel and fundamental insight: if Jesus' opposition to the Temple and its authorities is related to his status, then the polemic it generated is also to be explained in a similar manner. And that means that the Christian usage of such polemic has a social rootedness that is often not observed. But all of this is founded upon the possible link between Jesus' polemic and his *mamzer* status.

That Jesus' baptism was connected to his *mamzer* status and its undoing provokes thought and imagination. Let us assume that Jesus' baptism is somewhat political and let us also assume that it was concerned with a vision for Israel.[55] If so, it seems reasonable to me that Jesus took up, or began to take up, a new shape to his identity and that would have inevitably related to his previous status as a *mamzer*. The problem I see with this is that there is no evidence that I know of that suggests Jesus' status in his society changed as a result of his baptism. It is entirely possible, however, that Jesus' status in his own mind changed, even if other Galileans failed to accompany him in his new life.

Another feature of Chilton's proposals that I find to be potently suggestive is his notion that Jesus' *mamzer* status led to his inclusion of those otherwise excluded in Jewish society (K). While Christian tradition has often simply asserted that Jesus, by *fiat*, had a compassion and love otherwise unknown in Jewish society and while that perception of Jesus has recently been overturned, there has been little examination of the social basis for Jesus' inclusion of the unlikely of Jewish society – until Chilton's own suggestion (followed contemporarily by van Aarde). That is, while many have noted that Jesus' rejection led to his inclusion of others, most have shaped his inclusiveness on the basis of Jesus' view of God as loving or the kingdom as eschatologically inclusive. Chilton's suggestion is

---

55. On this, cf. my study, 'Jesus' New Vision within Judaism', in *Who Was Jesus? A Jewish-Christian Dialogue* (ed. P. Copan and C.A. Evans; Louisville, KY: Westminster/John Knox, 2001), pp. 73-96, here 78-81.

important to consider: a social foundation for Jesus' inclusiveness could well have been his experiences of exclusion because he was labelled a *mamzer*.

Finally, Chilton's suggestion that Jesus' *mamzer* status toughened his identity is to be considered successful (M). If we limit his toughness to his growing responses to his status, we fall short; but if we include his *mamzer* status as a contributing dimension to the development of a certain tough resolve to carry through with his mission to Israel, then we are probably on safe, if speculative, ground.

Significance: Christology from the Side

What then is the significance of Jesus' *mamzer* status? What are the implications of Jesus' opponents calling Jesus 'son of Mary' or an 'illegitimate child'? I suggest three implications, but first a word: it is one thing to suggest social implications for Jesus' life from his *mamzer* status. It is quite another to infer Jesus' self-perception or the perception of others from those accusations. It would be easy to guess; I'll try to keep our imaginations within the fold of three elements that are more or less secure once one concludes that Jesus was indeed considered by some to be a *mamzer*.

Jesus as teacher. There is no question that Jesus was perceived and received as a teacher of wit and wisdom. It should not escape our attention that the single most influential text in understanding Jesus as a *mamzer* is from the synagogue in Nazareth, and the setting for the accusatory questions and comment that this Jesus was after all the 'son of Mary' is that Jesus is teaching (Mark 6.2). The questions reveal the point: 'Where did this man get all this? What is this wisdom that has been given to him? What deeds of power are being done by his hands!' And the inference in 6.3 they make go to the problem with listening to this upstart teacher: 'Is not this the carpenter, the son of Mary and brother of James and Joses and Judas and Simon, and are not his sisters here with us?' Jesus' response deals with the same level: 'Prophets are not without honor, except in their hometown, and among their own kin, and in their own house' (6.4).

In other words, Jesus teaches with wisdom and in a way that draws others into his ambit of wisdom – and his opponents attack him *not on the basis of what he was teaching* but on the basis of his origins. Jesus is illegitimate; he should not be listened to. The charge of *mamzer* is an accusatory performative utterance designed to denounce Jesus and to draw crowds away from his authority and charisma. The Christology from the side is that Jesus has established himself as a powerful teacher and the way to dethrone his honor was by way of questioning his legitimacy.

Jesus as self-claimed authority and prophet. Many today would hesitate to accept the fullness of John's narrative in chapter 8 as carrying with it historical weight about the context for the accusatory words that Jesus was a *mamzer* (8.41, 42). The context, however, is generally credible: namely, that Jesus made self-claims about his authority to speak for God[56] – this is the claim of a prophet after all – and some of his contemporaries considered his claim fraudulent and deceptive and unsubstantial. If the words are more explicit in John 8 than what one might expect, the general substance behind them is credible: Jesus did make claims for himself (prophet, etc.) and others thought he was such and yet others thought he was not a prophet (e.g., Mk 2.1–3.6). His claim to have been sent by God (e.g., the 'I have come' sayings) and that those who know God would know him are all credible social settings for the historical Jesus – and therefore a charge that Jesus called into question the status of contemporaries is credible. If Chilton's thesis that Jesus' relations with the Temple authorities derives from their perception of his status, then we find confirmation of our point: the accusatory performative of calling Jesus a *mamzer* discredited Jesus' entire ministry and called *him* into question as a person worthy of teaching, preaching, prophesying, and ministering as he did.

Though hardly as secure as our first observation, a Christology from the side may well consider the label *mamzer* to indicate both that Jesus had called into question the legitimacy (spiritual) of some of his contemporaries and that question of them led to their questioning of Jesus' legitimacy (genetic). The accusation would also indicate in all likelihood that Jesus had made claims to have been sent from God, to have been authorized by God to utter his words, and to have been especially related to God. The accusation would have been designed to discredit the self-claims of Jesus about his authority and his prophetic vocation.

Jesus as of supernatural origins. I consider it only a slight possibility that the label *mamzer* reflects a claim on the part of Jesus, his family or his followers that he had supernatural origins. The birth narratives of Matthew and Luke, not to omit the astounding prologue to John, along with the early Christian snippets (e.g., Phil. 2.5-11; Hebrews 1) add up to an early Christian conviction that Jesus was no ordinary human being. However, that Jesus made claim to such origins in such a way that it drew out of others that he was, far from having a supernatural origin, one who was

---

56. In particular, see B.F. Meyer, *The Aims of Jesus* (London: SCM, 1979), and now J.D.G. Dunn, *Jesus Remembered* (Grand Rapids: Eerdmans, 2003), pp. 615-762.

actually illegitimate is beyond the evidence we now possess. To be sure, John 8.41-42 hints at such – and if taken as authentic could be utilized to lay claim that Jesus made claims of a supernatural origin – not unlike the virginal conception of Matthew 1, but that evidence is best left as quiet as it appears on such matters.

INDEX OF ANCIENT SOURCES

BIBLE

INDEX OF SUBJECTS